ADVANCE PRAISE FOR *THE MAGIC KEY*

"This book is an outstanding scholarly accomplishment and makes major contributions to several areas of practice and research. Most importantly, it reveals the obstacles and locked doors that have limited the educational success of Mexican Americans throughout their history in the United States, and it outlines how these doors may be unlocked. As a work of scholarship, it summarizes and synthesizes historical analyses, demographic data, and the latest qualitative and quantitative educational research. It makes important contributions to Latina/Latino Studies, gender studies, the sociology of race and ethnicity, and education research and policy. It deserves a wide readership and promises to have major policy impacts."
—JORGE CHAPA, PROFESSOR, INSTITUTE OF GOVERNMENT & PUBLIC AFFAIRS, DEPTS. OF LATINA/LATINO STUDIES AND SOCIOLOGY, UNIVERSITY OF ILLINOIS AT URBANA–CHAMPAIGN

"*The Magic Key* gathers some of the best thinkers in higher education and offers a rare multi-dimensional and multi-data source investigation into Mexican American student success. One message in particular from Sally Alonzo Bell's "Personal Narrative" stuck with me—people matter—mentors, teachers, a parent who cares. While we must address the broad cultural, policy, and institutional barriers, we also have got to remember the direct and powerful role that individuals can and must play. The larger the network of support wherever it can be created is the magic key when it comes to creating greater equity for Mexican Americans. Our strategies must combine strategic efforts to change policy while also building allies and networks of support that help create success in the interim and work to create the pressure for policy changes in the long-run."
—ADRIANNA KEZAR, PROFESSOR, UNIVERSITY OF SOUTHERN CALIFORNIA ROSSIER SCHOOL OF EDUCATION, CODIRECTOR, PULLIAS CENTER FOR HIGHER EDUCATION

"Many years ago my father, a tractor operator, told me that education was the one thing nobody could ever take away from me. Similarly, my mother, a single parent, in the 1950s operated an *escuelita*, a neighborhood school where for 50 cents a week she would teach children how to read, write, and do math. In their own ways, my parents, who never graduated from high school, intuitively knew the value of *la llave májica*, the magic key of education to get out of poverty and find success in American life. Because of their example, *consejos y apoyo*, I was able to find the determination to earn the magic key.

"In this well-researched collection of essays, a cadre of established academics as well as a newly emerging generation of scholars, masterfully employ rigorous methodological approaches to extend theoretical insights and to highlight and debunk deficit perspectives that have worked against Latino/a students' success. We are left with a sense of hope that the magic key need not be elusive and can be placed within the reach of every Latino/a student."

—LAURA RENDÓN, PROFESSOR, EDUCATIONAL LEADERSHIP AND POLICY STUDIES, UNIVERSITY OF TEXAS AT SAN ANTONIO

"Each chapter undoubtedly includes a thoughtful and provocative critique that contributes to a deeper understanding of the U.S. educational legal policy, racialization, and structural inequality faced by Mexican Americans in the educational trajectory. I commend the authors for their important contributions to the status of Mexican Americans and other Latino/a students' education in the United States."

—JEFFREY F. MILEM, ERNEST W. MCFARLAND DISTINGUISHED PROFESSOR, UNIVERSITY OF ARIZONA COLLEGE OF EDUCATION

"Ruth Enid Zambrana and Sylvia Hurtado have assembled a truly impressive collection of essays to address the future education of Mexican American and other Latino students. Applying an innovative framework and the most recent cutting-edge scholarship, this book is a must-read for educators, policy makers, and anyone interested in the educational future of the country."

—AÍDA HURTADO, PROFESSOR OF CHICANA AND CHICANO STUDIES, LUIS LEAL ENDOWED CHAIR, UNIVERSITY OF CALIFORNIA, SANTA BARBARA

The Magic Key

Book Thirty-Eight
Louann Atkins Temple Women & Culture Series

The Magic Key

The Educational Journey of
Mexican Americans from K–12
to College and Beyond

EDITED BY RUTH ENID ZAMBRANA
AND SYLVIA HURTADO

University of Texas Press ⟡ *Austin*

Requests for permission to reproduce material from this work should be sent to:
    Permissions
    University of Texas Press
    P.O. Box 7819
    Austin, TX 78713-7819
    http://utpress.utexas.edu/index.php/rp-form

♾ The paper used in this book meets the minimum requirements of
ANSI/NISO Z39.48-1992 (R1997) (Permanence of Paper).

Library of Congress Cataloging Data
The magic key : the educational journey of Mexican Americans from K-12 to college
and beyond / edited by Ruth Enid Zambrana and Sylvia Hurtado. — First edition.
    pages cm
    Includes bibliographical references and index.
    ISBN 978-1-4773-0370-2 (cloth : alk. paper)
    ISBN 978-1-4773-0725-0 (pbk. : alk. paper)
    ISBN 978-1-4773-0726-7 (library e-book)
    ISBN 978-1-4773-0727-4 (non-library e-book)
1. Mexican Americans—Education. 2. Education—Social aspects—United States.
3.Minorities—Education—United States. 4. Discrimination in education.
I. Zambrana, Ruth E., editor. II. Hurtado, Sylvia, editor.
    LC2682.M35 2015
    371.829′68073—dc23
                                                                    2015004428

doi:10.7560/303702

This book is dedicated with deep admiration to all Mexican American pioneras and contemporary men and women who have with strength and courage tackled the higher education system successfully. Their success has opened doors of opportunity for future generations who will continue to enter into unwelcoming spaces but know they can resist and succeed. We also acknowledge all the educational administrators, teachers, and scholars who, in a long period of national retrenchment, which has rekindled racial tensions in this country and on university campuses, continue to challenge the "lens of failure" and propose new strategies of resistance, hope, and support for Mexican American students in the educational pathways.

Contents

Foreword

PATRICIA GÁNDARA
CIVIL RIGHTS PROJECT
UNIVERSITY OF CALIFORNIA, LOS ANGELES

In reading through the chapters of this volume, one is tempted to conclude that the more things change, the more they stay the same. Certainly, some of the particulars are different: Mexican-origin males and females have changed places since the 1970s so that today they are the mirror image of each other's college representation of forty years ago. Women are now about 60 percent of the college freshmen and getting about 60 percent of the college degrees, whereas it was men who garnered this larger share forty years ago. And today a larger percentage of the Mexican-origin population is immigrants or the children of immigrants, which changes the college-going dynamic in important ways. But the major challenges facing this population have not changed greatly. Poverty, unequal K–12 schooling opportunities, low parental education, and low expectations of Mexican-origin youths' abilities and educational prospects remain endemic.

Even though we have recognized for some time the barriers that keep these young people from going to college, and especially from completing college degrees, little has been done to address these barriers. In fact, it is fair to say that as the population has grown, there has been an erosion of those policies that fostered the first large wave of Mexican American (and other "minority") youths' entry into higher education during the civil rights period of the 1960s and early 1970s. Active recruitment and targeted financial support for these youths largely dried up with the passage of anti-affirmative-action legislation in some key states and the belt-tightening of budgets for higher education across the nation.

It has been widely touted that Mexican Americans are *going* to college in higher percentages than ever (in fact, even at slightly higher rates than of White students), but this statistic can be misleading. Mexican American students go to very different "colleges" than other students, primarily two-year institutions, from which they only rarely transfer to a four-year college and get a degree. As a result, degree completion is inching up very slowly, and the gaps in completion between Mexican-origin students and other groups are actually getting wider (see chapter 3). And, too many of these students are left with heavy debt but no degree to show for it.

Forty years ago the undereducation of the Mexican-origin population was a minor problem from a national perspective. Today it is a national disaster in the making. In this sense, things have indeed changed. Latinos generally, and Mexican Americans more specifically, are occupying a larger role in the nation's present and future. "Hispanics" (two-thirds of whom are Mexican-origin) have grown by 600 percent since 1970, from 9 million to 53 million persons in 2012. In California and Texas, the two states with the largest numbers of Mexican-origin youth, these young people now constitute more than half of all students in the public schools. It matters very much how they fare; they will be the backbone of the economy in the Southwest (and increasingly in other urban areas around the country) in a few short years. And they are the least likely of all major subgroups to complete a college degree. Studies in California project that as a result, the state by 2025 will be *at least* a million college degrees short of meeting its labor force requirements, and Texas is similarly poised for a significant shortfall in college-educated workers.

So, why have things changed so little in terms of policies that could stimulate and increase the educational level of Mexican Americans? The civil rights era was not only a period of opening doors to spaces that had been virtually closed to Hispanics, such as elite higher education, but also a period of *investment* in education. The states built public schools to meet the needs of the burgeoning postwar baby boom, and they built colleges and universities to satisfy their growing aspirations for postsecondary education. But beginning with the recessions of the mid-1970s and early 1980s and a more conservative federal government, both the states and Washington, DC, began to pull back. The 1973 Supreme Court decision *San Antonio Independent School District v. Rodriguez* found that education was not a fundamental right protected by the U.S. Constitution, thus laying the foundation for a growing inequality in the nation's public schools. Without legal protections against vastly inequitable funding of schools in poor communities versus those in wealthy areas (because poor children were not found to have a *right* to equal schooling), schools serving the Mexican American population have been routinely underfunded. The antitax crusade that began in California in 1978, following on the heels of the mid-1970s economic recession, and that subsequently swept the nation, left declining funds to support public services such as schools. And increasing income inequality (the top 1 percent hold about 23 percent of the nation's wealth compared to the bottom 90 percent, who hold less than half[1]) means that while the wealthy hold on to more of their income, the poor get poorer and their neighborhood schools become even more unequal, more segregated, and more bereft of the capacity to prepare students for college. Immigration from the Southern Hemisphere, especially Mexico, also began to increase sharply in the early 1980s, and so more students in need of equalizing opportunities were crowded into the schools that were least equipped to provide those opportunities. As always in our history (as recounted by Victoria-María MacDonald and Jason Rivera, chapter 2), as immigration grew, the outcry to close the borders and punish those who came here seeking to take the jobs of "real Americans" became louder. Anti-immigrant sentiment over the last several decades has been closely tied to anti-Mexican sentiments, with many people seeing them as one and the same (although historically this is not the case). All the more reason to not open our pocketbooks for the schools and services that would serve "those children." It is especially ironic that Americans' negative attitudes toward immigration have mounted in the face of a growing body of research that finds that immigrant students often outperform their native-born peers in schooling because of the "immigrant optimism" that their families bring with them.

Thus, while we have known for a long time that poverty and inadequate schooling are core causes of failure to enter and complete higher education, there has been little motivation on the part of many policymakers to attack these problems. Increased immigration also meant that parents of Mexican-origin students in the schools were more unlikely to have any experience with or understanding of the schooling system in the United States, or grasp the importance of returns on higher education. Increasingly heavy costs, a lack of understanding of the higher education system or how to finance postsecondary education, and the absence of individuals in the schools who could or would provide this information left many Mexican-origin families on the margins. Of course, it bears mentioning that since immigrants do not normally vote, their concerns are often overlooked by politicians seeking support in the next election.

In spite of this dreary history, there has been progress for Mexican-origin youth with respect to educational attainment, and this volume is filled with chapters that herald that success and illuminate the pathway to a better future for this population and, as a consequence, for the nation as a whole. Beginning with chapter 4, where the authors posit a new lens for examining the plight of Mexican-origin youth in higher education, the volume takes a turn toward the optimistic. The authors note the shift in the literature from an almost wholly deficit perspective that chose to blame the victim to a more critical lens in recent years that began to identify the structural determinants of the undereducation of Mexican-origin youth. Corroborating my own research (Gándara 1980, 1982, 1995, 1999b), others began to study and document the resilience of this population and the cultural *strengths* exhibited by these families. For example, in researching my book *Over the Ivy Walls*, I had been impressed by the stories told by Mexican mothers of their families' noble histories, pointing out to their children that they were *destined* to be successful because they came from a "*buena familia*." The mothers interpreted the often dire poverty in which the family was living as a temporary condition that did not define them or their aspirations. This formed the backbone of the resilience that these educationally successful Mexican-origin young men and women would take into the world of higher education. Similarly, as in chapter 5 of this volume, I, too, found that the gender stereotypes were not nearly so inflexible as often described in the literature, and both the mothers and the fathers of educationally successful Mexican-origin women were almost uniformly supportive of their daughters' educational aspirations, albeit in different ways. This, of course, is not to say that gender bias did not or does not exist in Mexican-origin families, but in those I have studied that saw themselves as upwardly mobile, the families clearly saw that their daughters were as worthy of support as their sons, and mothers were very influential in family decisions. It seems there is a "magic key" in these findings. Nurturing the aspirations of low-income Mexican-origin families may be one effective way to reduce gender bias—in favor of both sons and daughters. But as I will argue a little later, this must be in the form of social policies that provide *real* support for these youth and families, not simply exhortations to try harder to conform to Anglo-American ideals.

In fact, the challenge that is set forth in chapter 9 regarding the stagnation of progress for Mexican-origin men may also be addressed by this same strategy—supporting the aspirations of Mexican-origin males through more enlightened social and education policy. In my own research, I have concluded that the men are often more pragmatically driven than the women. Mexican-origin young men feel very keenly the duty to help support family and to declare economic independence early, even at the cost of their own education. Bringing home a paycheck and demonstrating both their independence and their ability to share the burden of family support are important markers of manhood. These expectations are often not quite as high for the women—though they may be expected to provide family support in other ways that can take time and energy that could otherwise be devoted to study. Nonetheless, like Ruth Enid Zambrana and Rebeca Burciaga (chapter 5), I found that one important way families supported their young women was in protecting them from too many household duties. The women I have studied, on the whole, have felt more freedom to choose education, and, being more protected (less independent), they were also less likely to get off the education track than their brothers. Luis Ponjuán and Victor B. Sáenz (chapter 9) argue that increasingly strict "zero tolerance" policies in public schools lead to disproportionate rates at which Mexican-origin males are suspended. This almost certainly factors into their estrangement from school, reducing their chances of graduating and going to college. At a time when costs of higher education were lower and financial support was greater, it was more possible for young men to demonstrate independence and even help the family in limited ways while also continuing their education. Today, this has become nearly impossible. It should also not be forgotten that while Mexican-origin women have outpaced the men in college-going and degree completion, they have not kept pace with women from all other major subgroups. Mexican-origin women remain the least likely to get a college degree.

Ultimately, the value of this book will rest not just on the description of the problems associated with the lower attainment of postsecondary degrees of the Mexican-origin population but also on the "magic keys" provided herein that may turn the situation around. As I noted at the beginning, little has changed with respect to policies that might make significant inroads, except to the extent that proactive, effective policies have been eliminated or reduced. Yet, as Frances Contreras asserts in chapter 10, the situation will not improve without better policies and greater investment of our resources.

Several authors allude to the dearth of teachers from the Mexican American community. There is now considerable evidence that more highly qualified Mexican-origin (and bilingual) teachers would make a difference in the educational outcomes of this population. Their better understanding of the resources that exist within these students' communities, their greater ability and desire to communicate with students' parents, their greater likelihood of investing their careers in these neighborhoods, and the important role they play as models of authority and educational accomplishment all make them highly desirable teachers. Why has there been no targeted national and state-level policy to recruit and support young Mexican-origin individuals to become teachers? Likewise, why has there been no concerted effort to recruit and support Mexican-origin individuals into the higher education faculty pipeline? Individual efforts exist at some university campuses, but this is largely a bootstrap operation that is headed by one or two people who are deeply committed at a personal level and who constantly struggle with limited resources.

As the United States has fallen further and further behind in the rankings for percent of population who are college graduates—now at about fourteenth—the reason for this is clear. Countries that have wanted to boost higher education enrollments and completion have supported their youth in getting a college education; tuition is free or nearly free, and oftentimes living stipends are also provided. And most of these thirteen other countries have poverty rates lower than ours. That is, college would be less of an economic challenge for more of their citizens. Those nations have seen completion of a college education as an important social policy priority and have made impressive and rapid gains. We have not. We have bemoaned the fact that we are dropping in the rankings but have done comparatively little to make it possible for a Mexican-origin (or other) low-income student to forgo a regular paycheck and dedicate him- or herself to higher education. If we were truly dedicated as a nation to equalizing opportunity and strengthening the national economy, we would make it possible for ambitious low-income students, of which Mexican Americans form a significant percentage, to go to four-year colleges and complete degrees without the constant worry of paying tuition or basic living expenses. The students would not have to choose between paying the rent and buying the books for class. And, we would not saddle future teachers, social workers, and other public service personnel with nearly insurmountable debt for the privilege of dedicating their lives to creating a better society.

Contreras (chapter 10) also challenges quasi-governmental bodies such as the President's Advisory Commission on Educational Excellence for Hispanics, of which I am a member, to do more to push for these policies. She is right. While the commission is only "advisory," it is important to remember that these are opportunities that should not be wasted. There is progress, but it is still too little and too slow to make a significant dent in the problem. It is my sincere hope that this book, by illuminating the challenges and suggesting ways to address them, will help push the college-completion agenda for Mexican-origin youth forward.

A Personal Narrative

SALLY ALONZO BELL, PHD, LCSW
PROFESSOR EMERITUS, DEPARTMENT OF SOCIAL WORK
AZUSA PACIFIC UNIVERSITY, AZUSA, CALIFORNIA

"Born and raised in East Los Angeles, fourth in a family of nine." This statement can be so misleading—hidden behind it are the struggle, anguish, pain, and often disappointment that are shared by Mexican American people in this society.

Both my parents were orphaned very young. My father was born in Michoacán, Mexico, and raised by an older sister in a very poor "rancho" that did not have running water, indoor plumbing, or electricity until the early 1960s. His poverty and rural existence denied him the opportunity of any formal education. Consequently, he taught himself to read and write in Spanish as a young adult. My father came to the United States at the age of fourteen, both to help send money to support his elder sister and three brothers and to fulfill his adolescent need for danger and excitement. He found life in the United States hard and unforgiving as an adult. He became an alcoholic, married young, and was widowed at thirty-five with three young boys. He married my mother, who was eighteen.

My mother was born in Mesa, Arizona, in the United States. She was orphaned by her mother at the age of six months, and orphaned by her father when she was six years old. Her old, rheumatoid, and arthritic paternal grandmother became her guardian. But, in all actuality, this tiny six-year-old became the caretaker and breadwinner. My mother and grandmother lived most of their lives in Mexico, suffering famine, drought, political unrest, and hunger. Since survival occupied all of my mother's energy, there was no time for a formal education, but somehow through desire and native intelligence, she taught herself to read and write in Spanish. At age eighteen she married my father, with hopes of finding a beginning, a new life, and most of all, being loved and cared for.

Family life became more and more difficult with the birth of each child.

My father continued to have longer and more frequent alcoholic binges, and consequently was less able to keep his various construction jobs as a bricklayer. All the while my mother was determined to keep her marriage and family intact. By 1948, my father's health, due to alcoholism, had deteriorated to the point that doctors warned him that he could die. He was frightened into sobriety for the rest of his life.

My father was convinced that his fate, as well as that of all Mexicans in America, was to be poor, landless, and subservient. Thus, he accepted his lot. My mother, on the other hand, had cloistered hopes and dreams that she began to project onto her children. For her generation and class, the optimum dream was a high school education. Every night she sat with each of us guiding us through our homework despite the fact that she did not know English and had little notion of what it was that we were doing. Two miracles began to emerge: the realization of the value of an education and my mother teaching herself to read, write in, and speak English. However, the abyss between the American culture and the Mexican culture proved too great.

Poverty, social class, and the lack of opportunity forced my mother to look to migrant work as a way to keep the family together and dare to dream of making enough money that eventually we could make a down payment on a house. My father left us in San Martin, California, choosing to live in a converted chicken coop (the "conversion" involved nothing more than throwing out the chickens), with no indoor plumbing, a wood-burning stove, and an icebox. He joined us three weeks later after realizing that we actually had made some money.

We did migrant work from 1950 to 1959, my siblings and I leaving school in May and returning in late October. Thus, school became a hardship; we were always behind, academically and socially. This took its toll. While we all did finish high school, I was the only one to go on.

My road to academia was not an easy one. While my mother valued school, she and my father perceived it as a luxury. And, as a luxury, it therefore was not work, so we were always expected to carry on our traditional roles and fulfill cultural expectations. What this meant for me was that I had to work in the home as well as outside the home in order to contribute to the well-being of the family. My parents were also suspicious of school and concerned that we would learn the loose ways of "Anglos," so I had to "sneak" literature that was not in the form of a textbook. My parents were also concerned that too much reading would hurt my brain and damage my eyes, so they would turn off the electricity at the fuse box at 11:00 p.m. Of course, you have to realize that because of house chores, part-time employment, and classes, 11:00 p.m. was when I often got around to studying. But necessity is the mother of invention; I learned to read under the covers with a flashlight, as they would check for light filtering from under the door.

School also posed its own obstacles. When I entered kindergarten, I spoke only Spanish, but the school went ahead and administered an IQ test, and a borderline mentally retarded label was promptly affixed. This hounded me until junior high school, when it occurred to someone that I was receiving excellent grades.

Junior high (Belvedere Junior High in East Los Angeles) was no fertile ground either; I had to fight tooth and nail to be allowed into the college track. Throughout this time no one, especially school counselors, spoke to me about college, but it was a notion that somehow floated in my head, placed there by these "bad Anglo" novels I had read.

Roosevelt High School in East Los Angeles was likewise no fountain of inspiration for Chicanos. There, my counselors, through their benevolence, advised me to take a vocational course—cosmetology. They felt that I would at least have a trade that I could support myself with, since my inability to finish high school and equal potential for an early pregnancy seemed clear. Fortunately, I did not take their advice. I took a college prep track, became a school council leader, joined the honor society, and earned many athletic awards (but no letter sweater, as we could not afford it).

I entered East Los Angeles Junior College in 1962 with a Roosevelt Alumni Scholarship, and then Helen Miller Bailey, PhD, "happened to me." She encouraged, cajoled, and inspired me and the few other Chicanos on campus. She helped me realize that my dream of a baccalaureate was more than a remote wish. During this time I received three honors, full scholarships to study a summer each in New York; Maryland/Washington, DC; and Puerto Rico. I received the Associate of Arts Degree in 1966 and received a Happy Latins Businessmen's Award. I transferred to California State University, Los Angeles (CSULA).

I attended CSULA from 1966 to 1967 and dropped out when I married. My family would not accept my marriage without my working full-time for at least one year and contributing financially to the household: "All this time in college and you go off and get married without our benefiting?" Under all this stress, my grades plummeted and I was forced to leave. In 1968, I married and resigned myself to working, helping put my husband through his senior year, and forgetting the silly notion of a baccalaureate. My husband graduated in 1969, turned to me, and said, "Now it's your turn." I was terrified and refused the idea. He persisted, dragged me to a school advisor, and got me reenrolled. I finished my senior year in 1970 with a 4.0. My baccalaureate was in Spanish Literature.

Through my husband's prodding, I applied to the Master's Program at UCLA's School of Social Welfare. To my surprise I was accepted! My parents' response was, "Haven't you already graduated?" The years 1971 to 1973 (like all of my college years) were politically active years for me. The struggle for minority enrollment and curriculum content required great commitment and energy. I received my master's in Social Welfare in 1973.

From 1973 to 1986 I worked for Los Angeles County in various departments, Mental Health, Health Services, and Social Services; my positions ranged from psychiatric social worker to administrator. My clinical work by choice has always been with Latinos in the barrios.

In 1977, I was blessed with the birth of a wonderful daughter. In addition to my academic and professional responsibilities, the responsibility of passing on to my daughter the beauty of her Latino culture, which is her birthright, is one I also take seriously.

In 1986 I joined the faculty of the UCLA School of Social Welfare as a Fieldwork Liaison. This was a very challenging experience, in that this school was struggling with issues of cross-cultural conflict in terms of both the student body and the faculty. I left in 1987 to begin my doctoral studies in Social Welfare in this same school.

While I would like to believe that my doctoral studies were undertaken in a supportive and nurturing environment, I found that my ethnicity and socioeconomic background continued to be pointed out as some sorrowful legacy to be overcome. This is why I am so determined to continue and succeed. My own personal aspirations aside, the statistical evidence is that the Latino population in the Southwest is the single fastest-growing ethnic group in the country. Without an infrastructure of professionals and leaders, this population, my people, will not participate in government, economic progress, social welfare benefits, educational opportunities (how many cosmetologists do we need?), and technological achievement, and will, rather than being represented, be overseen by a nonrepresentative minority.

I would like to be part of that leadership. I believe that I can bring my life experience, educational achievement, and maybe some inspiration to students who lack role models like my Helen Miller Bailey. Historically, the timing is critical for the development of Latino leaders and professionals—not only to bring our people into the American mainstream but also to revitalize this country in the face of military, economic, and technological challenges from the rest of the world.

Acknowledgments

For the first editor, Ruth Enid Zambrana, it has been close to three decades since a seedling idea emerged and this book journey began at UCLA. Early on in the 1970s, it seemed like obtaining a degree was filled with obstacles for underrepresented minority students. In particular, when I completed my own degree, I became a support person for a number of other Latino women and men who couldn't get through. Obviously, they were not lacking in intelligence and motivation, so I asked myself, "What is it?" One idea that became clear to me at that time was that I had embraced a fashionable myth: "If you have merit, you will be able to negotiate the dominant cultural systems." I soon realized that merit was not enough. The question emerged: what are the central factors that contribute to a Mexican American or historically underrepresented minority individual's ability to complete higher education?

Throughout my faculty career, I have experienced constant requests from underrepresented minority students to help them navigate the higher education system, and witnessed their lack of financial resources, lack of perceived support, and other obligations that precluded their ability to perform at their highest intellectual ability. From an institutional perspective, I continually struggled with the "other perspective," which views minorities as unprepared and incapable of fully participating in the mission of the university to strive for the highest academic excellence. They were viewed as "not very bright," as "affirmative action tokens," or as students to "put up with." Minority students were also perceived as hard to retain in the academic setting, and few faculty really understood the problem, except that perhaps "they were not that interested in education anyway." Thus, the impetus for this book emerged from my own personal observations over three decades of the need to empirically document the historical and contemporary experiences of Mexican American men and women and to describe their assets, strengths, and barriers in institutions of higher education. This book is timely, because it demonstrates vividly the strength and courage of Mexican Americans who have tackled the higher education system successfully. It is also timely because we are in a period of national retrenchment, which has rekindled racial tensions in this country.

The book has taken shape and taken on urgency over many decades. Thus, there are many individuals and organizations to acknowledge. First, I want to acknowledge funding from the UCLA Academic Senate Faculty Research Awards program (1985–1986) and the Institute of American Cultures Research Grant program, which supported the project from 1986 to 1990. Further, this project could not have been executed without the loyalty, dedication, and commitment of the respondents in my study of pioneering women, and of my graduate students in the UCLA Master's in Social Work program who collected the data—Yolie Flores (MSW, 1988), Brenda Francine Aquilar (MSW, 1986), and Evelyn Juanita Castro (MSW, 1986)—and all the other graduate Chicana students who contributed to this project. I also wish to express my deep appreciation to my two doctoral mentees, Dr. Sally Alonzo Bell and the late Dr. Claudia Dorrington (d. June 10, 2013), who were fiercely committed to making these data part of the national discourse through presentation and publication. I persisted throughout the decades in critically examining the literature and keeping abreast of Mexican American progress in education. In this effort three doctoral research assistants at the University of Maryland Consortium on Race, Gender and Ethnicity (CRGE) provided invaluable assistance: Tamyka Morant (College of Education), and Christina Perez and Dr. Ana Perez (Department of Women's Studies). I also wish to acknowledge the collaboration with Sylvia Hurtado, who was my co-thinking partner in helping to shape the book in ways that would be most valuable and relevant in the contemporary national higher education discourse, and with my coauthors, Drs. Rebeca Burciaga, Brianne Dávila, and Anthony De Jesús, from whom I also learned immensely about new constructs and new ways of thinking at the intersection of sociology, critical race theory, and education.

Unquestionably, the strong coordinating, administrative, and support skills of Dr. Laura Ann Logie, assistant director at CRGE, and her unwavering commitment were exceptionally instrumental in the timely completion of this project. Dr. Logie also engaged in research assistance and contributed to the dream of completing this book since her time as a graduate student. I am deeply grateful to her. Ms. Wendy Hall was a critical member of the team, and I also owe her a deep debt of gratitude. She engaged all the technical aspects of press requirements and produced a manuscript ready for copyediting. I also express a strong sense of gratitude to Ms. Theresa J. May, former editor in chief at the University of Texas Press, for her enthusiasm, support, and generosity with her time in shepherding the manuscript through all the initial phases of approval. I am deeply grateful to all the organizations, graduate students, and staff, especially at UCLA and the University of Maryland, that helped to fulfill the goal of bringing this book to fruition.

For the second editor, Sylvia Hurtado, understanding the experiences of Mexican American students was a driving force in my becoming a researcher in the first place. I think perhaps I sought to unpack my own experiences as a Chicana in a campus climate where the representation of both Chicanos and women was extremely low. In some ways, not that much has changed, and in our social and academic connections at every stage of our educational journey, we have much for which to be grateful. I would like to thank Frank Ayala, former assistant dean of students at Princeton University, for personal support and for making a space for and supporting the Chicano Caucus and other Latinas/os in college; Juan González, who gave me my first job at the Higher Education Research Institute, allowing me to prove my potential as a graduate student researcher; Sandy Astin for teaching me how to think like a researcher; and Walter Allen and Michael Olivas for supporting my career as a scholar. I want to thank my past and current graduate students for the knowledge and expertise they provide in moving important research forward so that it reaches the right audiences.

This book would not be possible without the involvement of the senior and next-generation Latina/o scholars featured here. Victor Sáenz, Luis Ponjuán, Nolan Cabrera, and Frances Contreras diverted their attention to focus their work on Mexican Americans specifically, and readily agreed to contribute. My colleague Adriana Ruiz Alvarado is a collaborator and sounding board about research and life in general. I also want to thank Patricia Gándara, a pioneer in the area of educational policy, reform, and equity, for writing the foreword in the midst of many other important deadlines. I also thank Ruth for walking into my office one day and suggesting that we coauthor on the topic of Mexican American education; working on this book has made me remember why I wanted to ask questions and find answers as a career.

Abbreviations

AACTE	American Association of Colleges for Teacher Education
ASU	Arizona State University
CIRP	Cooperative Institutional Research Program
DACA	Deferred Action for Childhood Arrivals
DREAM	Development, Relief, and Education of Alien Minors
ELLs	English language learners
ESEA	Elementary and Secondary Education Act
ESL	English as a Second Language
FACE	Fathers Active in Communities and Education
HEA	Higher Education Act
HERI	Higher Education Research Institute
HEW	US Department of Health, Education, and Welfare
HSGPA	High school grade-point average
HSIs	Hispanic-Serving Institutions
IFC	Inter-Fraternity Council
IPEDS	Integrated Postsecondary Education Data System
LULAC	League of United Latin American Citizens
MALDEF	Mexican American Legal Defense and Educational Fund
MEChA	Movimiento Estudiantil Chicano de Aztlán
MGC	Multicultural Greek Council
MMDLE	Multicontextual Model for Diverse Learning Environments
NAACP	National Association for the Advancement of Colored People
NAEP	National Assessment of Education Progress
NCES	National Center for Education Statistics
NCLB	No Child Left Behind

NHW	non-Hispanic White
NPSAS	National Postsecondary Student Aid Study
NWLC	National Women's Law Center
OMB	U.S. Office of Management and Budget
PEDS	Professional Education Data System
PIQE	Parent Institute for Quality Education
PWI	Predominantly White Institution
SES	Socioeconomic status
SHPE	Society for Hispanic Professional Engineers
STEM	Science, technology, engineering, and mathematics
TFS	The Freshman Survey
UCLA	University of California, Los Angeles
UM	University of Michigan
UMass	University of Massachusetts
UMD	University of Maryland
UNM	University of New Mexico
UW	University of Washington

PART I

SETTING THE CONTEXT

CHAPTER 1

Locked Doors, Closed Opportunities:
Who Holds the Magic Key?

RUTH ENID ZAMBRANA AND SYLVIA HURTADO

How racial barriers play in the experiences of Mexican Americans has been hotly debated. Some consider Mexican Americans similar to European Americans of a century ago that arrived in the United States with modest backgrounds but were eventually able to participate fully in society. In contrast, others argue that Mexican Americans have been racialized throughout U.S. history, and this limits their participation in society. The evidence of persistent educational disadvantages across generations and frequent reports of discrimination and stereotyping supports the racialization argument.
VILMA ORTIZ AND EDWARD TELLES, "RACIAL IDENTITY AND
RACIAL TREATMENT OF MEXICAN AMERICANS"

Renewed concern has been generated in the twenty-first century regarding the educational attainment of historically underrepresented groups[1] in institutions of higher learning. Mexican Americans are the most starkly underrepresented nationally with respect to access to and educational progress in institutions of higher education as students or tenure-track faculty.

The Obama administration has indicated a goal for the United States to once again become the highest-educated population in the world (Douglass 2010). The benefits of increased educational attainment serve to ensure not only economic equity but also a democratically engaged citizenry. College-educated individuals are less likely to end up in prison and more likely to vote in elections and contribute to the public good. However, this national goal cannot be achieved without attention to the large numbers of Mexican Americans who are enrolled in schools, seek access to higher education, and experience success in American colleges and universities.

For Mexican Americans, their growing numbers in higher education belie educational progress, as relative underrepresentation is perhaps most notable in regions where they are most largely concentrated, including California (Astin 1982; Hayes-Bautista 2004; Hurtado, Sáenz, Santos, and Cabrera 2008), and equity in attainments remains elusive. Among Mexican Americans/Chicanos,[2] a much-neglected population group in terms of research and policy, lower rates of retention in P–12 and in higher education pose challenges for educational administrators and personnel, and consequently pose serious issues for the progress of their communities.

Data indicate that Hispanics[3] will constitute 30 percent of the nation's population by the year 2050 (Ennis, Ríos-Vargas, and Albert 2011). Mexicans are by far the largest Hispanic-origin population in the United States, accounting for nearly two-thirds (64.6 percent) of the U.S. Hispanic population in 2011 (table 1.1) and 11 percent overall of the U.S. population (Gonzalez-Barrera and Lopez 2013).

The experiences of Mexican Americans warrant particular attention because they simultaneously are the largest of the Latino subgroups, have the longest history on American soil, and are the group with the lowest levels of educational attainment (Motel and Patten 2012). Before exploring the causes behind such adverse educational experiences, it is necessary to acknowledge that population growth is accompanied by greater heterogeneity in the Latino population. The percentage of Central Americans in the country has almost doubled since 2000, and close to 10 percent of the Latino population is now Puerto Rican (Ennis, Ríos-Vargas, and Albert 2011). Migration activity has also dispersed and has led to the establishment of new settlement locations in regions outside of those that already had large concentrations of Latinos (Flores and Chapa 2009), creating new precollege socialization contexts for students from different Latino subgroups. Moreover, the long history of settlement and migration since the colonial era suggests distinct variations in the characteristics of Mexican Americans today—some with many generations in the same region and others from more recent (im)migration experiences. For these reasons, it is important to disaggregate the Latino population by self-reported ethnic identity categories and other identity markers that intersect with ethnicity, such as race, class, and nativity, to increase our understanding of educational outcomes and experiences among Latino college students.

Recent changes in the demographic composition of the United States demonstrate that the population is becoming more diverse while staggering educational disparities grow more problematic. While investigators

Table 1.1. Statistical Portrait of Hispanics, Detailed Hispanic Origin: United States 2011

	Number	Percent
Mexican	33,539,187	64.6
Puerto Rican	4,916,250	9.5
All Other Spanish/Hispanic/Latino	2,373,901	4.6
Salvadoran	1,952,483	3.8
Cuban	1,888,772	3.6
Dominican	1,528,464	2.9
Guatemalan	1,215,730	2.3
Colombian	989,231	1.9
Honduran	702,394	1.4
Ecuadorian	644,863	1.2
Peruvian	556,386	1.1
Nicaraguan	395,376	0.8
Venezuelan	258,791	0.5
Argentinian	242,221	0.5
Panamanian	180,471	0.3
Chilean	148,532	0.3
Costa Rican	127,652	0.2
Bolivian	114,094	0.2
Uruguayan	60,764	0.1
Other Central American	40,001	0.1
Other South American	28,719	0.1
Paraguayan	22,876	<0.05
Total	51,927,158	100.0

Source: Pew Hispanic Center tabulations of 2011 American Community Survey (1% IPUMS).
Note: Hispanic populations are listed in descending order of population size; universe is 2011 Hispanic resident population. Hispanic origin is based on self-described ancestry, lineage, heritage, nationality group, or country of birth.

offer a number of different paradigms and theoretical explanations for why enrollment and retention in higher education remain low for Mexican American men and women, the historical and social contexts help to reveal the larger structural forces associated with these realities. All researchers conduct their studies within contexts that are bounded by historical time. The chapters in this book represent the educational trajectory experienced by Mexican Americans/Chicanos across a broad span of historical time frames.

All too often we omit history from empirical work in the disciplines of social science and education. Yet history informs and, more important, shapes group experiences and patterns, as well as helps us to assess progress or stagnation/retrogression. When examining educational trends and performance indicators, one can interpret data at face value and summarily determine that one group's status and/or performance is inferior to another's. On the other hand, one can interpret a group's performance as deeply embedded in a socially constructed historical context that includes educational legal policy, racialization, demographic changes, and structural inequality in access to resources. We seek to provide both depth and breadth to historical events by grounding this book in a historical record that has been mostly ignored. It is this historical narrative that provides an important context for a richer understanding of the higher education experiences of Mexican Americans. Historicity is a central anchor in intersectionality theorizing. Modes of historical incorporation are associated with the social and economic locations of underrepresented groups in U.S. society (Zambrana 2011). Our goal is to explore how historical events and consequent policy have depleted the accumulation of human capital over time and contributed to disinvestments in Mexican American peoples and their communities (MacDonald 2004).

Demographic Profile of Mexican Americans in the United States

A record 33.7 million Hispanics of Mexican origin resided in the United States in 2012 (Gonzalez-Barrera and Lopez 2013). This estimate includes 11.4 million immigrants born in Mexico and 22.3 million residents born in the United States who self-identified as Hispanics of Mexican origin. The size of the Mexican-origin population in the United States has risen dramatically over the past four decades as a result of one of the largest mass migrations in modern history. In 1970, fewer than 1 million Mexican immigrants lived in the United States. By 2000, that number had grown to 9.8 million, and by 2007 it reached a peak of 12.5 million (Pew Hispanic Research Center 2011). Since 2007 the Mexican-born population has experienced modest decline as the arrival of newer Mexican immigrants has slowed significantly (Passel, Cohn, and Gonzalez-Barrera 2012). Today, approximately 34 percent of Hispanics of Mexican origin were born in Mexico, while nearly two-thirds (66 percent) were born in the United States, half (52 percent) of whom have at least one immigrant parent.

The characteristics of Mexican immigrants have changed over the decades. Compared with 1990, Mexican immigrants in 2011 were less likely to be male, considerably older (median age of thirty-eight versus twenty-nine), and U.S.-resident for longer (71 percent had been in the United States for more than ten years, compared with 50 percent in 1990). On economic measures, Mexican immigrants have mixed outcomes or income patterns. Although median personal earnings increased by about $2,000 during the last two decades, the median household income of Mexican immigrants suffered a drop of more than $4,500. This reflects the effects of the recent economic recession that drove up unemployment rates in the nation, particularly among Mexican immigrants (Gonzalez-Barrera and Lopez 2013). More than half (52 percent) of Mexican Americans live in the West, mostly in California (36 percent), and another 35 percent live in the South, mostly in Texas (26 percent).

Of all Mexican immigrants residing in the United States in 2011, 53 percent were men and 47 percent women. In contrast, gender distributions included more females than males among the general U.S. native-born population and overall foreign-born immigrants in the United States (about 49 percent male and 51 percent female for both groups) (Stoney and Batalova 2013). The greatest difference between the two gender groups occurs in the first generation: 45 percent of Mexican immigrants are females, in contrast to 53 percent of non-Mexican immigrants. Only among a third of undetermined-generation Mexican Americans is the gender distribution similar to that of the non-Mexican-origin population (A. González 2001). Mexican immigrant women have lower workforce participation rates than men. Only 47 percent of Mexican immigrant women participated in the labor force in 2009–2010 (Brick, Challinor, and Rosenblum 2011). Significantly, second-generation Mexican American women are more likely to be employed (62 percent) than their first-generation counterparts (54 percent) (see table 1.2).

The Mexican American population tends to be younger than other racial and ethnic groups, with about 40 percent of the population under nineteen years of age. Educational trajectories of Mexican Americans are critically important to their future economic and social well-being. Mexican Americans have lower levels of education than other racial and ethnic groups and the Hispanic population overall. Compared to other Hispanic-origin groups, Mexican Americans are the least likely to have a bachelor's degree. Some 10 percent of Mexican Americans ages twenty-five and older compared with 14 percent of all U.S. Hispanics—and 19.9 percent of Blacks and 34 percent of non-Hispanic Whites—have obtained at least a bachelor's degree (U.S. Census Bureau 2012a). However,

Table 1.2. Demographic Profile of the Mexican American Population 2010

	Mexican Americans	U.S. Population	Hispanic/ Latino Population	Non-Hispanic Whites	Non-Hispanic Blacks
Reported in percentage unless otherwise indicated					
Gender					
Male	53.0	49.3	51.6	49.1	47.6
Female	47.0	50.7	48.4	50.9	52.4
Age median (in years)	25	37	27	42	33
Population by age					
<5 years	12.2	6.9	11.1	5.4	8.3
5 to 19 years	29.2	20.1	27.2	17.6	23.7
20–44 years	38.8	33.6	38.8	31.7	35.4
45–64 years	15.4	26.5	17.2	29.6	23.8
>65 years	4.5	12.8	5.7	15.7	8.7
Marital status					
Never married	40.0	31.1	40.0	26.2	46.8
Divorced/widowed/separated	13.6	18.1	14.7	18.7	21.2
Married	46.4	50.8	45.3	55.0	32.0
Nativity and citizenship status[1]					
Native	66.1	87.5	64.0	95.9	90.8
Foreign-born	33.9	12.5	36.0	4.1	9.2
Naturalized citizen	8.6	5.5	11.3	2.4	4.4
Not a citizen	25.4	7.0	24.7	1.7	4.7
Employment status[2]					
Employed	87.3	90.5	87.5	92.2	84.1
Unemployed	12.7	9.5	12.5	7.8	15.9
Median annual personal earnings[3]	$20,000	$29,000	$20,000	$32,000	$24,400
Family households[4]					
Two people	20.1	42.9	23.9	48.3	38.7
Three people	20.4	22.5	22.7	21.6	25.9
Four people	25.6	19.8	24.4	18.6	19.3
Five or more people	33.8	14.8	28.9	11.5	16.1
Poverty rate	28.0	15.9	25.9	10.9	27.9
Home ownership	48.1	65.0	46.5	74.0	43.0
Health insurance status					
Insured	67.5	83.7	69.3	88.3	79.2
Not insured	32.5	16.3	30.7	11.7	20.8

Source: U.S. Census Bureau (2012a).

[1] "Native" includes anyone who was a U.S. citizen or U.S. national at birth. Conversely, "foreign-born" includes anyone who was not a U.S. citizen or U.S. national at birth.

[2] Includes the civilian population 16 years and over.

[3] For all ages 16 and over with earnings.

[4] Households in which at least one member is related to the person who rents or owns the occupied housing unit.

native-born Mexican Americans are almost three times more likely to have earned a bachelor's degree than those born in Mexico—15 percent versus 6 percent, respectively (Gonzalez-Barrera and Lopez 2013). Table 1.3 displays educational attainment of populations twenty-five years of age and older by Hispanic subgroup and gender. Interesting patterns of more females earning bachelor's and advanced degrees are observed among all Hispanic-origin groups except Cubans.

In spite of a college degree, income inequities are observed by gender and racial/ethnic group. In 2007, the median income of male workers was generally higher than that of female workers for each race/ethnic group and at each educational level. Median income differed by race/ethnicity. For example, for those with at least a bachelor's degree, the median income was $71,000 for non-Hispanic White (NHW) males and $69,000 for Asian males, compared with $55,000 for Black males and $54,000 for Latino men. Among women, for those with at least a bachelor's degree, the median income was $54,000 for Asians, compared with $50,000 for Whites, $45,000 for Blacks, and $43,000 for Latino women (Aud, Fox, and KewalRamani 2010).

[handwritten marginalia: Women tend to graduate more]

The Magic Key

Why is this topic important? What do we know about Mexican American men and women and their educational journey through P–16?[4] The title of this book builds on the narrative of a first-generation college-bound Mexican American woman Zambrana interviewed in earlier research. When asked how her parents encouraged her to go to and stay in school, and what her inspiration was to persist and meet the challenges, she eloquently told the following story:

> My father took me to the fields where he worked and told me that I would not have to work in the fields if I stayed in school and studied hard. He said, "You will have the magic key, which is your education." He went on to explain to me that if I used the key I would not have to work in the job he worked at and [would] have a better life than he and my mom had. My father's story made me want to study more.

This belief, that their children can use education as a vehicle for social mobility, is inherent among Mexican American families. This value was common in the stories of three hundred college-educated women who

Table 1.3. Educational Attainment of the Population Age 25 Years and Over by Gender, Race, and Latino Subgroup 2011

	Total Hispanic	Mexican American	Puerto Rican	Cuban	Central American	South American	Non-Hispanic White	Non-Hispanic Black
Reported in percentage								
Both sexes	100							
Less than 9th grade	20.7	24.7	10.1	10.8	28.9	7.7	2.3	4.1
9th to 12th grade (no diploma)	15.0	17.0	13.4	7.4	16.5	6.8	5.3	11.4
High school graduate	29.8	29.7	32.2	32.2	28.6	28.8	30.9	34.8
Some college or associate degree	20.4	18.6	26.3	22.8	15.3	25.0	27.5	29.8
Bachelor's degree	10.0	7.3	12.3	18.0	7.8	21.6	21.6	13.2
Advanced degree	4.1	2.6	5.7	8.8	2.8	10.1	12.4	6.7
Male	100							
Less than 9th grade	20.7	24.2	10.9	9.4	30.1	7.0	2.5	4.1
9th to 12th grade (no diploma)	15.7	18.1	13.4	7.1	16.7	6.8	5.4	12.1
High school graduate	31.4	31.7	34.4	30.8	28.7	30.9	30.9	38.3
Some college or associate degree	19.1	17.0	24.9	22.5	14.8	25.1	26.2	27.6
Bachelor's degree	9.3	6.5	12.0	21.4	7.8	20.2	22.1	12.2
Advanced degree	3.8	2.4	4.4	8.7	2.0	10.0	12.9	5.8
Female	100							
Less than 9th grade	20.6	25.2	9.5	12.1	27.6	8.4	2.1	4.2
9th to 12th grade (no diploma)	14.2	15.9	13.4	7.7	16.4	6.9	5.2	10.9
High school graduate	28.2	27.6	30.3	33.6	28.5	26.7	30.9	32.0
Some college or associate degree	21.8	20.3	27.6	23.0	16.0	24.9	28.9	31.5
Bachelor's degree	10.8	8.2	12.5	14.7	7.8	23.0	21.2	14.0
Advanced degree	4.4	2.7	6.7	9.0	3.8	10.2	11.9	7.4

Source: U.S. Census Bureau (2012b).

were early pioneers (*pioneras*) in entry to higher education and subsequent academic and career positions. In other words, parents clearly understood the importance of digging preparatory roots to ensure economic stability and social mobility. The quote is symbolic of Mexican American parents' transmission of agency and aspirational capital to their children. It deeply disrupts the myths of lack of Mexican parental interest in and commitment to education for their children, and highlights the importance of resistance strategies among Mexican American youth who persist in spite of their challenges, particularly of racism, discrimination, and economic constraints.

Building on the work of early-career and senior scholars, we intend to create a counternarrative that reveals the forces and processes that have kept, and continue to keep, the body and soul of Mexican Americans together in the face of racism and inhumane treatment. Racial oppression is central to our focus on the dynamic interaction of social structure and human development (see Cobas, Duany, and Feagin 2009; Feagin and Cobas 2014; Telles and Ortiz 2008). Scholars have forged a new scholarly tradition to frame new thinking on the ways in which poverty, lack of educational attainment, and unemployment or underemployment in low-wage jobs can be attributed to the interplay of racism with ancestry, nativity, socioeconomic status, and gender.

We argue on multiple disciplinary fronts for the compelling need to produce knowledge regarding the racialized, ethnic, and gender-related educational experiences of Mexican American groups. First and foremost, Mexican Americans are the largest Latino subgroup (64.6 percent) and also continue to experience significant social and economic disadvantage at every stage of the life course. A vast amount of research has been conducted in the field of education that has, with few exceptions, focused on scenarios of failure, identifying individual and cultural attributes as predictors of low educational performance. In contrast, a more limited literature on scenarios of success or resilience exists that explores and describes how Mexican Americans and other Latinos have "beat the odds" (Portes and Fernández-Kelly 2008; Portes 2001). Emerging Mexican American and other Latino scholars forge new frontiers of knowledge production using counterstorytelling and an intersectional lens to redirect the field of educational inquiry to new ways of thinking about Mexican American educational engagement that can contribute to new policies and advance progress (Espino 2012, 2014; Ramírez 2013; Núñez 2014a, 2014b; Covarrubias 2011; Yosso 2005, 2006). In reviewing this corpus of work, an informed critic must ask how historical exclusionary practices, cultural stereotypes, bias and prejudice, and educational policies and practices have shaped past and contemporary patterns of educational performance, access to higher education, and long-term outcomes for Mexican Americans.

Purpose

The purposes of this book are multifold: to examine trends and generational patterns exhibited by Mexican American college students by historic era and by gender; to provide an alternative conceptual and analytic lens to broaden understanding of the factors that contribute to educational success among Mexican Americans; to present data from the civil rights era and contemporary era that provide a context for the lived experiences of Mexican Americans in P–16 educational pathways and for their perceptions of the college climate; and to proffer insights on emerging issues in the field of higher education and how policy and practice affect the educational attainment of Mexican Americans. We present new models and ways of thinking that can guide the next generation of research. An additional purpose of the book is to introduce the work of emerging Mexican American scholars who are generating new and promising knowledge pathways, devising critical lenses, and advancing scholarship about the changing circumstances that affect Mexican American men and women.

Throughout the book we provide multiple data sources, including historical archival data, national statistical trend data, and a mixed-methods empirical study of three hundred Mexican American women who graduated from college during the period 1960–1978, plus qualitative interviews and focus groups with contemporary Mexican American college students (2000–2010). In addition, several chapters rely on national data sources that provide a unique portrait of Mexican American men and women over time, particularly in their access to four-year institutions, building on the data archives from UCLA's Higher Education Research Institute (HERI) from 1971 to 2012. These sources pre-date federal data collection at the postsecondary level.

The questions that guide this book are sharply focused on what contributed to the persistence of Mexican American men and women in educational pathways; what strategies of resistance were/are used to overcome the odds through high school and on college campuses; what is keeping Mexican American men and women from entering higher education systems in larger numbers; and what barriers hinder completion of a college degree once they are in the higher education system. The vast amount of prior empirical work on Mexican Americans in the P–16 pipeline pinpoints culture as the culprit responsible for lower levels of participation in higher education institutions. Although systematic and unequal treatment of Mexican-origin students has been documented alongside their failures (Carter and Segura 1979; Haro 1983; MacDonald 2004), cultural factors are most often proffered as major determinants of these failures. Thus, the major focus of this book is to decenter the cultural-problem-oriented arguments and provide significant evidence of structural and normative climate issues and strategies of resistance.

The last three decades have advanced our understanding of the intersections of gender, race, ethnicity, nativity, and socioeconomic status (class), and their impact on access to higher education. Yet the reasons for lower participation of Mexican Americans are more complex in terms of structural inequality, which supersedes and frames gender and ethnic background/heritage.

The major premise that drives theorizing around these intersections is the importance of incorporating the historical forces that shaped access to higher education and their impact on the life course of individuals, families, and groups over generations (Barrera 1979; Almaguer 1994; Telles and Ortiz 2008). A broader intersectional lens, more fully developed in chapter 4, incorporates a historical and structural perspective to best capture those sociopolitical factors that provide an explanatory context for understanding contemporary patterns of educational performance and higher education completion. Drawing upon intersectional theorizing on how race, ethnicity, socioeconomic status (SES), and gender shape access to social and economic opportunity, this volume makes five explicit assumptions. First, historical incorporation and marginalized, unequal treatment have shaped the life circumstances and opportunities of Mexican American educational attainment. Second, race, ethnicity, SES, and gender are coconstitutive and mutually reinforcing dimensions that shape one's life chances, opportunities, and, in turn, experiences in the P–16 pipeline. Third, access to academic and technological resources predominantly limited by segregation is shaped simultaneously by the intersection of race, ethnicity, gender, and family SES, and is predictive of college entry, experiences in college, and college completion. Further, structural barriers, such as the increasingly resegregated conditions of urban majority/minority secondary schools, limit academic preparedness, and community colleges provide narrow pathways for four-year-college enrollment for Mexican Americans. Fourth, stereotypic representations of students as inferior permeate the attitudes of school personnel and contribute to perceptions of Mexican Americans as lacking the motivation or the ability to succeed academically (Cobas, Duany, and Feagin 2009). Last, institutional factors such as climate, policies, and attitudes of teachers and administrators in K–12 schools and colleges have contributed to the academic disengagement of Mexican American youth and adults, dampening educational expectations and aspirations for college entry and completion (Valenzuela 1999; Fuligni 2007; Solórzano and Ornelas 2002; Zambrana and MacDonald 2009).

Higher education is a principal pathway of access to the economic and opportunity structure, and of ensuring the right to claim one's benefits as a valuable citizen of U.S. society. History shows that education was denied to not only African American people but also Mexican American people, by means both de jure and de facto, by way of separate schools and academic departments with lower resources (Olivas 2006; MacDonald 2004). The social, political, and economic consequences of this denial came to a turbulent and public crisis during the decade of the 1960s. Important social movements, including the civil rights, health, and women's movements, spearheaded the convergence of social and political forces to address past inequities entrenched in institutionalized forms of discrimination and racism, which systemically ensured the exclusion of historically underrepresented groups[5] in systems of law, health, employment, and education.

Yet the educational agenda for Mexican Americans in the United States has remained relatively unchanged for decades, as evidenced by the ongoing White House Initiative on Educational Excellence for Hispanics (1990–present). The agenda calls for more access to educational institutions and increased educational opportunities at all educational levels. However, the empirical literature has both neglected the "lived experiences" of Mexican Americans and simultaneously stigmatized and stereotyped Mexican Americans for their outsider status (Zambrana 2011). The absence of historical accounts of access to higher education masks the historic patterns of racial inequality that have shaped past and current access to educational opportunity and completion of higher education. Access for Mexican Americans did not materialize until the late 1960s. One of the most compelling reasons why Mexican Americans have been unable to voice their socially driven intellectual concerns is the lack of academic voices, as they are underrepresented in major institutions of higher education as faculty, administrators, and students. In 2011, only 4 percent of full-time college faculty and 3 percent of full-time college professors were Hispanic (National Center for Education Statistics 2013). An important domain in assessing structural inequality in education is the construct of compositional diversity (Hurtado, Alvarez, Guillermo-Wann, Cuellar, and Arellano 2012). This notion underscores the representation of major institutional agents in the P–20 educational system. According to the American Association of Colleges for Teacher Education (AACTE) (2013), more than 80 percent of the bachelor's degrees in education awarded during the 2009–2010 school year were to non-Latino White students; only 4.2 percent were awarded to Latinos.

Data Sources: Drawing from the Voices of Pioneering Women and Contemporary Men and Women

We bring together and weave in data from the lives of pioneering women who completed college and beyond before 1980, and the voices of contemporary Mexican American men and women in college. Zambrana's interest in this topic was piqued in 1987, during a conference at Claremont Colleges, California. Participants at the conference highlighted the lack of information available on the experiences of Mexican-origin women, in contrast to the significant amount of literature available on the failures of Mexican-origin individuals, harping especially on stereotypic notions of the females (Zambrana 1987; A. A. Dávila 2001; Cruz 2002; Merskin 2007), particularly and startlingly their depiction as passive, traditional, and non–achievement oriented (Gutiérrez 2008). One of the pioneering study respondents clearly articulated the persistence of stereotypes as a major barrier to completion of higher education: "Yes, stereotypes that exist are harmful. Society doesn't expect Latino women to be task focused. They expect us to be more social, easily intimidated, and softer; not as goal oriented."

These respondents represent a particular historical cohort of women who were the beneficiaries of the educational and social gains made by the civil rights movement, *el movimiento*, and the women's movement. For all racial/ethnic groups, including Mexican-origin women, this time period (1960–1978) represents entry into the higher education system. They were the first generation of this historically disadvantaged Mexican American population to attain access to educational opportunities in significant numbers and experience social mobility.

Hurtado's research has focused on large-scale, national studies of the climate for Mexican Americans/Chicanos and other underrepresented groups in higher education, initiating studies that document trends in access and barriers to higher education completion. This focus has allowed an understanding of variability by diverse social identities (e.g., class, gender, and sexual orientation), institutional contexts, and historical differences among Mexican American college students. Still, only a handful of small studies speak to the resistance strategies of Mexican American students who successfully complete college degrees. Predominantly, the stories of success focus on foreign-born Latinos of Latin American origin and less on the generations of Mexican American students who labor and learn under the veil of historical myths of inferiority. Moreover, the nation's higher education data systems have not examined the ethnic groups that compose the Hispanic category. Only the Higher Education Research Institute (HERI) has consistently monitored ethnic group participation in its national surveys, revealing portraits of Mexican Americans relative to other Latino groups (Hurtado, Sáenz, Santos, and Cabrera 2008). The scholarship on Mexican American men and women remains marginalized and underrepresented in national data, and their lived experiences require insertion into dominant social science and education discourse.

The keen eyes of a number of scholars have provided intellectual challenges to narrow, culturally focused perspectives that exclude and fail to acknowledge the role of historical forces, and how existing institutional arrangements shape differential access by racial, gender, and ethnic groups. We wrote and edited this book on the premise that the educational progress of Mexican American women and men requires historical and structural contextualization incorporating broader and more nuanced analyses—access to resources and consequent social mobility are best explained within this contextualization.

Research and practice lend strong support to the need to discard cultural determinants as the sole explanatory lens for academic success and failure, and to investigate multiple social, familial, and institutional factors that jointly, across the life course, contribute to academic success, higher education completion, and career success. This book draws on an interdisciplinary, life course, and intersectional approach that offers an exhaustive and nuanced analysis to explain the educational trajectory of Mexican American women and men.

The major contribution of this book is its data-driven approach to extending theoretical insights into the Mexican American educational trajectory. To this end, the editors and contributors have collectively:

- Provided cogent insight into historical processes that have shaped and continue to shape the educational trajectories of Mexican American groups.
- Proffered counterarguments to cultural-deficit explanations (decentering) and highlighted the role of structural and historical dynamics.
- Built on prior work by extending the theorizing lens of the educational performance of Mexican Americans through the application of contemporary critical race theory, Chicana feminist theory, and intersectional and organizational climate studies to higher education.
- Emphasized the reproduction of inequality, and balanced individual and ethnic group agency to illustrate strategies of resistance, windows of opportunity, and the gaining of footholds in the educational progress of Mexican Americans.
- Used an assets-based approach to identify strengths and self-protective and self-enhancing mechanisms in the pursuit of educational progress.
- Conveyed student lived experiences to demonstrate their activism and advocacy throughout history, and their continuing vigilance toward inequality.

We share new findings that begin to create more dynamic views and new thinking about Mexican Americans, changing what we have previously thought, and in some cases reaffirming how little has changed. In other words, we engage in a process of recovering dynamic history and facts to inform Mexican American scholarship, its practitioners, other scholars, and allies, recognizing Chicano Studies as the vanguard of research and dissemination in the curriculum, and acknowledging that Mexican American scholarship is under attack (e.g., in Arizona's HB 2281 and A.R.S. §15-112).[6] This book resists suppression of vital knowledge that affirms and supports the voices of Mexican American men and women in their educational journey.

Organization of the Book

The book is divided into four sections: (1) setting the context, (2) conceptual understandings, (3) contemporary college experiences, and (4) implications for educational policy and future practices in P–16 pathways and beyond. The collection of chapters draws on the current work of scholars who are developing novel agendas around the education of Mexican Americans. Chapters stay true to period analyses and follow a chronological order, buttressed by unique sources of data to ensure that historicity is influencing interpretation—no other book offers this comprehensive approach toward understanding the Mexican American educational experience. We have designed four specific areas that deeply ground the life course experiences of Mexican American men and women who successfully completed higher education and postgraduate education degrees, and those who are currently enrolled in colleges and universities. Understanding the unique patterns and processes of the educational trajectory of a specific ethnic group—namely, Mexican Americans—demands examining historical features and the ways empirical data have been collected and used to explain patterns of educational underperformance. A significant body of knowledge has examined failure rather than success. Few studies have captured the educational milestones and moments that provide insight into how strategies of resistance were used to negotiate barriers to academic success. Our intent is to provide a richer, more comprehensive, yet nuanced, perspective on the varied structures associated with educational equity and the future progress of Mexican Americans.

Part I: Setting the Context

The first section addresses the historical incorporation of Mexican-origin peoples into the social and economic fabric of the United States, and provides trend analyses to illustrate the stages of progress in moving toward educational equity.

It is not widely known that different historical forces and prevailing ideologies have restricted access to mainstream educational institutions. Chapter 2, by Victoria-María MacDonald and Jason Rivera, offers an overview of the unique experiences of Mexican Americans from the 1600s to the present, indicating their attendance at alternative educational institutions throughout history. The chapter gives a historical narrative of more contemporary movements and the resulting investments in the education of Mexican Americans. Included is an account of the civil rights movement of the 1960s, which provided access to mainstream educational institutions, prompted philanthropic investments in the 1970s, and gave rise to the 1980s establishment of Hispanic-Serving Institutions (HSIs).

In chapter 3, key differences among Mexican Americans in their participation, from 1971 to 2012, in the transition from high school to college are examined. Sylvia Hurtado presents trend analyses to illustrate the modest increases of Mexican Americans who have entered institutions of higher learning and earned bachelor's degrees and beyond over the last several decades. This chapter provides additional context for the chapters that follow. One of the most significant changes has been the increase in the educational attainment of parents of Mexican American college freshmen (table 1.4). However, the contemporary enrollment patterns of Mexican Americans in four-year institutions are comparable to the enrollment patterns of non-Hispanic White students during the 1970s. Entering freshmen are attaining better course work in schools, at the same time that changes in access policies and aid are creating new barriers for the increasing numbers of students reaching college age—exacerbating financial concerns and constraining choices. This chapter refocuses on issues that will serve to broaden higher education opportunity for Mexican Americans, particularly at four-year institutions.

Part II: Conceptual Understandings

In this section authors present an interdisciplinary theorizing lens to foreground the multiple factors associated with the attainment of human capital in the United States and engage in in-depth analyses of major socialization mechanisms, such as family educational capital and K–12 school and higher education systems associated with the accumulation of educational advantage or disadvantage.

The study of the Mexican American educational experience has at its best been incomplete. In chapter 4, Ruth Enid Zambrana and Sylvia Hurtado offer intersectional theorizing[7] that integrates multiple domains of interdisciplinary knowledge to contextualize the life course experiences of Mexican American men and women who complete higher education. The authors examine and argue for an integrated and intersectional perspective that provides a comprehensive lens. This approach allows for an expanded understanding of the complex roles of family, socioeconomic status, and other institutional/structural factors associated with the completion of higher education. An analytic counterargument is made for viewing these factors not as individual attributes but as markers of power differentials and discrimination. This chapter critiques existing conventional theories in education that obfuscate the interplay of social class, gender, and social power in relationships between majority and minority groups, and maintains that an examination of structural and historical forces is key to analyzing the experiences of Mexican Americans. Moreover, it is necessary to expand our theoretical lens to include the larger

Table 1.4. Parental Education Levels among Latina/o Ethnic Groups, 1975–2006

	Mexican American/Chicano (%)				Puerto Rican (%)				Other Latina/o (%)	
	1975	1985	1995	2006	1975	1985	1995	2006	1995	2006
Father's education										
HS graduate or less	63.1	55.7	58.6	54.7	71.9	46.8	43.8	44.0	42.4	41.6
Some college or higher	16.8	17.9	19.0	18.4	9.4	12.8	21.1	19.6	17.1	17.9
College degree or higher	20.2	26.5	22.4	27.0	18.8	40.5	35.1	36.4	40.5	40.5
Mother's education										
HS graduate or less	70.9	62.4	61.8	53.6	78.7	49.8	42.4	35.2	44.8	37.7
Some college or higher	14.7	20.1	19.9	22.0	8.5	18.3	22.2	24.3	21.2	22.3
College degree or higher	14.5	17.6	18.3	24.5	12.8	31.9	35.4	40.5	34.0	40.1

Source: Hurtado, Sáenz, et al. (2008).

Note: The "Other Latina/o" category was first reported from the CIRP surveys in 1992 (see disaggregated tables in second half of report). "Postsecondary school other than college" and "Some college" were collapsed in "Some college or higher."

social and political macro forces, so as to appreciate how these forces have shaped the lives of Mexican Americans historically and continue to do so now.

In chapters 5 and 6, Ruth Zambrana and Rebeca Burciaga, and Ruth Zambrana, Anthony De Jesús, and Brianne A. Dávila, respectively, use data from a pioneering cohort of women (1960–late 1970s) to highlight successful features of the educational trajectory in both family and school life, and compare past and contemporary findings to assess whether the equity discourse around schools and families and their transmission of social capital has significantly changed.

Educational advantage is powerfully associated with social capital (resources and benefits received from class status networks). Chapter 5 synthesizes a significant body of work on the role that family capital has on educational performance, and challenges previous interpretations of the role of parental involvement in Mexican American families as being devoid of educational value. Zambrana and Burciaga argue that for understanding the role of the family in educational performance, outcomes must be understood within both the economic context of family resources and the structural inequality in school systems. Sufficient evidence confirms that family support, parents' expectations, and structural inequality, in confluence, shape the life course of Mexican American youth. Data are presented to demonstrate the role of the family in the success of Mexican American women, and how economic and social barriers are negotiated to ensure success. The unique theoretical contribution of this chapter is that it challenges existing epistemological assumptions regarding causality of academic underachievement by redefining culture as a dynamic and fluid group characteristic that interacts with structures of inequality.

In chapter 6, Zambrana, De Jesús, and Dávila theorize that the underachievement of Mexican Americans in school is largely due to inequality in schools, unevenly distributed resources, and differential treatment of students. In effect, power relations within the institutional structures of schools contribute to the disengagement and underachievement of Mexican American students in general, and Mexican American girls in particular. Important experiences that inspired and encouraged certain young girls are described, such as adult role models, which included teachers and extended family members, and ethnic-specific student organizations. In contrast, low expectations by teachers, lack of role models, scarcity of academic resources such as advanced placement (AP) classes, and low-resourced communities all work against the achievement of Mexican Americans and contribute to underperformance. These data provide insight into what worked for these women to move them forward, integrating more recent literature on youth in the K–12 pipeline and assessing the ways institutional practices have changed or remained the same. For the growing percentage of Mexican American youth who decide to go to college, issues of retention have taken center stage in the higher education literature.

Part III: Past and Contemporary College Experiences

In this section, past and current college experiences as facilitators or barriers are the focus. An extensive body of work is available on factors that promote college enrollment, retention, and graduation, but little has focused specifically on Mexican American men and women. Factors such as financial constraints; college adjustment in Predominantly White Institutions (PWIs); race, ethnic, and gender bias in college life; and academic difficulty due to inadequate preparation are principal areas of investigation.

In chapter 7, Nolan L. Cabrera and Sylvia Hurtado describe the experiences of Latino students at seven public universities, focusing on the voices of Mexican American/Chicana/o students. Specifically, it focuses on their perceptions of the campus racial climate, utilization of and reliance upon racial/ethnic-specific campus organizations, and perceptions of campus racial segregation. The participants tended to perceive a hostile campus racial climate and frequently relied upon Latino organizations. Despite the perception of high levels of campus racial segregation, the participants also had regular interactions across race/ethnicity. In chapter 8, Adriana Ruiz Alvarado and Sylvia Hurtado, using a relatively new database on Mexican American students' experiences with campus climate and with institutional barriers and support, examine key issues in areas associated with validation in the classroom, sense of belonging in college, and support for navigating college. They illustrate difficulties with climate, but also mediating processes that can be enhanced by faculty and staff in building inclusive classrooms and social environments.

Part IV: Implications for Educational Policy and Future Practices in P-16 Pathways and Beyond

Education is a critical asset for the social and economic integration of individuals into a highly industrialized society. Yet for Mexican Americans, educational progress has been slow in spite of the national focus on equity and disparity. The discourse of equity and diversity needs to be extended to ensure the inclusion of not only global citizens but also our domestic talent pool. In chapter 9, Victor B. Sáenz and Luis Ponjuán describe the educational future for Mexican American male students as being in a state of peril throughout the American education pipeline. This trend has been especially evident at the secondary and postsecondary levels in recent years. The question of why males are struggling to access and succeed in America's colleges is complex, and this chapter explores some of the social and educational factors, as well as familial and labor force demands, that may be driving this trend. Chapter 10 provides an overview of ways to implement a more informed perspective on Mexican Americans and integrate it into the policy arena, and suggests specific mechanisms that can be used to implement policy and engage in research. State and federal policy sectors have the potential to be an avenue for addressing the needs of this consistently expanding yet underserved segment of the student population. Frances Contreras examines some imperative policy issues for Mexican Americans and higher education. This chapter highlights select public policies that have served to support or hinder the progression of Mexican American/Chicano students through the P-16 pipeline. The emphasis in her data analyses is placed on policies related to college readiness, transition, and persistence. In particular, discussions of accountability policies (such as exit exams), inequitable curricular access, rising tuition costs, affirmative action policy, and shifts in financial aid policies are included to assess the effect that public policies have on Mexican American/Chicano student transition to and success in college. A specific set of policy recommendations is proposed to increase student preparedness and college completion.

Throughout the century, many important scholars in the history of education and educational policy have constructed a foundation upon which we can continue to build. These scholars have interpreted demographic data, explored histories, and conducted empirical research to explode common stereotypic notions of Mexican Americans (Vallejo 2012; Ortiz and Telles 2012; Solórzano and Delgado Bernal 2001; MacDonald 2004). Their studies have been vital sources of data that provide insights into how racial/ethnic oppression shapes life choices and limits the options of Mexican Americans (Telles and Ortiz 2008; Delgado Bernal, Elenes, Godinez, and Villenas 2006).

Research has provided frequently inadequate explanations for the ways in which the social system shapes Mexican American experiences through

CHAPTER 2

History's Prism in Education: A Spectrum of Legacies across Centuries of Mexican American Agency; Experience and Activism 1600s–2000s

VICTORIA-MARÍA MACDONALD AND JASON RIVERA

The fruit of secondary education is higher education, and in higher education Mexican-Americans are virtually unrepresented. A survey conducted at the University of California's Berkeley campus revealed that there were 231 Negroes and 76 Mexican-Americans in the student body of 26,083. At the Los Angeles campus there were 70 Mexican-Americans in an enrollment of 26,000.

FORD FOUNDATION, "A MEXICAN-AMERICAN
LEGAL DEFENSE AND EDUCATION FUND"

Competing ideologies over the purpose of U.S. public schools have always existed (Labaree 1997). Founding principles included democratic literacy for citizenship participation, preparation of a workforce for a strong economy, and the assimilation of immigrants into American culture and the English language (Kaestle 1983). For at least one population, Mexicans,[1] the promise of public education as a vehicle of upward mobility, realization of full citizenship, and constitutional safeguards under the Fourteenth Amendment has been largely a hollow promise. For example, as late as 1960, the median educational level of Mexican Americans in the Southwest was still only the eighth grade, four years behind their White, Black, and Asian counterparts there (Grebler, Moore, and Guzman 1970). Even after a civil rights revolution, desegregation, and decades of curricular, pedagogical, and federal school reforms designed to interrupt this educational disparity, Mexican American youth still underperform on key indicators of school achievement, such as standardized tests, high school completion, college entrance examinations, and graduation (Balfanz, Bridgeland, Moore, and Fox 2010; Orfield, Losen, Wald, and Swanson 2004; Perlmann 2010; Telles and Ortiz 2008; U.S. Department of Education 2010b). The role of institutional and structural racial discrimination in these outcomes, particularly evident in the shockingly high dropout rate, has remained virtually absent in the literature. In this chapter, we use the prism of history to chronicle across four centuries how agency and the persistent struggles waged to circumvent and challenge systemic obstacles facing Mexicans have been refracted through schooling. Although this legacy of resistance is rarely acknowledged in the literature, Mexican American leaders, parents, communities, and students have consistently fought for educational rights when they have been withheld or been inadequate. One of the consequences of this overlooked and still evolving history is its contribution to the characterization that Mexican Americans have not cared about, or resisted, subtractive educational practices. To the contrary, grassroots organizations and leaders have employed a wide variety of strategies, including the formation of women's and men's advocacy organizations, utilization of Mexican consuls to exert international pressure, and enrollment of children in alternative institutions such as Catholic, Protestant, or independent schools. Parents and students have marched, protested, penned petitions, litigated, and leveraged political and economic power for equitable policies and practices. In this chapter we bridge the past and present by deconstructing the deeply embedded historical ideologies, policies, and practices surrounding the role of Mexican Americans in U.S. society and education.

A historic reliance upon Mexican immigrants and their descendants as expendable and migratory labor and residential segregation enforced with racial covenants and other discriminatory practices virtually excluded Mexican American children from high school and then college in the first half of the twentieth century (Foley 1997; García and Yosso 2013; Montejano 2010; Ong and Rickles 2004; Ramos 2001; Romero and Fernandez 2012). Further, the absence of Mexicans as an officially recognized category in federal and state classifications until the 1970s,[2] and the dominance of scholarship that privileged a male, Anglocentric history, prolonged the invisibility of Mexicans as part of the U.S. narrative. In the 1970s, an increasing number of historians, mostly of Mexican descent, challenged this dehistoricization and began to document and revise an incomplete and often flawed history, an ongoing process each generation of historians continues.

The role of social class and education among Mexican Americans has been little discussed in historical monographs and is included here to provide a more comprehensive portrait of the range of educational access and achievement. Although a small slice, we have identified through primary (including oral histories) and secondary sources the presence of what we term a "Mexican American Talented Tenth." The term "Talented Tenth" is based upon W. E. B. DuBois's conception of an elite, highly educated leadership class in early-twentieth-century African American society (DuBois 1903). The middle- and upper-class Hispanics who were permitted access to the "White" schools (segregation was never monolithic), an estimated 10 percent of the pupils present in "White," "American," or "Anglo" public schools, were of Mexican descent. Factors such as lighter skin color (phenotype), "American" surname (typically based upon marriage with Anglos), higher economic or political status, and claims of pure Spanish ancestry permitted access and upward mobility in education and workplace. Acknowledgment of this privileged group is emerging in recent historical literature (Barajas 2012; García, Yosso, and Barajas 2012; Whitaker 2005). The legacies of this segmentation are revealed in the work of contemporary scholars documenting how phenotype can significantly impact access, equity, and upward mobility in educational and workplace settings (Hannon, DeFina, and Bruch 2013; Ortiz and Telles 2012; Telles and Murgia 1990). In contrast to this Mexican American Talented Tenth, the vast majority of Mexican Americans prior to the civil rights era were forced to actively resist White attempts to maintain dominance and suppress educational advancement (San Miguel, Jr. 1987, 2013). Our focus here is on the estimated 90 percent who underwent subtractive and discriminatory experiences in schooling (Valenzuela 1999), while acknowledging the contestation that expanded access to more inclusive levels across the twentieth century.

The strategies and practices of contestation from the Spanish colonial era forward unfold in nine chronological sections: (1) Legacies of *Casta*, Catholicism, and Differentiation of Educational Opportunity in the Spanish Colonial Era (1500s-1821) and Mexican Independence (1821-1848); (2) Schooling under Mexican Independence; (3) Conquest, Segregation, and Resistance (1848-1924); (4) Understanding Mexican Educational Marginalization and Segregation in the Era of Xenophobia, Eugenics, and Scientific Racism; (5) Incubating a Civil Rights Generation: K-20 (1920s-1950s); Tackling K-8 Segregation and Secondary School Exclusion; (6) World War II and Its Legacies: Stimulus for Latino Civil Rights; (7) Higher Education from the Progressive Era through World War II; (8) Fighting for Our Rights: Impact of the Chicano *Movimiento* on Education; and (9) Post–Civil Rights to the Present.

Legacies of *Casta*, Catholicism, and Differentiation of Educational Opportunity in the Spanish Colonial Era (1500s–1821) and Mexican Independence (1821–1848)

The educational origins and trajectory of Mexican Americans stem from broad preconquest cultural, religious (Catholic), legal, political, and economic values and factors that were adapted in the New World. One significant Iberian concept, *limpieza de sangre*, evolved into the *sistema de castas* (caste system)[3] in its adaptation through the transatlantic passage to New Spain racial hierarchical orders. *Limpieza de sangre* (cleansing of the blood, or purity) stemmed from the Crown's wish to ensure that only individuals free from Jewish or Muslim blood or heresy would occupy the highest tiers of Spanish society (Martínez 2008). In the Spanish American colonies, including what is now Mexico and the southwestern part of the United States, *limpieza de sangre* slowly transformed over the centuries of early conquest in the 1500s and 1600s into an increasingly rigid and hierarchical racialized *sistema de castas*. Widespread racial miscegenation based largely upon unions (forced and free) between Native American women and Spanish men occurred in the initial decades of conquest.[4] This multiracial society expanded considerably when African freed persons and slaves were also brought as laborers to New Spain. According to Martínez (2008), Peninsular Spanish values of honor, status, and prestige were thus mapped onto Spanish, Native American, and Black blood, "influencing colonial power relations, individual and group identities" (166–167). The classic authors on *castas*, Mörner (1967) and Lipschütz (1944), and contemporary scholars such as R. A. Gutiérrez (1991) and M. E. Martínez (2008), emphasize the enormous variety and fluctuation of terminology utilized across time and generations, and via political and religious legal rulings. Lipschütz, the Chilean sociologist who originally coined the term "pigmentocracy" in 1944, emphasized the link to Whiteness and status in the colonies among *casta*. Gutiérrez (1991) explained, "The whiter one's skin, the greater was one's claim to the honor and precedence Spaniards expected and received. The darker a person's skin, the closer one was presumed to be to the physical labor of slaves and tributary Indians" (198–199). The embedded colonial favoritism for light-skinned peoples continues to have implications for today's Mexican American students despite centuries of racial mixing (Ortiz and Telles 2012).

Broadly, one's legal and social status was calculated based upon the three principal racial groups present at the point of contact between Europeans and indigenous peoples in Latin America and Africa—Whites,

Native Americans, and Blacks. Additional factors that were calculated to determine rank included legitimacy through Catholic baptism versus illegitimate birth, and generational origin in New Spain. As Mörner (1967) points out, legal and social classifications were not parallel. European Spanish-born *peninsulares* (Spanish-born Spaniard or Mainland Spaniard) occupied the highest legal and social status. *Criollos* (creoles), individuals born in New Spain of pure Spanish parentage, represented the next level. Native Americans ranked next on the legal scale; but *mestizos*, mixed Spanish-Indian peoples, ranked socially immediately below *criollos*. Mestizos (and those in accompanying derivative categories based on race mixture) are the foremothers and forefathers of today's Mexicans and Mexican Americans. Contemporary scholars often utilize the term *mestizaje* in critical studies and with a different interpretation (Banks 2006), but it stems from these colonial origins. In some regions, Africans held higher social status than Native Americans based upon the prestige of their Spanish owners or urban occupation (Mörner 1967; M. E. Martínez 2008). African slaves, free Blacks, and *mulatos* (from forced and free unions between Africans, Native Americans, or Spaniards) legally remained at the lowest tier. The status of Afro-mestizos and other mixed-race individuals continued to decline in the seventeenth and eighteenth centuries in New Spain, drawing from centuries-old biases against Blackness under Moorish conquest (Sweet 1997).

During the first centuries of Spanish colonization, three general forms of schooling at the elementary level emerged, reflecting the ideologies of the *sistema de castas*: settlers' schools, mission schools for Native Americans, and nonformal education. The settlers' schools provided cultural and linguistic continuation for children of the highest *castas*. The Spanish language, Catholic religion, and culture were embedded throughout the curriculum and via the teachers' knowledge of Iberian customs and culture. Among the earliest schools of this era was a Franciscan classical school and preparatory seminary founded in 1606 in St. Augustine, Florida (MacDonald 2004).

Mission schooling for Native American/American Indian children and youth took place within the walls of the large network of Catholic missions established largely on land that became Texas and then California in the 1700s. Native American children were often placed in the missions under the tutelage of missionary priests at the ages of seven or eight, segregated by gender, and subjected to cultural and linguistic subtraction. Within the walls of the mission, students were taught the superiority of Catholicism to other forms of religion, the Spanish language, and a gendered curriculum based upon Spanish views of the Native Americans' roles as subordinated colonial workers. Girls placed under the strict care of a female guardian, and locked in at night in a nunnery for safekeeping against predatory Spanish soldiers, learned sewing, weaving, and cooking. Even as privileged women of high *casta* in Mexico City were denied advanced learning, much more so were Native American girls or mestizas. Boys learned agricultural, woodworking, and other utilitarian skills. Some priests selected the brightest boys for accelerated and classical education to enter the universities and become priests or leaders. However, in some cases, such as the famous Pueblo Revolt of 1680, the mestizos (sometimes called *ladinos*) utilized their educational skills to rebel against the colonizers. Higher education for this population was increasingly viewed negatively, as reflected in a Spanish colonial *dicho* (saying), "*Mestizo educado, mestizo colorado*" (an educated mestizo is a red devil) (Burns 1908; Gallegos 1992).

The remoteness of New Spain's lands and the limited mobility of soldiers and settlers resulted in sporadic access to formal education, particularly in the northern regions that comprise today's southwestern states of the United States. As a result, families often utilized what print culture was available in their homes, such as Catholic prayer books or legal documents, to impart literacy. For instance, Apolinaria Lorenzana, who later became a teacher, recorded, "When I was a young woman in California, I learned alone to write, using for this the books I saw, imitating the letters on whatever white paper I found discarded. Thus I succeed in learning enough to be make myself understood in writing" (Ruiz and Korrol 2005, 7).

The Spanish colonial period established a hierarchical link among education, racial purity, economic status, and curriculum whose legacies are still evident in modern form. Colonial-era privileging of European Whiteness in the *sistema de castas* translated into a classical educational curriculum to prepare a very small number of young men to enter the universities and become ruling colonizers or priests (Nieto-Phillips 2004). At the University of Mexico in Mexico City, admission was increasingly restricted to ensure the dominance and superiority of Spaniards. M. E. Martínez (2008) noted that in the 1630s the Crown "prohibited the matriculation of Indians, mulattos, and illegitimate mestizos and made them ineligible to hold university degrees" (152). Thus some mestizos, Native Americans, and other racial mixes at the lower levels of the *casta* system were blocked from full access to the educational landscape. Instead, many, if they were provided with schooling at all, received handicraft and skilled labor training.

Schooling under Mexican Independence

When Mexico declared independence from Spain in 1821, its many democratic reforms (such as eliminating the *casta* system) ironically narrowed the number of educational options that had been available under the colonial regime. The Mexican government's secularization of the missions greatly weakened the Catholic Church's role in schooling. Because they were lucrative financial entities, the new government withdrew subsidies for missions and ordered the return of Church-controlled lands to the public domain (Martinez and Alire 1999). The Republic of Mexico's 1824 Constitution stipulated public education and normal schools for teacher training, but the distance and isolation of the far northern territories from Mexico City, coupled with limited finances and political instability, compromised the ability of the fledgling nation to carry out its democratic educational reforms (Berger 1947). Some of the government's efforts were successful, however. In 1834, for example, the Mexican government sent twenty teachers to open schools in Alta California. Further, the Sisters of Charity ran the Young Ladies Seminary in San José, and in San Francisco, the Church of Saint Francisco School remained active (Menchaca 2001). Overall, an estimated one thousand children in California were being educated during the Mexican Independence Era in a variety of Catholic, private, and public schools (MacDonald 2004).

The Republic of Texas, established in 1836 and annexed to the United States in 1845, also created ambitious plans for public education, condemning the Republic of Mexico for its failure to establish public schools. However, economic difficulties and political instability also constrained Texas from carrying out a concrete or systematic public school system until much later under statehood. Overall, the brief period of Mexican independence revealed the persistence of Catholic schools as favored educational institutions and the beginning, at least on paper, of public support for secular schools in the new Republic of Mexico and the short-lived Republic of Texas. The long intertwined history of Catholicism and schooling would clash with the Protestant Anglo-based public education introduced when the southwestern territories were annexed to the United States through the Mexican American War (1846–1848) and the Gadsden Purchase (1853–1854). However, the limited funds available for public schooling during Mexican independence gave Anglo settlers coming from the eastern part of the country the false impression that education was little valued. Cultural conflict between the arriving Anglo-Protestant settlers and new Mexican Americans surfaced in muted terms during the 1830s and 1840s, but escalated during the Mexican American War and into the 1850s and beyond. Anglos arriving in Texas and California brought with them negative stereotypes of the character, religion, and racial composition of Mexicans. In general, Mexicans were disparaged as "greasers," immoral, sexually degenerate, indolent, "mongrels," "papists," and potentially subversive political elements during times of international discord (De León 1983; Horsman 1981). These beliefs, coupled with an era of extreme anti-Catholicism in the United States, contributed to the marginalization and dismissal of alternative forms of education for Mexicans in favor of the Anglo-Saxon Protestant, middle-class public school reform movement of the mid-nineteenth century (MacDonald 2001). In this chapter, education is contextualized and woven into the larger narrative of Mexican American history. One of the unsettled issues across this history is the differential treatment accorded to a small group of "honorary white" (López 1997) Mexicans by the dominant White population. MacDonald (2011b) has named this group a "Mexican American Talented Tenth," documenting that Mexican segregated schools were always partially integrated by students from this population and from those whose parents actively resisted segregation.

✕ Conquest, Segregation, and Resistance (1848–1924)

Beginning in the mid-nineteenth century, the United States began an era of expansionism, supported ideologically by the notion of "Manifest Destiny"—that the spread from the Atlantic to Pacific coasts of the United States was God-ordained for Anglo Protestants. This ideology, linked to the desire for more land, ultimately provided justification for the Mexican American War of 1846–1848. As a result of the war, the United States gained more than one-half million square miles of land, which, along with 300,000 square miles acquired in the Gadsden Purchase of 1853, increased U.S. territories to include the current states of Arizona, California, Colorado, New Mexico, Nevada, and Utah, in addition to the Texas annexation in 1845.

The defeat of Mexico, ratified in the 1848 Treaty of Guadalupe

Hidalgo, rendered Mexicans as colonized peoples on their former land. Articles VIII and IX of the Treaty articulated the rights and responsibilities of the approximately 100,000 Mexicans who had been conquered and were given one year to choose to become U.S. citizens or remain Mexican nationals. The terms of the treaty stipulated that Mexicans would be lodged in the United States' "White" race category. According to Menchaca (2001), many individuals who were Native American/Spanish mestizos chose "White" to avoid the discriminatory American "Indian" classification. As territories entered U.S. statehood, their constitutions largely granted suffrage only to Mexicans considered of the White race. For instance, California enfranchised "every white, male citizen of Mexico who shall have elected to become a citizen of the U.S." (del Castillo 1990, 66). The technical legal classification of "White," however, never matched the social treatment of Mexicans. According to Gómez (2007), "off-white" captured the new social reality of Mexicans in the American racialized hierarchy, residing somewhere below Anglo Protestant Whites and above Blacks and Native Americans. Although the Republic of Mexico had technically ended the *sistema de castas* as part of its independence and the adoption of a democratic ideology, Mexicans, in their new jurisdiction, found themselves once again subject to state classification based upon race and ethnicity.

The status of Mexicans remaining north of the Rio Grande thus decreased rapidly through a series of formal and nonformal policies and practices, including the devastating loss of land by families who held Spanish land grants but could not prove ownership through titles. The U.S. Congress's passage of the California Land Act of 1851 and the subsequent 1862 Homestead Act granted license for squatters to secure lands and resulted in the reduction of many older Mexican families to bankruptcy as a result of protracted legal battles to preserve their land (Pitt 1966). Important distinctions existed, however, among the new territories in the power of Mexican-descent communities to hold on to their political and economic power.

The tangible aspects of the American conquest codified in citizenship and property law represented only some of the dramatic changes for Mexicans in the nineteenth-century Southwest. Educational policies during this era varied depending upon the local economic and political power of the Mexican-descent population. Texas is an illustrative example of shifting educational conditions during the nineteenth century as Anglos garnered power and increasingly imposed educational policies inimical to Mexican interests. As a republic (1836–1845), Texas had attempted a public school system, with little success. In 1854, the state established a permanent system of common public schools. Only two years later, in 1856, and again in 1858 (Eby 1918; Gammel 1898), new constitutional amendments were added stipulating that "no school shall be entitled to the [monetary] benefits of this act unless the English language is principally taught therein" (Eby 1918, 336). Targeted at Mexicans, the policy to eliminate the Spanish language and, by proxy, culture marked the beginning of a continuing and persistent practice to this day to assimilate children through the elimination of their familial language and to create monolingual English-speaking citizens. Mexican parents with resources responded to this act and the virulent anti-Catholic sentiments that Protestant Anglo settlers brought to the Southwest by enrolling their children in Catholic schools or establishing their own independent private schools (San Miguel, Jr., and Valencia 1998).

According to San Miguel, Jr. (2013), Catholic schools were popular among Mexicans in the Southwest for three reasons. First, Catholic schooling was seen as a form of preserving their identity because of the closely intertwined nature of religion and Mexican culture. Second, the Catholic Church permitted the speaking of Spanish in school. Thus, instead of imposing culturally "subtractive" measures upon Mexican children, defined by San Miguel, Jr., and Valencia (1998) as ones that "inculcate[d] American ways, but also . . . discourage[d] the maintenance of immigrant and minority group cultures" (358), Catholic teachers permitted "additive" measures, such as bilingual or trilingual language instruction. Third, unlike coeducational U.S. public schools, Catholic schools were largely single-sex, an important culturally congruent practice.

Between 1848 and 1900, dozens of Catholic schools for boys and girls were established in Texas (MacDonald 2004). Female teaching orders that came to Texas from Europe in the nineteenth century played a pivotal role in spreading education, particularly for Mexican girls and young women. In general, European religious orders brought with them linguistic fluency and a cultural acceptance of multilingualism, in contrast to the monolingual English Anglo-Saxon culture. The promulgation and acceptance of linguistic diversity bolstered a positive academic environment. For instance, the Ursuline Academy of San Antonio, founded in 1851, taught traditional academic subjects, and all students were required to learn Spanish, English, and French, "not only by theory, but by practice: the pupils were required to converse in these languages in the respective classes" (Castañeda 1958, 292). The Incarnate Word in Brownsville, Texas, was founded in 1853 for girls between the ages of five and eighteen.

While many of these schools for girls undoubtedly included the ornamental arts of sewing, music, and etiquette, as could be found in the southern and northern U.S. states, they provided solid academic educational opportunities. Tuition requirements, however, did slant student enrollment toward an upper-income population, contributing to the building of a Mexican American Talented Tenth (MacDonald 2011b). For instance, boarding students at the Ursuline Academy were reputed to come from the wealthier class of Mexicans, but the sisters also opened a "free day school principally for the benefit of Mexican children" (Castañeda 1958, 292). Simultaneously, Texas Bishop Odin also enthusiastically championed Catholic education for boys.[5]

Protestant denominations, particularly the Presbyterian Church, also saw Texas specifically and the Southwest in general as a missionary enterprise. Tejanos enrolled their children in Protestant schools for several reasons: lack of alternatives (particularly during the frontier decades), perceived advantages for their children learning English from Anglo teachers, or anticlerical sentiments toward the Catholic Church that dissuaded them from sending their children to Catholic schools (Yohn 1995).

During the first years of statehood in California, 1850–1855, Catholic schools continued to educate Mexican Americans and were often provided with public funds. The Spanish language was also permitted, and numerous public schools were bilingual. However, the 1855 revised school law removed public funds for religious schools, and English was ordained as the only language of instruction in the California public schools (MacDonald 2004). During the immediate postwar decades, fluidity characterized the status of Mexicans and their educational experiences. Elite families from the preconquest era, identified as *Californios*, *Tejanos*, and, in New Mexico and Colorado, *Hispanos*, or broadly *Los Ricos* (the wealthy/rich ones), had been accorded a special status with Anglo settlers due to class, adopted nomenclature of "Spanish Americans" versus Mexicans, intermarriage with Anglo settlers, and phenotype. As these families experienced downward social mobility, captured poignantly, albeit romantically, in María Ampara Ruiz de Burton's classic novel *The Squatter and the Don*, the power to control public educational policies and practices decreased. As the next section illuminates, waves of new immigrants from Mexico arrived during a complex and long period of international strife between the United States and Mexico, encompassing the Mexican Revolution of 1910, U.S. involvement in Mexican politics, and concern over the country's alliance with Germany during World War I to invade the United States and retake Mexican lands, as proposed in the famous 1917 Zimmerman Telegram between Germany and Mexico. One impact of these pro-tracted struggles was increased hostility toward Mexicans residing in the United States, whether citizens or new immigrants. As in Texas, a small number of Mexicans initially controlled a considerable portion of the land and political power in California at the time of American conquest, but rapidly experienced downward mobility and numerical marginalization, particularly with the draw of the California Gold Rush (Pitt 1966).

Understanding Mexican Educational Marginalization and Segregation in the Era of Xenophobia, Eugenics, and Scientific Racism

The numerically largest and most diverse immigration surge in U.S. his-tory (roughly 1880–1920) had almost finished when the Mexican Revo-lution of 1910 triggered the flight of hundreds of thousands of Mexicans north to the United States. The sheer number of Mexican newcomers in a short period of time and their rural, working-class backgrounds fueled a reactionary nativist movement against immigrants (Ngai 2005). The Johnson-Reed Immigration Act of 1924, including the National Origins Act and Asian Exclusion Act, did not, however, exclude peoples from the American continent, including Mexico and Canada, an exception that catered to the needs of agribusiness and manufacturers. Immigra-tion restrictionists angrily denounced this clause of the immigration act (R. A. Gutiérrez 1991). The rise of so-called scientific evidence also bol-stered Anglo attitudes embracing the alleged genetic inferiority of Mexi-cans and other non-White populations. The impact of these macro events and the continued view of Mexicans as transitory migrant and agricultural or manufacturing laborers—rather than future citizens—promoted fur-ther marginalization and increased segregation of children into "Mexi-can" schools.

African American students in the eleven former Confederate States of the South were placed in de jure segregated schooling based upon strict racial classification grounded in the "one drop" of Black blood rule. In contrast, Mexican American children were placed in "Mexican" or "Americanization" classrooms or entirely separate schools as a result of "custom" or "color of the law" beginning in the early 1900s. However, in the five southwestern states where Mexicans predominated (Texas, Cali-fornia, Arizona, Colorado, and New Mexico), statutes or constitutional measures requiring or permitting the segregation of Mexican Americans did not exist (Donato and Hanson 2012). As Sánchez and Strickland described in 1948, the decision to place students in a White or Mexican school was "arbitrary and capricious" (22). The practice of segregating Mexican American pupils, or what Valencia (2008) calls the "no-statute" phenomenon, was conducted outside of the legal structures, rendering its identification and demolition particularly difficult for litigators. Tuck (1946) observed in the 1940s how the extralegal nature of these practices posed a difficult challenge: "Rather than having the job of battering down a wall, the Mexican-American finds himself entangled in a spider web, whose outlines are difficult to see but whose clinging, silken strands hold tight" (198).

Anglo administrators justified this practice because of English-language deficiencies, objections from White parents to having their children schooled with allegedly "dirty and diseased" Mexicans, and other pretenses (San Miguel, Jr. 1987). Underlying these rationales was an ideology among Whites that most Mexican children belonged to a different and lower class, in a system based upon the political economy of southwestern agriculture (Montejano 2010), and should be excluded from the American polity (Ngai 2005). Nomenclature of schools is telling in this regard. Schools in Texas and California with mostly White children were called "American," while children of Spanish or Mexican descent were segregated into "Mexican" schools. Although historians have recently emphasized that a select number of Mexican children were always permitted access to de facto segregated "Whites only" elementary spaces in the pre-civil rights era, restrictions became more severe in high schools, which enrolled and graduated fewer Mexican children.

The Aoy Preparatory School in El Paso, Texas, is illustrative of the transition, in the late nineteenth and early twentieth centuries, from parent-created grassroots bilingual schools to racialized and segregated "Mexican" public schools. Mexican parents founded the Aoy School in 1887 and hired Olives Villanueva Aoy (1823–1895) as a bilingual private school-teacher for Spanish-speaking pupils. The next year, the El Paso, Texas, public school board incorporated the school into its system, retaining Mr. Aoy and hiring his two English-speaking assistants (San Miguel, Jr. 1987). However, by 1905, Mexican children were mandatorily separated by language and race: "All Spanish speaking pupils in the city who live west of Austin Street will report at the Aoy School, corner of 7th and Campbell, English speaking Mexican children will attend the school of the district in which they live" (*Report of the Public Schools of El Paso, Texas 1905–1906*, 35). Increasingly, students in Mexican schools were required to spend three years in the first grade until they reached English proficiency. This discriminatory system, which consigned non-English-proficient Mexican children to unnecessary grade repetition, was utilized throughout the Southwest (G. Gonzalez 1990; Wollenberg 1976). Furthermore, this delaying tactic, called "retardation," coupled with the use of discriminatory intelligence testing, resulted in many students reaching the end of compulsory school attendance and going to work before they could attend "White" junior or senior high schools (MacDonald 2011b).

During the first four decades of the twentieth century, Mexicans in the United States experienced increased racialization, hostility, and segregation. In the Progressive Era, in what were initially characterized as "Americanization" schools or classrooms, several factors, including demands by White parents and communities, led to widespread segregation of Mexican children. The Mexican schools in this early era were almost entirely taught by White English-speaking teachers, and students were punished for speaking Spanish. Few children continued on to high school, and in many elementary schools, administrators added sixth, seventh, and eighth grades within the building rather than permit students to attend the "White" junior high school. As discussed in the next sections, parents and communities fought back against marginalization of their children's educational opportunities in underresourced schools, racial segregation, and exclusion from secondary education (San Miguel, Jr. 2013).

Incubating a Civil Rights Generation: K–20 (1920s–1950s); Tackling K–8 Segregation and Secondary School Exclusion

By the 1920s, children born in the United States, largely to parents who had fled the Mexican Revolution, were coming of age. Through parental vigilance, their own persistence, and activism, this group, dubbed the "Mexican American Generation," accrued sufficient educational, political, and economic power to push for their civil rights (M. García 1989; G. J. Sánchez 1995). The Treaty of Guadalupe Hidalgo's stipulation that Mexicans belonged to the "White" race drove the overall legal strategy to fight segregation. Scholars such as Foley (1997) have argued that utilizing Whiteness as a basis for racial integration represented a "Faustian Pact," which would impede Mexicans in their long-term civil rights quest. Other scholars, such as Blanton (2006), have framed this "whiteness strategy" more sympathetically in terms of the limited pre-1950s political and economic capital of Mexican Americans. For example, during the Great Depression of the 1930s, approximately one-half million Mexicans were repatriated, including countless U.S. citizens who would thereby be separated from their families (Ngai 2005). Regardless of the scholarly debates, the record of Mexican school segregation and desegregation has until the last decade been largely overlooked in the history of U.S. educational discrimination.

The denigration and racialization of Mexicans in the pre-1930 decades contributed to the rapid response of school districts to White parental pressure for separate buildings or classrooms. In some cases, students were diverted to basements, or buildings no longer used for White students. Mexican American parents utilized the assistance of Mexican consuls, lawyers, and community organizations to contest the placement of their children into these largely inequitable, poorly resourced, and educationally deficient "Mexican schools." Furthermore, except for the "Chosen Few," students were blocked from continuing on to the "White"-identified junior or senior high schools (MacDonald 2011b).

Emerging work documents how, prior to the use of litigation, parents of Mexican nationality utilized the Mexican consuls to reject and contest U.S. society's ideological construction of a Mexican race barred from full participation in the nation's public institutions. Between 1912 and 1931, U.S. State Department records reveal, parents filed almost a dozen complaints concerning the racial segregation of their legally White children into Mexican or Black public schools and their exclusion from secondary schools. Guzmán and MacDonald (2013) argue that despite sustained protests from parents that reached all the way to the U.S. secretary of state, governors, ambassadors, and attorney generals, and from there down to the local level via the consuls, most students remained segregated, excluded, and/or subject to physical and verbal harassment and hazing. The limits of diplomacy in these situations indicate that despite transnational political pressures, embedded notions of the non-White racial identity and inferiority of Mexicans prevented acknowledgment of their legal White racial status and blocked full exercise of their constitutional rights.

In the earliest known legal case over these rights, *Adolpho Romo v. William E. Laird et al.* (1925), a Mexican American parent sued the Phoenix, Arizona, school district for placing his children in the Tempe Normal Training School with student teachers instead of fully trained teachers. Judge Joseph S. Jenckes agreed that the board's practice of essentially segregating Mexican students rather than giving them opportunities equivalent to those of other children to attend the regular public schools violated the students' rights, and he ruled for the plaintiffs. However, the precedents established by *Romo v. Laird* and two subsequent desegregation cases were limited by jurisdiction to only the level of the school/district/county/ state named in the suit (L. K. Muñoz 2013).

A significant lever for Mexican American advocacy and reform during this era was the League of United Latin American Citizens (LULAC), founded in 1929 in Corpus Christi, Texas. LULAC supported several school desegregation cases decades before the *Brown v. Board of Education* decision of 1954. The first case LULAC supported, *Del Rio Independent School District v. Salvatierra* (1930), alleged that children in this south Texas community were unconstitutionally segregated by the "color of law" and that the construction of another "White" school, while maintaining Mexican American children on the other side of town, would ensure further segregation. Although Salvatierra won at the district court, the Texas Court of Civil Appeals overturned the decision. Judge J. Smith, presiding, basing his decision on the right of a school board to utilize "educational reasons," in this case, the language needs of Mexican children, permitted the school district to continue its construction of another school far from the Mexican American community (Valencia 2008). Utilizing the "special language needs" of Spanish-speaking children as a premise for segregation in the lower grades was a practice common throughout the Southwest.

In *Roberto Alvarez v. Lemon Grove School District* (1931), the first successful Mexican American school desegregation case, pursued through a class action suit, parents fought the attempt of a California school board to move Mexican students into a Mexican residentially segregated area and utilize a building locally called La Caballeriza (the stable) because of its use for animals. Parents of the schoolchildren denied entrance to the regular schoolhouse formed a committee, Comité de Vecinos de Lemon Grove (Lemon Grove Neighbors Committee), hired lawyers, and successfully fought the case. San Diego Superior Court judge Claude Chambers ruled that school boards had no right under California law to segregate Mexican American children. Contrary to the school board's premise that the segregated school would provide opportunities for English language learning and Americanization, the judge reasoned that these goals could not be accomplished without integration among White non-Spanish-speaking pupils (Alvarez 1986; Valencia 2008).

The lawsuits of the 1920s and early 1930s, while not all fully successful, demonstrated the esteem in which education was held among Mexican Americans and their willingness to challenge the dominant community's resistance to their social acceptance and legal "White" status in a racialized U.S. society. To date, historians have not uncovered school desegregation lawsuits during the 1930s Great Depression, when job scarcity and repatriation movements most likely discouraged resistance. Each of these early pre-Depression cases had only local jurisdiction; however, they represented the inception of the use of litigation among Mexican Americans as a strategy for equitable schooling opportunities.

World War II and Its Legacies: Stimulus for Latino Civil Rights

The harsh Depression era slowly vanished with the onset of World War II and the creation of jobs in military defense industries. Mexican Americans—volunteers and draftees—were racially integrated into the military forces and numbered an estimated 500,000 (Rivas-Rodriguez 2005; del Castillo 2008). The global experiences of Mexican American soldiers serving abroad and fighting alongside White citizens outside of the de facto segregated Southwest stimulated a nascent civil rights movement. Veterans who had heroically risked their lives and seen family members and friends sacrifice theirs for the larger cause of maintaining democracy abroad recognized the hypocrisy of homeland discrimination. Furthermore, the U.S. government recognized the risk of alienating Mexico, its neighbor on the southern border, which might ally with fascist or other totalitarian regimes. Programs and policies such as the Good Neighbor Policy, at the federal level, and state-level commissions were created to curb anti-Mexican discrimination, particularly in the manufacturing industries, but also other arenas (Bernstein 2011; Foley 2010; Gugliemo 2006). Furthermore, Mexican American veterans were imbued with a renewed sense of their rights as part of the U.S. body politic and became more proactive in securing improved access to constitutionally protected rights and governmental services. Litigation and grassroots community organizing into advocacy organizations such as the GI Forum positively impacted the upward mobility of Mexican Americans through education.

The first post–World War II victory for Mexican Americans in education was a constitutional challenge to school segregation. A class action suit, *Mendez et al. v. Westminster School District* (1946), supported on appeal by an amicus curiae brief from the National Association for the Advancement of Colored People (NAACP), was filed on behalf of more than five thousand students in this California district. Of particular significance was the judge's finding that the students' rights should be protected under the Equal Protection Clause of the Fourteenth Amendment (Valencia 2005). The State of California's initial requirement in 1863 of separate schools for "Negro, Mongolian, and Indian children" (Wollenberg

1976, 13) left nebulous the status of Mexican children. The segregation of Black, Asian, and Native American children was eventually removed from the California statutes; Mexicans, however, continued to be segregated without a code stipulating inclusion in or exclusion from White schools. In *Mendez et al.* the judge finally ruled that Mexicans were White and ordered them integrated into the "American" schools. Furthermore, the judge also ruled that separating Spanish-speaking children from their English-speaking classmates denied them access to learning the English language. In particular, Judge McCormick invoked the democratic spirit of the post–World War II era, arguing that separating children "foster[s] antagonisms in the children and suggest[s] inferiority among them where none exists," and that, instead, "commingling of the entire student body instills and develops a common cultural attitude among the schoolchildren which is imperative for the perpetuation of American institutions and ideals" (*Mendez et al. v. Westminster School District* [1946]).

Encouraged by the success of *Mendez et al.*, activists in Texas backed the class action lawsuit of six-year-old Minerva Delgado. In *Delgado v. Bastrop Independent School District* (1948), plaintiffs claimed that Mexican-descent students were routinely denied entrance to so-called White schools. One of the key figures involved in this case was George Isidore Sánchez, a prolific and exceptional Mexican American educator, activist, and leader of the era. One of the key points that lawyer Gus García had to demonstrate in court was that segregating Mexican children, although not enacted by statute, was a custom and could be tried in a court of law. Plaintiffs were successful in *Delgado*, although the judge ruled that Spanish-speaking children could still be segregated in the first grade for pedagogical reasons. Although neither *Mendez et al.* nor *Delgado* overturned *Plessy v. Ferguson* (1896), the U.S. Supreme Court case upholding the separate but equal doctrine, thereby ending de jure segregation throughout the country, the cases' legacies were notable for at least three reasons. First, they led to the *legislative* termination of school segregation in their respective states of California and Texas (discriminatory practices continued for at least another decade). Second, the discriminatory and unsound rationale of English-language deficiency, the "pedagogical cloak" for segregation, was finally declared indefensible. Third, through *Mendez et al.* the equal-protection-of-the-law clause of the Fourteenth Amendment became a successful test for future litigators in *Brown v. Board of Education* (1954).

Higher Education from the Progressive Era through World War II

During the late 1800s and until World War I, college participation in the United States among all adults was still small (less than 5 percent) in proportion to the entire population. Among Tejanos, Californios, and Hispanos in the late nineteenth and early twentieth centuries, the sons and daughters of these elite (but downwardly mobile) classes often attended private Catholic colleges. These schools offered a smooth continuity with the Spanish language, culture (sex segregation, for example), and religion. Many of these Catholic colleges started first as academies to provide college preparation before they reached collegiate status and accreditation. The most prominent included Santa Clara College in San Jose, California (1851); College of San Miguel/St. Michael's College (1859), chartered again in 1874 as College of the Christian Brothers of New Mexico; Notre Dame College, San Jose, California (1868); and Our Lady of the Lake in San Antonio, Texas (1895) (MacDonald and Garcia 2003).

Distancing themselves from the segregated practices in Texas and California carried out by White school officials who viewed Mexican Americans as racially inferior, unclean, and in need of Americanization, Hispanos in New Mexico and Colorado emphasized their distinct heritage as something to be *affirmed* in the public schools. One prominent example of the economic and political clout of Hispanos was their creation of a public bilingual teacher training institution. In 1909, the state legislature of New Mexico founded the Spanish-American Normal School at El Rito. The legislature charged the institution to educate "Spanish-speaking natives of New Mexico for the vocation of teachers in the public schools of the counties and districts where the Spanish language is prevalent" (*Nineteenth and Twentieth Annual Reports* 1911, 19, 144; *Twenty-Seventh and Twenty-Eighth Annual Reports* 1918, 30). The school continued through the 1930s as a normal school and then was absorbed into the New Mexico higher education system and is now called Northern New Mexico College, an accredited baccalaureate institution (MacDonald and Garcia 2003). Similarly, the New Mexico Normal School, founded in 1893 in Las Vegas, New Mexico, became New Mexico Normal University in 1902 and New Mexico Highlands University from 1941 to the present.

Few scholars have focused on the role of Mexican American women in teaching or on larger questions regarding the intersection of gender, schooling, and Mexican girls and women. Vicki Ruiz pioneered the inclusion of women in Mexican/Chicano history, with a larger focus on social, economic, and political history.[6] However, emerging scholars have begun to engage the role of Mexican women in pre–civil rights community activism, their involvement in World War II defense industries, and their emergence as public and private school teachers (C. E. Orozco 2009). Women attended teacher training institutions, Catholic colleges, and junior colleges during the era of segregation, an area warranting greater exploration. The first junior college opened in 1901 in Joliet, Illinois; junior colleges quickly became popular commuter institutions for students as affordable alternatives to four-year residential schools. Parents of Mexican girls also preferred junior colleges because their daughters could live at home and study nearby, making it possible to safeguard ethnic cultural traditions. Some schools were vocational/technical in nature from their origins, and others offered both skilled training programs and academic preparation for transfer to four-year schools. In Brownsville, Texas, a predominantly Mexican American community, many high school students advanced to the Junior College of the Lower Rio Grande Valley, founded in 1926. In 1931, its name was changed to Brownsville Junior College and then Texas Southmost College in 1950, the appellation in use today. In Corpus Christi, Texas, the state founded Del Mar College in 1935 as a vocational/technical school, a role it has continued in until the present. Catholic colleges, teacher training schools, and junior colleges/community colleges thus appear to have educated the majority of both male and female Mexicans and other Latinos in the pre–World War II era.

The Morrill Land Grant Act of 1862 provided monies for each state to open land grant universities for all students. The 1890 Act, in the age of Jim Crow, provided federal funds for southern states to open segregated Black institutions. As in the K–12 public school system, Mexican Americans were not legally excluded from public colleges or universities, but de facto, their presence was discouraged. Extracurricular activities were another site for oppression and discrimination. Sororities and fraternities barred students on public university campuses, except for a limited few who possessed "honorary Whiteness." Undeterred, many Mexican and Hispano students formed their own organizations (MacDonald 2011a).

The admittance to higher education of Mexican Americans, increasingly middle-class and aided by philanthropic organizations and their own determination, widened in the pre–World War II era. However, local customs, the relatively weak social and political clout of Spanish-speaking citizens, and other intangible factors negatively impacted access and the nature of the college experience. Perhaps the greatest factor blocking college entrance was the insufficient number of Mexican Americans who could complete eighth grade and attend secondary schools. For most

Mexican Americans during this era (1848–1940), eighth grade was the highest level reached due to segregation, racism, and a political economy based on the inexpensive agricultural labor of Mexicans (Donato 1997; G. Gonzalez 1990).

Early Mexican college students were pioneers. They provided leadership and talent to nurture the formation of the later Chicano/Puerto Rican civil rights movements of the 1960s and 1970s. Unlike the late nineteenth-century participation of Mexicans from older elite Hispano and Californio families, students from middle- and working-class families were finally entering college (MacDonald and Garcia 2003). In the 1930s, for example, Mexican American students at UCLA created the first known Mexican college student organization in the United States, called the Mexican American Movement (MAM). Felix Gutiérrez, a club member and student, founded the first Mexican student newspaper, called *The Mexican Voice*, and served as its editor from 1938 to 1944 (Navarro 1995; M. García 1989; Sánchez 1995).

Mexican American participation in southwestern state flagship universities was minimal during this era, a historical underrepresentation that lasted into the early 1970s. The University of California, Berkeley, opened in 1869 with forty students. Between 1870 and 1872 the university established a "Fifth Class" composed of Mexican students, and almost two dozen enrolled in a preparatory college program. According to historians León and McNeil (1992), when the preparatory department was abolished two years later, it resulted in the "virtual disappearance of Spanish surnamed students at the University of California" (194). The University of Texas at Austin opened in the fall of 1883, and apparently Manuel García was the first Mexican American to graduate (Kanellos 1997). Little is yet known about other Latinos in the Texas university system during this early era, when only 1 percent of the undergraduates in Texas universities were of Mexican descent (Carter 1970).

During the 1940s and 1950s a growing number of Mexican Americans enrolled in higher education. The GI Bill, or Serviceman's Readjustment Act of 1944, provided educational benefits, and Latino veterans (the majority of them male) took advantage of these perquisites. In fact, some two-year colleges, such as the San Luis Institute (1943) in San Luis, Colorado, were created as a result of veterans' demands (Donato 2007). At the University of Texas at Austin, Mexican American veterans who were excluded from fraternities formed their own clubs, such as the Laredo and Alba Clubs, and used their status as veterans to advocate for educational and veterans' rights (MacDonald 2011a). Oral histories of Mexican

American veterans of World War II at the Oral History Project Archive at the University of Texas at Austin and Library of Congress reveal the transformational role of both military service and soldiers' subsequent ability to use the GI Bill to attend college free of tuition costs, while receiving, among other benefits, stipends for books and housing. We still know little about the educational impact of World War II on Mexican American young women, although some scholars have investigated the defense industry experiences of the iconic laborer "Rosita the Riveter" (Santillana 1989). A small number of Mexican American professors began to teach in the universities during the 1940s and 1950s, serving as mentors and role models for the coming generation of activists.

Eclipsed by the stunning *Brown v. Board of Education* (1954) case, rendering separate but "equal" Black schools unconstitutional, a second highly significant U.S. Supreme Court case in 1954 was *Hernandez v. State of Texas*. In this case, the court ruled that Mexican Americans and other racial groups "beyond the racial classes of white or negro" were also protected under the Equal Protection Clause of the Fourteenth Amendment (*Hernandez v. Texas*, 347 U.S. 475). As the civil rights movement took off in the next decade of the 1960s, an ideological shift occurred among Mexican Americans, who rejected many of the assimilationist views and claims to Whiteness of the World War II generation and instead embraced indigenous origins, Chicano nationalism, and radicalism over a gradualist pace of change.

Fighting for Our Rights: Impact of the Chicano *Movimiento* on Education

The conservative climate of Cold War 1950s American society was slowly rocked, first by the beginning of the African American civil rights movement, and then by a firestorm of multiple social revolutions. The Free Speech Movement, launched at the University of California, Berkeley, by Mario Savio in 1964, was followed by urban riots, beginning in 1965 with the Watts Riot in Los Angeles, anti–Vietnam War protests on college campuses, and a series of ethnic, gender, and racial rights movements that accompanied, and, in some instances, followed, the Black civil rights movement for equal rights under the law. Within these tumultuous decades, Mexican Americans, politicized as Chicanos, sparked their own forms of protest. A key difference between the Mexican American Generation activists and the more radicalized Chicanos of the 1960s and 1970s generation lay with a prioritization of working-class barrio communities and rural migrant workers and youth. The pre-civil rights Mexican American Talented Tenth, whose class and other attributes often permitted entrée to Anglo establishments, was now largely dismissed as elitist. Instead, slogans such as "Brown Power" and "Viva La Raza" emphasized the grassroots nature of Chicanismo and pride in Native American heritage and *mestizaje* (Montejano 2010; Pycior 1997). A continuing characteristic across both generations was the marginalization of Mexican American women's roles as active players in educational rights. As with Black women who found their efforts and work underplayed, although some Chicanas became members of the visible Brown Berets, most were "foot soldiers" in the *movimiento*. They worked behind the scenes making copies of leaflets and petitions, cooking, and organizing while their brothers took more visible roles (A. M. Garcia 1997).

The persistence of subtractive language policies and curricula, the small number of Mexican American teachers and administrators (less than 3 percent in 1968 in the Los Angeles Public Schools), the tracking of Mexican students into vocational classes, and the lingering segregation of schools led to more successful and widespread agitation for collective and legal rights for educational equity. Largely a high school and college youth movement, these activists concluded that the solution to their social plight lay with "massive protests, disruptive boycotts, strikes, and even riots" (J. Gonzalez 2000, 174). Among the notable Mexican American civil rights actions were the 1968 Los Angeles high school walkouts, or "blowouts." Chicano students at four East Los Angeles high schools staged massive walkouts. Dramatized in documentaries and an HBO film, students demanded guidance counselors who encouraged them to pursue college, Mexican American teachers and history classes, bilingual classes for new arrivers, and the elimination of punishment for speaking Spanish on school grounds (Esparza and Olmos 2006; Public Broadcasting Service 1996). Although the walkouts elicited a negative response from the Anglo community, resulting in arrests and crackdowns, the school district eventually gave in to some demands, and parents formed their own Mexican American educational committee to monitor reforms (García and Castro 2011; Behnken 2011; I. F. H. López 2003; Rosales 1996). The Los Angeles walkouts spread to other towns, such as Crystal City, Texas, as word of their success spread through newly created youth networks (Navarro 1998).

Mexican American leaders and organizations believed that Lyndon B. Johnson's election to the U.S. Senate and then ascension to the presidency after John F. Kennedy's tragic assassination in 1963 would result in federal recognition and programs for the economic and educational mobility of Mexican-descent peoples. After several disappointments and protests, in 1967 President Johnson finally established the federal Interagency Committee on Mexican Affairs and appointed the first Mexican American to the Equal Economic Opportunity Commission (Pycior 1997). Educational discrimination could also now be addressed through Title VI of the Civil Rights Act.

In the late 1960s and early 1970s, the Health, Education, and Welfare Department (HEW), in conjunction with the U.S. Commission on Civil Rights, undertook almost a decade of investigatory hearings and reports to address and rectify discrimination against Mexican Americans in K–12 education (U.S. Commission on Civil Rights 1968, 1971a, 1971b, 1972a, 1972b, 1973, 1974). A significant early piece of legislation was the Bilingual Education Act, passed by Congress in 1968. Initially the act was voluntary and for districts that submitted proposals. With the 1974 U.S. Supreme Court case *Lau v. Nichols*, however, the provision of educational services for English language learners, of any nationality or ethnic background, was mandated.

While inclusion of Mexican Americans in Great Society programs was initially slow, litigation was also successful in these decades. The Mexican American Legal Defense and Educational Fund (MALDEF) was created in 1968 with the assistance of the NAACP and funding from the Ford Foundation (Ford Foundation 1968). Millions of dollars from the Ford Foundation provided funds to train more Mexicans in the law profession, hire lawyers, and file lawsuits against schools denying Mexicans equitable educational opportunities or financing. In post–*Brown v. Board of Education* Mexican American desegregation cases, claiming Whiteness as a strategy was discarded. As historian Guadalupe San Miguel, Jr. (2001), explained, when school districts attempted to utilize Mexican children to achieve racial balance in Black schools, the original strategy of Mexican American lawyers to classify students as "White" finally backfired. In one federal district court case, *Cisneros v. Corpus Christi Independent School District* (1970), the judge ruled that Mexican Americans were "an identifiable ethnic minority group" and could thus benefit from *Brown* school desegregation cases. In a subsequent ruling at the nation's highest court, *Keyes v. School District Number One, Denver, Colorado* (1973), the Supreme Court also stipulated that Mexican Americans had the constitutional right to be recognized as a separate minority (Valencia 2008).

While segregation and linguistic and cultural discriminatory policies and practices were being tackled at the K–12 level, significant reforms occurred in higher education for Mexican Americans. One tangible result from Chicano student protests was the creation of Chicano studies and research centers. San Francisco State University's Ethnic Studies Department (encompassing African, Native American, Asian, and Raza Studies), established in 1969, is generally considered the first such academic department and center in U.S. higher education. Newly minted Mexican American PhDs produced research, created professional organizations, and started scholarly journals to revolutionize a traditional Anglocentric academic culture. The Ford Foundation, considered radical among many conservative politicians, particularly President Richard Nixon, played a central role in funding both Black and Mexican research centers and individual scholars (MacDonald and Hoffman 2012). In addition to Ford, other private philanthropies, such as Rockefeller, funded programs supporting Mexican American studies or scholars (MacDonald, Botti, and Clark 2007). The Mexican American experience is now a legitimate field of study, and there are academic journals, courses, and university departments devoted to research on Mexican history and culture (L. H. Flores 2001; Rochin and Valdes 2000; Quinones 1990; I. M. Garcia 1998; Soldatenko 2009).

The outcome of the civil rights movement among Chicanos affected most areas of society, including K–12 and higher education. Mexican Americans in the United States, unlike other minority or immigrant groups, have experienced a continuous influx of new immigrants for over one hundred years. The consequences of this continuous transnational movement over the border are the replaying of educational challenges during cycles of nativism, anti-immigration sentiment, and monolingualism, alternating with toleration and specialized programs for newcomers during labor shortages and flush economic times.

Post–Civil Rights to the Present

In the post–civil rights era, Mexican Americans face two unique challenges, impacting education, based upon demographic change and shifting political identities in relation to other Hispanic/Latino groups. While they are still numerically dominant among all Latino populations (64.6 percent), the 1977 Statistical Directive 15 of the U.S. Office of Management and Budget (OMB) collapsed all Latino groups under the federal identification term of "Hispanic." As a result, the specific historical legacies and contemporary needs of Mexicans, versus other Hispanic subgroups, are elided in ways that may have unintended negative consequences for practices and policies.

For instance, the overall educational achievement and outcomes of the broader Latino/Hispanic population can vary greatly by subgroup, generation, and place of birth. Mexican American children and youth, even those born in the United States, consistently rank low on most of these indicators, but only some school district, state, and federal-level data are broken down by subgroup. In the critical area of high school dropouts, for example, the National Center for Educational Statistics (NCES) reports that 7.7 percent of sixteen- to twenty-four-year-old White youth in 2007 were dropouts. In comparison, among *all* Hispanic youth, the percentage in this age group was 19.9 percent, but 34.3 percent for those born outside of the United States and 11.5 percent for American-born youth. Mexican American dropout rates vary from almost one-quarter of all Mexican youth regardless of place of birth (22.2 percent) to 38.8 percent for foreign-born (U.S. Department of Education 2010b). Because many Mexican young men, in particular, come to the United States for labor without entering U.S. high schools, researchers caution that the dropout rate of Mexican-born individuals is inflated (Fry 2003).[7]

Without historical or contextual understanding, educational data can also mask differing achievement levels that require nuanced policy or curricular interventions. Cuban secondary-school-age youth, for instance, have lower dropout rates than Whites, whether U.S.-or foreign-born. Five percent of Cuban children drop out of high school, revealing how distinct historical legacies can shape contemporary achievement levels (U.S. Department of Education 2010b). Cuban refugees fleeing Castro received numerous educational services and compensatory programs upon their arrival in Miami in the late 1950s and early 1960s, as part of the middle- and upper-middle-class "Golden Exiles." Subsequently, Cuban refugees garnered a level of political and economic strength that has not diminished over the last fifty years, and has translated into educational capital generationally (MacDonald 2004). In summary, data utilized for justifying, funding, and creating programs for Hispanic youth can easily mask the specific needs of Mexican American children if pan-Latino calculations are used instead of uniformly parsing the data by subgroup. Despite their long-term residency in the United States versus newcomers from some Central and South American countries, Mexican American children rank among the lowest in terms of preschool participation, SAT and other standardized tests, and high school and college completion (U.S. Department of Education 2010a).

As the number of Mexicans, the largest Latino subgroup, rose dramatically between the 1990 and 2010 censuses, not only in historically familiar states but in the American South, the far West, and Mid-Atlantic states as well, anti-immigrant groups employing nativist rhetoric passed exclusionary legislation (Wortham, Hamann, and Murillo 2001). Voters in 1990s California, for example, eradicated bilingual education in the state and also voted for measures requiring teachers to report students they believed were undocumented to federal immigration authorities (Suarez-Orozco and Paez 2002). In the early 2010s, reactionary measures emerged again in sectors of the country as diverse as Arizona, where the Tucson School Board outlawed Mexican American history classes, to the state of Georgia, whose board of regents of higher education banned undocumented students from attending the top five public universities in addition to denying them in-state tuition rates at lower-tier state institutions.[8] Mexican Americans responded to these measures with several counterefforts learned through a long history of demanding their rights. Communities marched in rallies during the 1990s and the following decades, asserting their rights to reside in this country and their children's rights, under the U.S. Supreme Court's ruling in *Plyler v. Doe* (1982), to receive free public schooling, regardless of documented status. Furthermore, the right to receive English-language services without home languages being denigrated, and to resist marginalization at all levels of school and university systems, is not taken for granted among Mexican Americans.

As this volume goes to press, higher education access for undocumented high school students, known as "Dreamers," is being expanded. The DREAM Act, which stands for Development, Relief, and Education for Alien Minors, was first introduced in the U.S. Congress in 2001 as a bipartisan effort to permit students who were brought to the United States as young children without their knowledge and have resided continuously to become eligible for a pathway to citizenship. Bills to pass the DREAM Act have continually failed at the federal level, but as of November 2013, fifteen states had passed their own forms of the DREAM Act, with varying stipulations. A key financial benefit for DREAM Act students is to be eligible for in-state tuition and grants, a perquisite denied as undocumented youth.

On June 15, 2012, President Obama utilized his executive privilege to sign a memorandum, Deferred Action for Childhood Arrivals (DACA), implementing a policy that would delay deportation of students wishing to take advantage of the DREAM Act. While new calls for immigration reform are poised to tackle these issues in the long term, many Mexican students remain in limbo until permanent reforms are put into effect.

From the first encounters between Spaniards and Native Americans, Mexican Americans have demonstrated the high value they place upon education as a means of economic, political, and social maintenance and upward mobility. Equitable opportunities and access to quality educational facilities have posed a formidable challenge to Mexicans in U.S. history, despite generational improvements over time and the passage of equal rights legislation (Telles and Ortiz 2008). The Mexican American community, living, for the most part, near an international border more than two thousand miles long and possessing a long history of acceptance and rejection in the United States, has displayed persistence, resistance, courage, and sacrifice in its response to discrimination. Whether the goal concerned the freedom to speak Spanish in schools without punishment, or to resist the eradication of hard-won gains incorporating Mexican American history into the school curriculum, Mexican American communities have never taken for granted their constitutional rights. Through collective action, lawsuits, lobbying, petitions, and other measures, they have not remained silent, but reminded the United States that for a healthy democracy to function, all of its citizens, not only a select few, must be part of the polity.

comparison to the percentage of Asian American students (86.1 percent). While White and Asian high school graduates have typically been more likely to attend four-year colleges immediately after high school, in recent years, Hispanic freshman enrollment has been growing faster at four-year colleges than enrollment in two-year colleges (Fry 2005b).

These trends suggest that many colleges and universities are experiencing a transformation in their student bodies, and the young age of the Latino population portends steady and continued growth in higher education. Given these general trends, however, we do not know how Mexican Americans have fared in this growth trend of Latina/o enrollments in higher education. The purpose of this chapter is to explore changing historical contexts (historicity) and intersections of ethnicity, gender, and class to address the following questions: What are the changing characteristics of Mexican American/Chicano students entering four-year colleges over the decades? Have Mexican American men and women made progress, or are there new issues to attend to in the current era? Central to these questions is the need for adequate data by context (four-year colleges in this case), ethnicity, gender, and class over time to better attend to issues in the future.

This chapter examines forty years of trends among Mexican American/Chicano students entering four-year colleges, highlighting the unique features of this group relative to other Latinos and the general population. The data show a unique portrait of how Mexican American first-time, full-time students have changed at four-year institutions over the decades. Reports reveal that among eighteen- to twenty-four-year-olds in college, Hispanics are now the largest minority group at four-year colleges (Fry and Lopez 2012; Fry and Taylor 2013). More than half (56 percent) of Hispanic eighteen- to twenty-four-year-old college students were attending four-year institutions, compared to 66 percent of Black and 72 percent of White students. Moreover, students who begin at four-year colleges are more likely to attain a baccalaureate degree than students who begin attendance at a community college (W. Velez 1985; Alfonso 2006). The lack of large-scale data and the availability of only small-scale studies on Mexican Americans, however, prevent us from understanding those attending community colleges compared with other groups and how their experiences may differ—a topic that is also a limitation of the trend data in this chapter. Specifically, the data presented here capture Mexican Americans transitioning from high school to four-year colleges, including their characteristics, concerns, and aspirations, with a specific focus on gender differences. These data help to identify continuing issues that

Mexican Americans/Chicanos face at college entry and shed light on the changes and contemporary issues that may help institutions advance students along college pathways toward degree attainment and realization of their aspirations.

Focusing on a specific ethnic group in the transition from high school to college allows for examining the intersectionality of gender, race/ethnicity, and class, and their alignment with historical context, in a way that few studies on higher education are able to do. At the same time that we may see progress regarding Mexican Americans' entering higher education, there continue to be multiple inequalities at work that require more nuanced analysis to identify new challenges that play out differently for men and women, and according to class differences within the population. Anthias argues that

> hierarchical relations linked to social divisions are emergent and subject to historical contingencies depending on different constellations of power in different time/space frameworks. This means social categorizations are not equally positioned or salient at all times. . . . The approach has to be historically sensitive as there are new and emerging constellations of disadvantage. (2013, 14)

Reviewing data on Mexican American students over time allows for identification of these new challenges. However, this perspective also complicates the assessment of progress for minoritized groups and requires monitoring by gender, class, and specific ethnicity over sociohistorical time and policy contexts in order to understand how specific groups are uniquely affected.

Data on Students from High School through College: Where Are the Mexican Americans?

Colleges and universities participating in the Cooperative Institutional Research Program (CIRP), a major survey research and campus assessment activity, began to monitor first-year students using The Freshman Survey (TFS) in 1966. In 1971, CIRP introduced two Latina/o ethnic categories, where students could designate their racial/ethnic identity as Mexican American/Chicano or Puerto Rican. The numbers of both Latina/o ethnic groups were small in the early years, and we are not clear how nationally representative the population was at the time, because

CIRP data have historically monitored these ethnic groups separately, rather than in one general Hispanic category, as is typical in the institutionally based data collection of the U.S. Department of Education. Current student-level data from the National Center for Education Statistics (NCES) focusing on school-to-college/workplace and beyond have more consistently included specific Latino ethnic categories, but these are underutilized by researchers.

The U.S. Census Bureau has provided basic educational attainment information by Latino ethnicity since 1970 and, beginning in 2010, provided much more detail about ethnic origin than in the past (Ennis, Ríos-Vargas, and Albert 2011). The data consistently show that although Mexican Americans are the largest Latina/o ethnic group, their overall educational attainment has historically lagged significantly behind that of Cuban Americans and other racial/ethnic groups, and began to lag behind Puerto Ricans as early as 1980 (U.S. Census Bureau 2011). However, many studies in education have focused on Latina/os in general, which obscures these differences among Latina/o ethnic groups that are shaped by immigration history, social mobility, and distinct social and political contexts. Random samples of students followed from high school to college did not always have separate ethnic categories for Latina/os and therefore could not provide sufficient data about Mexican Americans/Chicanos or other Latina/o subgroups in national federal data sets (Dey et al. 1997). More recent federal data collections have oversampled Latina/os and provided sufficient numbers of Mexican Americans, enabling researchers to study such issues as college choice among Mexican Americans and other groups. In these longitudinal studies of student movement from high school to college, researchers have found lower probabilities of Mexican American enrollment at four-year colleges compared with other Latina/o ethnic groups, and potential indirect effects of income differences that influence enrollment via academic preparation (Núñez and Kim 2012; Núñez and Crisp 2012).

Table 3.1 shows the national databases on students that include data on Latino ethnic categories but are still underutilized in examining the Mexican American experience in particular. Most of these data are publicly available and can be accessed online at the NCES website, and more specific information can be merged with identifiers for students that can be obtained through special licensing procedures. It may be that researchers are still unaware that these data exist, with samples on Mexican Americans ranging from approximately 242 (Baccalaureate and Beyond survey) to 7,524 (National Postsecondary Student Aid Study) being available for analysis. These are longitudinal databases, some of which begin in middle school and go through higher education and/or work history (e.g., NELS, HS&B), while others reach into postgraduate degree attainments (e.g., Baccalaureate and Beyond). While these are important for tracking a particular cohort of students and predicting outcomes, they are not suited to trend analyses across cohorts.

Colleges are required to report the numbers of students entering, enrolling in, and graduating from their institution by race/ethnicity and gender to the Integrated Postsecondary Education System (IPEDS) at the National Center for Educational Statistics (NCES). IPEDS data collection on Hispanic students did not begin until 1972, and these data have never been collected or reported in ways that would permit understanding Mexican Americans as distinct from other Latino ethnic groups. Even with a major revision in IPEDS data collection that occurred in 2007, there are no data by Latino subgroups for the population of America's college students. Thus, while these data are ideal for trend analyses of Latina/o enrollment and degree completion, they are not ideal for understanding these trends specifically for the Mexican American student population.

Individual colleges and universities have typically collected race/ethnicity information in greater detail to comply with federal affirmative action guidelines regarding the need to increase specific targeted groups. State systems have also collected such data to ensure that institutions are addressing the needs of underrepresented groups that are growing and will be the future taxpayers who support state economies. Campuses were interested in learning more about their students with regard to access and success, and collaborating could produce new data for their own institution, as well as contribute to national normative data through the CIRP. Participating colleges and universities began to monitor first-year students with The Freshman Survey (TFS), and CIRP used a stratified sampling scheme to ensure that different institutional types participated across the nation. Institutions could be included in these national reports if they surveyed the majority of their first-time, full-time freshmen. The student survey not only collected data on Mexican American/Chicano and Puerto Rican students, but also allowed a student to check more than one race/ethnicity—an innovation that allowed institutions and researchers to understand multiracial and multiethnic identities since the early years. When federal data collection began, student data were collected from institutions by gender and race/ethnicity, which allowed the weighing and norming of CIRP data to ensure representation of all first-time, full-time students by gender. To date (2014), however, because of federal data limitations in institutionally collected data, the national data cannot offer comparable data from all institutions on Latino ethnicity, and it is impossible to link the national data on Mexican American/Chicano and Puerto Rican students, or Other Latinos (added as a category in 1992), to the national CIRP surveys. This partially explains why there is so little focus on Mexican Americans in studies using data that are generalizable across institutions, even though these students are now present in greater numbers in higher education.

Method and Data Sources

Each year, the TFS data are collected according to an institutional sampling strategy (based on selectivity, control, and type of institution) that ensures broad representation of four-year institutions to reflect a national, normative profile of the American freshmen entering all four-year private and public colleges and universities. Institutions are instructed to administer the survey at freshman orientation to capture student expectations for college and predispositions (e.g., political and social views) in order to permit institutions to monitor changes in students' expectations over their college careers. The comprehensive survey allows for examination of student demographic characteristics, precollege behaviors, and values, as well as college plans and expectations. Depending on the year when comparable survey items were available, Mexican American student respondent sample sizes in the TFS (prior to weighing) ranged from 598 in 1971 to 12,100 in 2012. Further, all data are adjusted to represent the freshman population by gender, and all reports have typically included breakdowns by gender from the Higher Education Research Institute (HERI).[2] This information has been disaggregated by racial/ethnic groups for specific studies, and used to predict college completion (Arellano 2011; DeAngelo, Franke, Hurtado, Pryor, and Tran 2011), examine student change over the college years (Gurin, Dey, Hurtado, and Gurin 2002), and compare trends with Latina/o ethnic groups and non-Hispanic White students (Hurtado, Sáenz, Santos, and Cabrera 2008). A special survey report was generated for all Latinas/os and Mexican Americans/Chicanos by gender specifically to provide highlights for this chapter, updating a previous report on Latina/o first-year students at four-year colleges (Hurtado, Sáenz, et al. 2008) and extending the trends to include more recent historical events in the nation. Comparison data across groups on many items are available in the prior report.

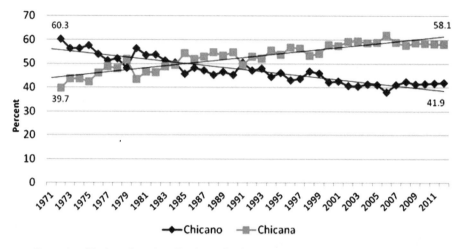

Figure 3.1. Mexican American Freshmen by Sex, 1971–2011
Source: Data archives, Higher Education Research Institute, UCLA; The Freshman Survey, available at http://www.heri.ucla.edu/cirpoverview.php.

Portraits of Mexican American/Chicano Freshmen over the Decades

Changing Gender Disparities

Focusing on data on Mexican American/Chicano freshmen begins to paint a portrait of these students entering four-year colleges over time. The earliest entrants were the product of the larger civil rights and social movements of the era, as *el movimiento* opened many doors of higher education for the first time to groups targeted for increased representation. Figure 3.1 shows the representation of Chicanos and Chicanas in college, and, as was the case at most colleges, the representation was decidedly male—60.3 percent, compared with only 39.7 percent female. By 1976, no doubt as a result of the women's movement in the early 1970s, majority White women had achieved equal representation and had begun to surpass males among four-year college first-time, full-time entrants (Pryor, Hurtado, Sáenz, Santos, and Korn 2007). However, for Mexican Americans/Chicanos this change in female representation did not definitively occur until almost the mid-1980s. Except for an anomalous year, 1991, where representation was equal, the trend continued, and since the early 1990s the gender gap has accelerated. By 2012, the proportion of Mexican American men (41.9 percent) compared with women (58.1 percent) had become nearly the reverse image of the gender gap of the early 1970s. College enrollments for all Latinas/os have increased, but clearly the number of first-time, full-time Chicanas has increased at a faster rate than that of Chicano males, resulting in a more pronounced gender disparity among Mexican American freshmen than, for example, among White non-Hispanic students and other Latina/o ethnic groups (Hurtado, Sáenz, et al. 2008). This reversal of representation of Chicanas relative to Chicanos is an example of how the attributes of social categories are fluid rather than fixed, and are subject to differences in time periods (Anthias 2013). From early concerns about the representation of women, the new narrative has changed to a focus on the issues particular to racial/ethnic males (Ponjuán and Sáenz, chapter 9). However, just because women are now more represented in higher education, it does not mean that Latinas are experiencing greater privilege because of their success in school (Núñez 2014a). They face unique barriers: Latina students are less likely than Latinos to enroll in selective higher education institutions, to be satisfied with college, or to leave home for college or graduate school (Núñez, McDonough, Ceja, and Solórzano 2008; Ramírez 2013). This latter point will be reexamined more specifically for Mexican American men and women in a subsequent section.

First Generation in College

Students with college-educated parents have more advantages in access to college, navigating transitions, and eventually attaining college degrees (McDonough 1997; Lareau 2003; DeAngelo et al. 2011). Over time, we can expect that more students entering college will have college-educated parents, as the general population becomes more educated. However, the United States has also fallen from first to twelfth place in the world in terms of the proportion of college graduates, prompting President Obama to set a goal for the nation to once again have the most college-educated population in the world by 2020 (Obama 2009). In a previous report, we indicated that Other Latina/o and Puerto Rican students were significantly more likely to have parents (either a mother or father) with a college degree than Mexican American students; and that all Latina/o students' parent education levels were "just barely catching up" in 2006 with 1975 levels of parental education reported among non-Hispanic White students (Hurtado, Sáenz, et al. 2008, 6). This relatively low percentage of students with college-educated parents among Latinos, and Mexican Americans in particular, clearly indicates that institutions must provide them with assistance and knowledge about transitioning to college. At the same time, however, colleges need to recognize the community cultural

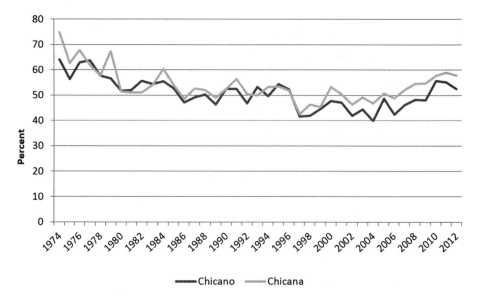

Figure 3.2. First Generation* in College, Mexican Americans by Sex, 1974–2012
Source: Data archives, Higher Education Research Institute, UCLA; The Freshman
Survey, available at http://www.heri.ucla.edu/cirpoverview.php.
*Reporting that either parent had less than a high school diploma, or
postsecondary other than college.

wealth that students bring (Yosso 2005) and strive to cultivate critical resilience through educational practices that empower Mexican Americans
for success in college (Campa 2010).

The trend line for Mexican Americans who are the first generation in
college by gender is featured in figure 3.2. In these data, students were
classified as first generation in college if they reported that their parents
had not attended college or had only received up to a level of a high school
diploma or some postsecondary experience other than college. Surprisingly, the trends suggest that we are witnessing not a steady decline in the
number of first-generation college students among Chicanas/os as we had
in the first twenty years, but rather a steady increase since the late 1990s.
Moreover, females are somewhat more likely than males to be the first in
their family to go to college, particularly in recent years.

What could be driving this trend toward more first-generation college
students at four-year colleges? Recent immigration of Mexican Americans
relative to other groups may explain this trend, but it is only a partial explanation, since only 35 percent of all Mexican-origin individuals are recent immigrants. One major historical point is that since the mid-1990s,

there have been concerted challenges to the use of affirmative action in the courts and voter referenda in several states that prohibit the use of race/ethnicity or gender in college admissions at public institutions (Garces 2012). This happened in states with large numbers of Latina/o students, such as California, Washington, Florida, and Texas. Admissions policies changed to include more emphasis on student rank-in-class (as in the Top Ten Percent Plan in Texas and Eligibility in the Local Context in California), opening up opportunities in some high schools that do not typically send students to college, and for women, who typically make better grades than men in school. First-generation status may also be a proxy for other qualifications that indicate students have overcome significant adversity to get to college, which is also given consideration in admissions at many public and private colleges that have moved away from strict formulas based only on academic qualifications. These admissions challenges culminated in a series of Supreme Court decisions (such as *Grutter v. University of Michigan* and *Fisher v. University of Texas*) and have reinforced the use of broader definitions of diversity and changing admissions criteria to de-emphasize race/ethnicity. Another way to look at class issues is to examine distinctions among Mexican Americans by level of family income. In the next section, a pattern similar to that of first-generation status was evident: There were increases in the proportion of Mexican American first-year students from low-income families over time (shown in figure 3.3), perhaps as a consequence of more campuses under race-neutral constraints emphasizing low-income status in student admissions at four-year colleges.

Students from Low-Income Families

Low-income students complete college at lower rates and take longer to graduate than their higher-income counterparts even when students' academic performance, precollege and college experiences, and institutional factors are controlled for (Franke 2012). The disparity in college completion between students from different income categories has actually increased over the last thirty years (Bowen, Chingos, and McPherson 2009). Although degree attainment at four-year public institutions increased from 65 percent in 2001 to 70.3 percent in 2009, degree attainment decreased from 57.4 to 54.8 percent for low-income students (Aud et al. 2011). This suggests that over time, low-income students' chances of completing college are actually declining, and it is within this historical context that we see an increase in Mexican Americans from low-income backgrounds gaining access to higher education.

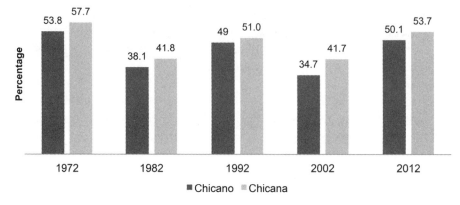

Figure 3.3. Mexican American Freshmen at 4-year Colleges from Low-Income*
Families by Sex, 1972–2012
* Low-income calculated at the poverty threshold for a family of four, multiplied
by 200%, in respective years. No thresholds were posted for 1972, so 1973 poverty
threshold was substituted. Federal poverty thresholds for all years are posted at
U.S. Census (2013) website. Data reported to nearest income category, as on The
Freshman Survey, Higher Education Research Institute, UCLA, http://www.heri
.ucla.edu/cirpoverview.php.

Figure 3.3 shows that more than half of Mexican Americans entering
four-year colleges came from low-income[3] households in 1972, and the
same is true for 2012. Specifically, 57.7 percent of women and 53.8 percent
of men were from low-income families in 1972, and in 2012 those numbers
show only slight declines to 53.7 percent and 50.1 percent, respectively.
Further, Chicanas were typically more likely than men to come from low-
income households, and this was particularly true in 2002, when the proportions were lowest at 34.7 percent for men and 41.7 percent for women.
This dip in 2002 is significant, in that this was the cohort admitted immediately following the terrorist attacks on 9/11. It may indicate a relative
lack of willingness to take low-income Mexican American men in comparison to women in the wake of 9/11. However, there was a subsequent
increase in the proportion of low-income Mexican Americans over the
next decade. As stated earlier, one of the reasons for increasing numbers of
low-income Mexican Americans may be that admissions criteria are now
more likely to take into consideration low-income status along with high
school performance as evidence of achievement in the face of adversity,
particularly in states prohibited from considering race/ethnicity or gender
in admissions. However, it may be that recent increases in the allocation of
federal Pell grants has also led to increasing numbers of Mexican Ameri-

cans taking advantage of additional federal funds to attend four-year colleges, particularly in light of a weak economy that cannot accommodate large numbers of young workers who require skill development. These increases in the proportion of low-income students suggest the need for additional institutional financial, academic, and social support to understand the specific issues that low-income Mexican Americans face and improve their chances of completing college. The next section addresses intersectionality of ethnicity and gender when it comes to financial issues in college.

Financial issues play an important role in not only deciding which college to attend but also decisions about whether to remain in college. Table 3.2 displays data on differences between Mexican American men and women's financial concerns and the location of the first four-year college they have chosen to attend. Confirming information about Chicanas

Table 3.2. Financial Concerns among Mexican American Freshmen and Location of First Four-Year College Attended

	Chicano (%)			Chicana (%)		
	1972	1992	2012	1972	1992	2012
Concern about financing college						
None (I am confident that I'll have sufficient funds)	26.1	20.6	19.5	10.5	12.3	11.3
Some (but I probably will have enough funds)	47.2	56.8	62.9	59.7	53.7	62.4
Major (not sure I will have enough funds to complete college)	26.6	22.6	17.6	29.7	34.0	26.3
Work expectations during college*						
I expect to get a job to help pay for college expenses	36.9	39.1	51.3	41.5	46.6	63.2
I expect to work full-time during college	—	6.1	10.1	—	6.9	14.2
Proximity of the college to home						
Less than 50 miles	38.6	45.6	58.3	48.5	45.5	58.1
More than 50 miles	61.4	54.4	41.7	51.6	54.5	41.8

Source: Data archives, Higher Education Research Institute, The Freshman Survey, CIRP, http://www.heri.ucla.edu/cirpoverview.php.
Note: Dashes indicate item was not on the survey in 1972.
* Percentage reporting there is a "very good chance."

coming from lower-income families, the data show that they were substantially less confident than Chicanos about their ability to have sufficient funds to finance college in 1972, 1992, and 2012. Across these years, the proportion of Mexican American students who expected to get a job to help pay for college expenses also increased, with 63.2 percent of women and over half of men (51.3 percent) expecting to do so in 2012. Chicanas were also more likely to report that they expected to work full-time during college (14.2 percent) than were men (10.1 percent) in 2012, almost twice the percentage of Chicanas who reported this expectation in 1992. The latter changes were likely due to the recent effects of the Great Recession, which disrupted family financial security, with household wealth declining the most and the poverty rate increasing the most among Latina/o families compared to families of any other racial/ethnic group in the period 2006–2010 (DeNavas-Walt, Proctor, and Smith 2011). Illustrating intersections between gender and ethnicity, the data show that Chicanas appear to be uniquely affected by economic issues and assume greater financial responsibility for college expenses.

The data show a clear trend among both Mexican American men and women to attend colleges close to home and a declining proportion who were attending college over fifty miles from home. This sets the stage for specific institutions located near these communities to take on the overwhelming job of accommodating increasing numbers of Mexican American high school graduates. Hispanic-Serving Institutions (HSIs) have more than 25 percent Latina/os in their student bodies. These institutions are more likely to enroll large numbers of low-income Latina/o students, students with lower high school grades, and those who choose to live near home, presumably to lower college costs (Cuellar 2012). In terms of the latter, while Chicanas were more likely to attend college close to home in 1972, in 2012 they were as likely as men to choose a college within fifty miles of home (approximately 58 percent for both groups). The inclination of Mexican American students to save costs by living at home may be due to their parents' aversion to loans. However, researchers have identified a potential undermatch problem in college selection among Latina/os, where many more are qualified to go to a more selective college than actually attend—which, in turn, actually lowers the probability of baccalaureate degree completion (Bowen, Chingos, and MacPherson 2009). In the face of rising tuition costs, students need to be savvy about strategies to finance college and understand how to calculate their real costs, rather than respond to college "sticker prices," to choose the best colleges. While finances play a definitive role in both choice of college and persistence over the long term, much can also be said for Mexican American student motivations, or *ganas.*

Degree and Career Aspirations

High motivation and aspirations are generally positive traits for entering college students. Social cognitive theory establishes that strong self-efficacy and well-thought-out goal-setting can increase students' academic achievement, because goals specify the requirements for personal success. Self-efficacy, which incorporates beliefs about one's abilities and perceptions of situations, plays a central role in the exercise of personal agency because of its impact on thought, affect, motivation, and action (Bandura 1991). Previous work has identified lower self-efficacy/esteem particularly among low-income Latinas (Zambrana and Zoppi 2002), notably with regard to their academic ability compared to Latino males and non-Hispanic Whites of both genders over the years (Hurtado, Sáenz, et al. 2008). This is in spite of the fact that Latinas have higher high school grade-point averages than Latino males and non-Hispanic White males at college entry (Hurtado, Sáenz, et al. 2008). The data indicate that this is still the case: In 2012, 70 percent of Mexican American/Chicano males rated their academic ability in the top 10 percent compared with the average person their age, whereas only 57.8 percent of females rated themselves this highly. Chicanas remain more modest about their abilities relative to men, and the question that arises is whether this has been a consistent disadvantage in college and postcollege goals. In terms of students' aspirations, this does not seem to be the case.

Increasing numbers of non-Hispanic White and Latina/o students have been seeking master's degrees over the past four decades, perhaps mirroring workplace changes in requirements for many entry-level positions. Figure 3.4 displays postbaccalaureate degree aspirations for Mexican Americans entering four-year colleges at three time points: 1972, 1992, and 2012. Chicano males have dramatically increased their aspirations for master's degrees—from 27.4 percent in 1972 to 42.9 percent in 2012. And while the aspirations of Chicanas have also steadily increased, a somewhat smaller proportion of women aspire to a master's as their highest degree, increasing 6.2 percentage points to 39.9 percent in 2012. However, a more compelling trend among freshmen has been a drop in the number of Latino males interested in advanced graduate or professional degrees (Hurtado, Sáenz, et al. 2008), which is precisely mirrored in Chicano male data presented here—a higher proportion of the early

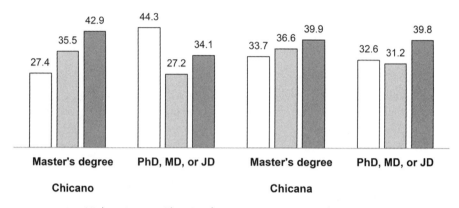

Figure 3.4. Highest Degree Objective for Mexican American/Chicano Freshmen (%).
Source: Data archives, Higher Education Research Institute, UCLA; The Freshman Survey, available at http://www.heri.ucla.edu/cirpoverview.php.
Note: Students indicated the highest degree they intended to obtain anywhere.

entrants to higher education aspired to advanced degrees (44.3 percent in 1972 versus 34.1 percent in 2012). This is largely due to a drop in the number of males interested in medical and law degrees, which has not been offset by a small increase (only 2.5 percentage points over forty years) in the number aspiring to doctoral degrees (22.5 percent in 2012). Although both men and women in 1992 experienced drops in interest in advanced degrees, Chicana students' interest in advanced graduate and professional degrees, in contrast to that of males, has increased from 32.6 percent in 1972 to 39.8 percent in 2012. Further analysis showed that this proportional increase among Chicanas was largely driven by the number aspiring to doctoral degrees (both PhD and EdD degrees), which changed from 15.7 percent in 1972 to 25.5 percent in 2012. From a social cognitive theoretical standpoint, this adoption of high goals sets the stage for personal action and behaviors that affect achievement and personal decisions along the educational pathway.

However, what could explain these declines in degree aspirations for presumably relatively lucrative professions, particularly among males? First, a review of students' career choices at college entry shows there is increasing interest in nonphysician health professional careers, engineering, and business careers for Mexican American students entering college (see table 3.3). Many of these careers do not require more than a master's degree. Second, the bans on affirmative action in key states (Texas,

Washington, Florida, and California) have resulted in declines in graduate and professional school admissions for underrepresented groups (Garces 2012) and the inability to target aid for Latina/os. These policy changes may have dampened interest among freshmen as certain professions became increasingly expensive to finance and admission to training for them became more competitive. Career areas are changing as well: Shortages in certain fields have created the promise of demand for skilled workers and financial returns immediately after the baccalaureate (e.g., in nursing and

Table 3.3. Top Ten Career Aspirations among Mexican Americans

In 1971:

Chicana	%	Chicano	%
Education (elementary)	19.1	Lawyer	12.8
Education (secondary)	12.5	Business	8.8
Health professional	7.1	Doctor (MD or DDS)	7.9
Artist/writer/journalist	6.3	Engineer	7.9
Doctor (MD or DDS)	5.6	Education (secondary)	7.8
Social worker	5.3	Military	7.0
Nurse	3.5	Research scientist	4.4
Lawyer	2.7	Artist/writer/journalist	4.3
Business	2.2	Social worker	2.5
Research scientist	2.2	Farmer or forester	1.9

In 2011:

Chicana	%	Chicano	%
Doctor (MD or DDS)	9.0	Engineer	16.8
Business	8.8	Business	12.9
Nurse	8.6	Doctor (MD or DDS)	7.4
Health professional	7.5	Artist/writer/journalist	6.4
Artist/writer/journalist	6.4	Health professional	5.8
Social worker	3.9	Lawyer	3.2
Education (elementary)	3.8	Education (secondary)	3.0
Education (secondary)	3.8	Nurse	2.1
Lawyer	3.6	Research scientist	1.9
Engineer	2.9	Military	1.5

Source: Data reported as students' probable career from The Freshman Survey, data archives of HERI, UCLA.
Note: Students reporting "Undecided" or "Other career" were excluded from these percentages, even though these were among the top ten listed.

engineering). Over time, education careers (teaching and administration) dropped in importance among Chicanas in favor of other professions, and engineering made the top-ten list in 2011. It is interesting to note that in 2011, just below tenth place on the list for Chicanas (not shown in table 3.3) are careers such as research scientist and college teaching, indicating potential areas that converge with Chicanas' increasing advanced degree aspirations. Meanwhile, engineering as a career moves to first place among Chicano males, and nursing makes its debut on the top-ten list of career aspirations. Mexican Americans' aspirations are motivated by job opportunities, and the fact that many are still first-generation college students suggests that earning power is key in shaping their aspirations. Among Chicano males, aspirations for a military career dropped significantly in importance, as did those for a research scientist career, although both remain careers among Chicanos' top ten aspirations. Careers such as farmer/forester or social worker dropped completely off the top-ten list, as neither is especially lucrative and such professions are subject to downsizing based on changes in the economy. Mexican Americans' aspirations undergo further revision as they face the limitations of their high school preparation in relation to college expectations, become exposed to many new knowledge areas through course work, develop their social and personal identities in college, and encounter institutional agents in faculty and staff who help them navigate college and support them toward a career path.

Implications for the Future: New Challenges and Opportunities

In terms of new constructions of intersectionality that take into account multiple social identities, context, and historical time (Anthias 2013), this chapter has been able to identify critical areas that necessarily complicate the question of whether Mexican Americans are making educational progress. First, previous research has shown that Latinas/os are more likely than any racial/ethnic group to be among the first in their family to set foot in college (Hurtado, Sáenz, et al. 2008), and the trends show that this is particularly true of Mexican American students and females within this community. This was true not only in the early 1970s, but also in 2012, raising the issue of whether real progress has been achieved and/ or whether we should be optimistic that substantial numbers of Mexican Americans are now using four-year colleges for upward social mobility. All other groups have witnessed declines in the proportion of first-generation college students. However, intersections among gender, class, and ethnicity are evident over time: Chicanas entering college as the first in their family to go to college went from nearly 75 percent to 58 percent, which is still a substantial portion of young women who must find guides among faculty, staff, and peers to navigate college. As a consequence of parental education and low income, higher numbers of Chicanas than males expect to work during college and are concerned about their ability to finance college.

Chicanas also tend to have lower self-assessments about their academic abilities than Chicano males. This occurs even as their achievement and goal aspirations are increasing and changing to consider entering the most challenging male-dominated fields. Instead of looking only at the progress of women in terms of access to college, we have to acknowledge continuing inequalities that Chicanas face compared with other groups and also ask more complex questions. For example, in spite of greater challenges associated with socioeconomic class, what particular strategies of resistance are unique among Chicana women that allow them to beat the odds and continue to aspire to college completion and admirable career goals? This is an important area for future study.

While previous research indicated Latinas were less likely to go far from home for college, this has decidedly changed for Chicanas: They are now equally as likely as males to go farther away from home to attend college, at least since the 1990s. This is another area where examination by gender and specific time periods for a specific Latina/o subgroup was important. As time changes, the gender disparities disappear or shift and take on more complexity, requiring more nuanced analysis to reveal areas where inequity is reproduced and other areas that show promise of progress. For example, living away from home may be a sign of progress, indicating Chicanas are choosing more selective institutions in 2012. In this case, however, previous research could not detect the more alarming trend across the historical period: Overall, both Mexican American men and women are less likely to go farther away from home to attend a four-year college than in the past. A recent report confirmed that between 1995 and 2009, Black and Latina/o students' access has improved, but they are less likely to be represented in more selective institutions even as enrollments have grown at those institutions—an undermatching of student ability with type of college attended (Carnevale and Strohl 2013). "Since 1995, 82 percent of new white enrollments have gone to the 468 most selective colleges, while 72 percent of new Hispanic enrollments . . . have gone to the two-year and four-year open-access schools" (9). Moreover, undermatched students were less likely to graduate from the less selective colleges they attended, even though they had the ability to do so. This indicates that larger sociostructural issues are at play in limiting access, increasing racial stratification of institutions, and affecting eventual outcomes, particularly for Mexican Americans, whose progress lags behind other Latina/o ethnic groups. These include not only economic issues that affect families, but also actual policies and practices that ban considerations of race and gender in admission to selective colleges. Additional disaggregated data and policy reports should include information on Mexican Americans by gender to broadly monitor these trends in the future. Current data and reporting on Latinas/os continue to ignore the differences among the ethnic subgroups.

At the micro level, we should be attentive to gender-specific stress factors and intersubjectivities unique to the underrepresentation of Mexican Americans, which include issues such as discrimination and stereotyping, social and emotional support networks, and availability of the institutional support that alleviates academic, social, and financial concerns. Earlier work indicated that even the highest-achieving Chicanos at college entry tend to have more difficulty in social adjustment to college compared to other Latina/o groups (Hurtado, Carter, and Spuler 1996), an issue that is also intertwined with coming from first-generation and low-income families. Having Latina/o role models (faculty and staff) and cultural support programs that build networks for Chicanas/os in unfamiliar environments can go a long way in easing the transition to college for students who are the first to attempt a baccalaureate degree in their family.

The fact that one in four Chicanas aspires to a doctoral degree at this early stage of college entry suggests that there may well be changes in the research workforce and professoriate that will include more Chicanas in the future, if they find support along these pathways. Changes in Mexican American career aspirations are subject to the economic era, as well as changing gender roles that have occurred over time. For example, they may be uniquely impacted by period effects such as the longest war in U.S. history and also recovery from the Great Recession in recent years (DeNavas-Walt, Proctor, and Smith 2011). Both of these major events have had a marked effect on Mexican American communities in terms of what students do after high school. Increasing postsecondary participation rates at the undergraduate and graduate levels may be due mainly to the inability of the economy to accommodate large numbers of young, inexperienced workers.

The increase in men's and women's aspirations for health-related professions also portends great opportunity for diversifying the scientific workforce, but only if Mexican Americans successfully navigate introductory course work in science, technology, engineering, and mathematics (STEM). Students are more likely to increase or sustain their commitment to graduate school and career development if they have access across the life course to opportunity structures, including undergraduate research programs, internships, supplemental instruction, departmental clubs and organizations, and institutional and faculty support and mentorship (Eagan et al. 2013; Hurtado, Eagan, Tran, Newman, Chang, and Velasco 2011). Most of the growth in new jobs is predicted to occur in STEM fields, and ensuring that Mexican Americans have the academic preparation and opportunities to be successful in college will be key to their progress in these fields of study. The fact that student interest in STEM majors is the highest it has ever been suggests that academic preparation may be improving in schools but that competition may be higher in college. Engineering and health professions schools and majors must do more to retain the diversity of talent. It is important to note that there is currently a flurry of activity as institutions work to improve their STEM programs due to new grant monies available at the federal level (National Science Foundation and National Institutes of Health) and from private foundations for curricular reform. While a few of the foundation grants stipulate that colleges must include underrepresented groups in their sponsored initiatives, we should assess the extent to which these reforms assist Mexican Americans and other historically underrepresented groups in college. Both women and racial/ethnic minorities are severely underrepresented in engineering and the physical sciences, and, although numbers are growing in the biological sciences, they have yet to ascend the employment hierarchy to jobs that promise the greatest rewards. However, individuals from underrepresented groups who attain success could open pathways for others to follow.

As with all historical periods, we find both windows of opportunity and other times that have constrained choices among the growing numbers of Mexican Americans seeking access to higher education and careers after college. Further study on Mexican Americans is important and necessary, since they continue to lag behind other Latina/o groups and non-Hispanic Whites; and continuing to study only the general Latina/o population can mask these differences and hinder our evaluation of progress. Existing data from federal and state sources should be analyzed using a lens of critical intersectionality, directed toward the whole life course of those studied, with attention to circumstances that make a difference (or con-

PART II

CONCEPTUAL UNDERSTANDINGS

CHAPTER 4

An Intersectional Lens: Theorizing an Educational Paradigm of Success

RUTH ENID ZAMBRANA AND SYLVIA HURTADO

Presently, many behavioral and social scientists hold the deficit thinking model in disrepute—arguing that it ignores the role of systemic factors in creating school failure, lacks empirical verification, relies more on ideology than science, grounds itself in classism, sexism, and racism, and offers counterproductive educational prescriptions for school success.
RICHARD R. VALENCIA, *DISMANTLING CONTEMPORARY DEFICIT THINKING*

The goals of educational opportunity, equity, social mobility, and diversity—what do these terms mean for Mexican American progress and completion of schooling and higher education, and what does the achievement gap portend for the social and economic well-being of the United States as a nation? The *achievement gap*, as educational inequity has been labeled, recalls for the American public the question of access to the basic right to a quality education, whether in compulsory P-12 or voluntary participation in sectors of higher education necessary for high-skill jobs. Gaps in educational performance have been stark and indisputable markers of how historical exclusionary practices and social disinvestments have shaped Mexican Americans' educational opportunities and progress in their educational journey. The causes of these disparate outcomes cannot be understood without theoretical framing that devotes attention to myriad social and institutional factors that reproduce inequity, permit incremental social mobility, and transform conditions for Mexican Americans throughout their educational trajectory.

An examination of the foundational knowledge base on Mexican Americans and educational success in the mainstream literature shows a *culturally circumscribed framework* that seriously delimits the power to explain factors associated with academic achievement. Therefore, several important empirical questions guide the analytical review in this chapter in understanding the factors associated with educational progress among Mexican Americans: Why has *culture* become the default signifier of educational failure for Mexican Americans and the larger aggregate of Latinos? How do we explain achievement and success among Mexican Americans? What new theoretical developments and approaches can help us best explain the educational trajectories of Mexican Americans? Our ultimate goal is to shift the discourse on Mexican American education, subvert the master narrative of cultural deficit and blaming individual victims, break disciplinary silos, and link individual with group and organizational/institutional contexts.

The overall goal of this chapter is to engage the multiple bodies of scholarship that contribute to understanding the pathways of educational success, with particular attention to integrating sociohistorical and institutional contexts that shape the conditions for Mexican Americans in education. To that end, this chapter has four major purposes: (a) to briefly critique major theorizing assumptions in existing conventional theories of performance and educational attainment that obfuscate historical social and power relationships between White dominant and Mexican American groups; (b) to examine the role of structural inequality and institutional barriers throughout the educational pipeline as central constructs in reproducing inequality for Mexican Americans; (c) to proffer an intersectional theorizing lens to engage a theoretical discourse that decenters individual attributions as major predictors of success as opposed to outside and institutional context; and (d) to integrate multiple Mexican American identities, and institutional contexts, and extend the intersectional lens to address its use in specifically higher education outcomes. In doing so we can extend and fill in gaps of knowledge about the factors that matter most in successful completion by Mexican Americans of educational milestones in P-16 and beyond. We proffer a more comprehensive and nuanced accounting through the use of an intersectional lens, one that accounts for coconstitutive student identities of race, class, ethnicity, and gender and power relations between majority and subordinate minority groups.

We focus on Mexican Americans, as they represent the largest and most maligned group and as a result have experienced *generations of exclusion* (Telles and Ortiz 2008). Our scholarly investments are driven by shifting ethnic- and gender-centered discourses that all too often essentialize the Hispanic/Latino ethnic category, erasing the experiences of Mexican American men and women. Ultimately, the intellectual outcome of this chapter is to develop an approach that not only identifies the re-production of inequality, but also reveals the transformative moments that are shaped by the dynamics of actors within educational contexts that reverse long-standing oppression and privilege in each historical epoch. Our first step in the development of a more comprehensive theoretical approach is to critique existing paradigms that frame the problems and solutions for the education of Mexican Americans.

The Contours of Conventional Paradigms of Success: Disjuncture in Lived Experiences

In past and contemporary periods, the prevailing explanatory framework in the field of education has been the *culturally deterministic approach*, wherein ethnic values regarding education were assigned a causal role in educational performance. The paradigm of cultural determinism has been unyielding in its narrow conceptions of individual attributes assigned, such as lack of parental value on education, as a major cause of educational failure. This master narrative is deployed to focus on individual and ethnic group deficits, and dismisses structural inequality and institutional factors that strongly shape educational outcomes (Espino 2012).

Critically important is the dominant discourse on Mexican-origin groups, which is rooted in traditional theory that rests on a restricted and static notion of social history, and the ways in which problems have been ascribed to culturally coded difference (Baca Zinn 1995). In these narratives and many others, the grounding of theory is based on the documentation of historical observations without acknowledging how structural forces shaped the lives of Mexican American communities (Almaguer 1994; Barerra 1979). More to the point, conventional sociological theory has treated race, gender, and class as secondary factors in its analysis of nondominant culture group differences, a practice that strongly supports a Eurocentric view, a social problem orientation, and a culturally deter-ministic fallacy (Palmer 1983, 154; Bonilla-Silva 2006). Conventional thinking dominates the intellectual discourse on Mexican Americans and other Latinos, as it both reflects and is rooted in a superior/inferior binary that obscures the relationship among power, institutional investments, and the production of knowledge (Zuberi and Bonilla-Silva 2008).

The legacy of conventional research has promulgated a master narra-tive of basic deficiency theories, which contend that historically under-represented racial/ethnic minority groups occupy an inferior economic, social, and political position because of some cultural deficiency within the minority group itself. For example, Mexican American families have been characterized as highly traditional and as using nonadaptive family structures that are in conflict with the requirements of upward mobility in an industrialized Western society. Further, their gender role structure has been described as ruled by a rigid patriarchy or the myth of machismo and inflexible gender roles (Valencia 2010). These deficit models thrive because the majority of studies are conducted with low-income families, and results are all too frequently misinterpreted and generalized to an entire group regardless of socioeconomic status. A careful review and critique of mainstream literature on Latino families, the majority of the evidence for which is derived from Mexican American samples, challenge the claims that families have a patent on male dominance, and highlight the variations in family patterns and gender role behaviors (Zambrana 2011). Research that utilizes deficit framing typically relies on victim-blaming and offers programs and policies dedicated to correcting deficiencies (Valencia 2010), ignoring structures and power relations that perpetuate inequality.

A school of thought has developed alongside, and in opposition to, traditional theorists that debunks the myths of ethnic causality and simplistic explanations that point to parental values and attitudes as an explanation for educational underperformance (Valencia 2010). Rather, these theorists argue that institutional forces assume varying degrees of relevance, and interact in diverse ways throughout the life course of a family, and in the school and community, to expand or constrict access to the social and economic opportunity structure. Mexican American families experience a disproportionate burden of low material resources that creates pathways of disadvantage and diminishes their access to the opportunity structure (e.g., quality of health services, employment opportunities, and access to educational institutions).

Families as Resources: The Role of Material Advantage in Educational Performance

Beyond the critical body of interdisciplinary work, we also draw from the sociology of family. The study of the educational pipeline is firmly entrenched in the study of families, as parents are viewed as the major gateway or gatekeeper to educational performance and success. Significant limitations of these studies include samples that are predominantly of low-income Mexican-origin families, which proffer a limited view of socioeconomic variation in family socialization processes and family assets. Ample evidence suggests that Mexican-origin families exhibit values that provide cohesiveness to the family structure and reliance on each other for emotional encouragement and support, and extended family structures that vary by generational status and socioeconomic status (SES) (Landale, Oropesa, and Bradatan 2006; Espino 2014). New avenues of inquiry have been pioneered by the examination of family and institutional factors, and how the intersection of race, ethnicity, gender, and SES is associated with academic and professional success (Covarrubias 2011; H. Garza 1993; Molina 2008; Zambrana, Dorrington, and Bell 1997).

Family size, family structure, and socioeconomic status critically shape a child's access to early learning activities and future academic achievement (Lee and Burkam 2002). A two-parent family structure is considered most favorable for providing positive learning and schooling experiences. This advantage is accentuated when both parents have a decent standard of living, knowledge of their role as advocates in the school system, and the emotional energy and economic means to provide extracurricular opportunities for their children. Several scholars contend that we cannot study Mexican American family processes, gender socialization, and development without taking into account the role of material conditions and community resources (García-Coll et al. 1996; Baca Zinn 1995; McLoyd, Cauce, Takeuchi, and Wilson 2000; Lareau 2003, 2014). In an in-depth comparative ethnographic study of African American and White families to assess different child-oriented educational practices, Lareau (2003) found that middle-income, college-educated parents have more economic resources to provide multiple access points to the opportunity structure—such as academic tutoring and sports—to promote cognitive growth and nurture specific talents, which are associated with accomplishing future goals. These resources also allow them to engage in parenting practices that stress communication, negotiation, logic, and reasoning. Furthermore, values of assertiveness and competitiveness are associated with high parental education level in all cultures. Generally, parents with higher education and marketable skills tend to be more economically and psychologically prepared to engage in early learning activities and skill-building with their children, and to be actively involved in their education regardless of racial/ethnic grouping. In contrast, low-income, non-college-educated parents are less likely to effectively engage in their children's early learning due to a lack of access to information, and to help with homework due often to low literacy and math skills. These impediments, combined with language barriers, discrimination by school counselors and other personnel, economic necessities requiring parents to work two or more jobs, and transportation problems, preclude attendance at school meetings (Auerbach 2002; Loza 2003; Zambrana and Morant 2009). High-income Mexican American and other Latino parents do not face these challenges, and are more likely to send their children to high-performing schools, live in neighborhoods with higher-resourced schools, and have children who engage in extracurricular academic activity. Nonetheless, low-SES parents also have much family capital and proffer important assets to their children to help them remain in school and enhance academic preparation for a competitive application for college entry.

Data show the unique ways in which Mexican American parents socialize children to navigate the educational process. In a study of Mexican American families and their interactions in the home, Delgado Gaitan (1992) shows how parents draw upon material resources and social networks to facilitate their children's educational experience. Further, parents offer their children emotional support, often referencing their own personal experiences to communicate their aspirations and motivate their children. Montoya (1994) identifies "masking our inner selves" as a defensive strategy parents teach their children in order to navigate racism within schools and society. She states, "There is sometimes the feeling of moving between different worlds, of putting on one face and taking off another" (5).

In an attempt to shift away from the deficit-driven frameworks applied to economically underserved ethnic communities, Yosso (2005, 2006) posits a theoretical model of community cultural wealth, which she argues encompasses the various forms of capital that are abundant in communities of color and can be used in order to resist oppressive forces. Yosso (2005, 2006) has identified six forms of community cultural wealth:

1. Resistant capital: acknowledging when Latinos challenge inequity and/or subordination;
2. Linguistic capital: where communication through different languages and/or styles is seen as an asset;
3. Navigational capital: one can learn to maneuver social institutions and barriers;
4. Social capital: resources that are accessed through social networks;
5. Familial capital: acknowledges the strength of cultural and/or family knowledge and histories; and
6. Aspirational capital: acknowledging that aspirations and hope are motivating factors despite challenges.

Among the six forms of capital, familial capital highlights the way cultural knowledge is developed, maintained, and encouraged by kinship networks and fosters a commitment to community well-being. Although Yosso focuses on all Latinos, her model's applicability to Mexican Americans is evident in more recent scholarship in higher education that is being expanded on by emergent scholars. These scholars have weaved together a theorizing lens that incorporates and constructs intersectional and social capital theory to create counternarratives around factors associated with successful pathways to higher education (Espino 2012, 2014; Cabrera 2014; Núñez 2014a, 2014b).

Cultural and social capital theory (Bourdieu 1986; Bourdieu and Passeron 1977) was developed as a theory of social reproduction—explaining how the rich sustain opportunities for their children and the poor reproduce poverty in their children's life trajectory. In framing the problem as one of social reproduction, however, researchers neglect moments of resistance and success in transcending these social and cultural norms. How can we explain, for example, the relatively high proportion of Mexican Americans from low-income, first-generation families gaining access to four-year colleges over the decades (see chapter 3)? This fact disrupts the reproduction hypothesis and opens possibilities for understanding alternate forms of capital, including what Yosso (2005) calls resistant capital. More important, educational solutions based on this social reproduction narrative seek to remedy deficits using interventions to provide social and cultural information missing from low-income students' families rather than addressing the real problem of power and/or lack of empowerment. Alternately, Yosso (2005, 2006) acknowledges that inequality is reproduced, and at the same time identifies the transformative resources within communities and families that foster resistance and strength among Latino children in the educational process. Conchas (2006) also identifies the mechanisms by which familial and nonfamilial capital (peer norms and behaviors within school structures) work to produce achievement among Mexican American urban youth, in spite of discrimination and neglect.

The scholarly discourse on Mexican American family socialization and educational processes requires shifting the lens to account for an understanding that the transmission of values is filtered through gender differences, racial/ethnic origins, class background, and historically unfair treatment in the host society. Critical to placing Mexican Americans at the center of analysis is an understanding of their multiple social identities as marginalized and privileged, depending on the source of oppression (e.g., racism, sexism, classism). Critics have also stated that many intersectional studies that do well in documenting how life experiences lead to multiple forms of identity are often limited in that they undertheorize the role of power in different settings, and how it shapes life chances (Cho, Crenshaw, and McCall 2013). The power hierarchy is often institutionalized as structures, norms, and legitimizing myths that shape daily life and forms of epistemology (Espino 2012). The next sections detail intersectional approaches that recognize these essential components.[1]

Emerging Scholarship on the Intersections of Race, Ethnicity, Class, and Gender

A major barrier to creating a discourse reflective of the lived experiences of Mexican Americans has been the resistance (or blindness) by leading education scholars to the emergence of major embedded and interlocking systems of oppression around race, ethnicity, gender, and SES arising from a history of past racial relations in the United States. Mexican American racial and/or social identity continues to be a contested issue. History and legal policy demonstrate that Mexican Americans were classified as *Black or Other Race* up until 1960. Different historical periods have shaped the social identity of Mexican Americans in terms of imposed identity definitions by dominant cultural institutions, such as the United States Census Bureau, and by individual perceptions associated with geography and peer group. Not unexpectedly, fluid constructions of identity in the twenty-first century are associated with individual ambivalence, level of political consciousness regarding the benefits of being White, family socialization, and the ever-changing national diversity discourse on race and mixed-race ethnicity (Bonilla-Silva 2006; Ortiz and Telles 2012; G. A. Martinez 1997; C. E. Rodríguez 2000). Ample criticism has been leveled against conventional theorizing models for their short-sightedness and limited power to further our understanding of factors associated with the social and economic mobility of racial/ethnic groups in the United States (Cho, Crenshaw, and McCall 2013; Zambrana 2011; Zuberi and Bonilla-Silva 2008; Telles and Ortiz 2008). These challenges are exacerbated by the lack of consensus on definitions for "ethnicity" and "class." New understandings regarding culture as an asset, rather than a predictor of inequality, are being inserted into the discourse of academic success (Yosso, Smith, Ceja, and Solórzano 2009). Similarly, "class," or "socioeconomic status," is a term that has received extensive attention at different moments in intellectual discourse.

Acknowledging race and class categories challenges existing ideal notions of meritocracy and upward class mobility. Class is deeply embedded in a framework of economic resources, which influences educational standpoints, achievement, values of work, and expectations for social mobility. Long-standing empirical work furnishes strong evidence of the relationship between class status and educational standpoints (belief in the value of education). In general, a fairly high positive relationship is reported between social class and parental emphasis on ideals, critical thinking, and the development of special abilities, rather than an emphasis only on obtaining a better job (Allen and Solórzano 2001; Lareau and Horvat 1999; Lareau 2003, 2014). A significant counterargument to conventional individualistic theories of success and meritocracy is that the relationship between social class and educational standpoints can be generally conceived of as linear, with increases in education level associated with increases in SES, and in turn increased access to social and economic opportunity structures (Guinier and Sturm 2001). We argue that the educational standpoint on value of education does not differ considerably across SES groups, but rather access to educational and social resources differs by SES and impacts educational outcome. Yet within the discourse on unequal opportunity and treatment, gender and Mexican American ethnicity were marginal to the civil rights demand of equal treatment and inclusion in the national discourse on educational achievement and success.

Late twentieth-century Chicana scholars demanded the insertion of Mexican American women into the Chicano movement and into the feminist discourse. Cuádraz (2005) noted that theoretical developments in the 1990s took several important turns in the study of Chicanas in higher education. Scholars incorporated "feminist theory (particularly that of women of color), social reproduction literature, postcolonial studies, and cultural studies, employing innovative and methodological frameworks to explore the issues of educational attainment for Chicanas" (224). These developments brought together and explored gender, social agency, strategies of resistance, and community and institutional contexts. And yet, despite the progress in theorizing after three decades of research on Chicanas and higher education, Cuádraz (2005) concludes with some questions: Has theory been decolonized? Does it go far enough in "interrogating the centrality of power, culture, and ideology to understand how the variegated experiences of Chicanas are shaped in institutions of higher education? And how are we translating across theory and practice?" (228). A reading of contemporary empirical literature and trend data suggests that this body of groundbreaking theory linked with action has yet to be operationalized, as Chicanas are still not faring well in institutions of higher education relative to other groups, and continue to confront the effects of gender, class, and racial/ethnic stereotyping and discrimination (C. E. Rodríguez 2000; K. P. González 2002; Gándara and Contreras 2009). Yet continued investigation of the role of gender in Mexican American progress in higher education has revealed a reversal in prior data trends. More recent trends reveal that Chicano males now face specific and unique forms of discrimination in education, and have experienced a reversal of opportunity relative to Chicanas in educational progress. This poses new questions for further studies on changes in men's and women's experiences relative to distinct domains of power, especially in academic settings.

Schools and Colleges as Institutions That Maintain or Change the Status Quo

Educational institutions are powerful in the socialization and intellectual and cognitive development of Mexican American children. The quality of institutional agents and academic resources along the P–12 pathway, such as advanced placement (AP) classes and computers, is associated with and deeply affects structural inequality over the students' life course. Extensive studies have been conducted on the persistence of institutional barriers to learning and educational performance—namely, the prevalent stereotypic attitudes held by educators regarding their students' ability, resulting in lower expectations; lack of support systems, such as financial assistance; and lack of Latino role models, such as faculty and administrators who can provide mentorship and emotional support during students' higher education experiences (Escobedo 1981; Azmitia, Cooper, Garcia, and Dunbar 1996; Cooper 2001; Gándara and Bial 2001; Reese, Balzano, Gallimore, and Goldenberg 1995; Zambrana, Dorrington, and Bell 1997). Research on the high school experiences of Mexican Americans continues to confirm that high schools provide inadequate preparation for college, low teacher expectations, and too little information and communication about college options, which hinders academic achievement and erodes self-confidence and a sense of belonging and pride in heritage and ethnic identity. Researchers have identified academic tracking as the primary way schools structure inequality in America (Oakes 2005; Malagon 2010). Academic tracking ensures that large numbers of African Americans and Latinos from low-income families rarely attain social mobility through education. Tracking shapes the educational experiences of Mexican American students, and males in particular, as they are often concentrated in special education and vocational training and targeted for disciplinary sanctions (Malagon 2010). This results in Mexican American students' receiving unequal access to college preparation, and in some cases, unwelcoming classroom environments and tense interactions with teachers. Malagon (2010) uses evidence from a study of Chicano male continuation high school students to argue that they experience a binary of neglect and hypersurveillance from teachers and school staff. B. Dávila (2014) exposes Latino student interactions with special education teachers, which include disregard, bullying, and low expectations. Tracking is influenced by not only measures of performance in students' earliest years, but also teachers' judgment of students. Solórzano (1997) argues that stereotyping is often relied upon in order to justify teachers' unequal treatment of students in high schools. Racial profiling in schools also reinforces rationales for tracking systems, and affects the academic performance and identity development of Mexican American students (Conchas 2006; Noguera 2003; Pizarro 2005).

Some scholars have also contended that community colleges, where the majority of Mexican Americans begin college, serve as a form of tracking in higher education; they were built to offset demands for access to more elite institutions, and the role of counselors is to discourage students from pursuing baccalaureate degrees (Karabel 1972; Alba and Lavin 1981; Dougherty 2001). Research specifically on Latino community college students confirms that many who begin college with intentions to transfer to a four-year institution do not transfer within the time frame of most studies (Crisp and Núñez 2011). Controlling for individual and institutional factors, predominantly first-generation, low-income Latino community college students who intend to transfer are placed in vocational curricular tracks (rather than academic tracks) that reduce the likelihood of ever transferring to a four-year institution. However, educators can assume, and have assumed, more empowering roles to assist Mexican American students in navigating systemic barriers.

Research demonstrates the importance of the presence of role models and other institutional agents in the development of Mexican American and other racial/ethnic minority youth. Stanton-Salazar (1997, 2001, 2010) provides the theoretical construct of *institutional agents*, people in key positions with a high degree of social and cultural capital, and the ability to mobilize resources on behalf of low-income youth. Essential to this process is the critical consciousness that institutional agents possess, which is dedicated to empowering youth. Expanding on this work, Espinoza (2011) offers a model of pivotal moments that present low-income youth pathways to higher education. She argues that students' disposition toward schooling is transformed by pivotal-moment educators who establish trust with students and transmit academic knowledge. Key personnel can make a difference in students' lives in their transition to college. New complexities identified include a reversal of opportunity for college enrollment of Mexican American men compared with women—a key illustration of how historicity can alter conditions. However, both groups continue to face structural, representational, intersubjective, and experiential challenges that sustain oppression, but appear to have become more unique to each gender. Thus, what may largely be attributed to individuals are really responses to larger social dynamics that shape forms of oppression experienced by Mexican American students. From a life course perspective, family material assets are associated with educational choices and educational and social resources that affect life chances and access to the opportunity structure.

Drawing from existing and emergent theory, we examine and argue for a more interdisciplinary, intersectional perspective to formulate a broader theorizing discourse of educational processes and outcomes among Mexican Americans. This approach allows for an expanded understanding of the complex role of historical conditions and their associations with family, socioeconomic status, and structural and other institutional factors associated with the successful completion of various educational milestones in the P-16 pathways and beyond to the long-term career trajectory. What is more, it is necessary to expand the theoretical lens to include new frameworks that address the larger social and political macro forces, so as to fully appreciate how these forces have shaped the life course of Mexican Americans in the United States.

Key Features of an Intersectional Approach to Mexican American Education

To advance our understanding of Mexican Americans, research may be improved by operating with explicit critical assumptions that contest conventional explanatory paradigms about inequality and social location. We propose the use of an intersectional lens that includes four foundational critical theorizing assumptions:

1. History shapes lived experiences that, in turn, are reflected in dominant/subordinate group relations, which shape access to resources, and policies and practices that maintain subordination of groups and hinder social mobility. Every study is historically situated, and although eras, issues, and struggles have changed, the mechanisms of oppression can be similar in outcome, resulting in only incremental progress for Mexican American communities.

2. Racial/ethnic characteristics are mutually constituted and embedded in power relations. *Power-based relations* are defined as "hierarchical, stratified (ranked), centered in power—benefiting and providing options and resources for some by harming and restricting options and resources for others" (L. Weber 2010, 23). Power-based relations make invisible the structural factors that contribute to restricted resources and options. They uphold a paradigm that attributes success and upward mobility to the assumptions and legitimizing myths embedded in discourse, such as individuals "pulling themselves up by their bootstraps," a shared definition of meritocracy, or the existence of a color-blind society (Bonilla-Silva 2006).

3. Gendered and racialized social constructions are made visible and filtered to and through the American public imagination via primary mechanisms of socialization, such as schools, media, and science. The major argument here is that the marking of Mexican Americans as a *racialized other* has consequences that limit access to economic opportunity structures, such as P–16. Racialized social constructions of Latino subgroups as poor and culturally stagnant are inserted into social science research and reinforced in educational and college systems, creating negative identity markers with severe social consequences (Amaro 1995; Bettie 2003; A. Hurtado 1996; Sandoval 2000; de la Torre and Pesquera 1993; Cobas, Duany, and Feagin 2009).

4. Social agency is a critical concept for understanding the lives of individuals and the transformation of institutions. Social agency can take the form of individual resistance or collective action (which has historical roots in a community), to consciously alter the reproduction of inequality (Espino 2012; Yosso 2005, 2006).

These explicit deconstructionist features have been central in advancing the knowledge production of the interdisciplinary field of Chicana/o Studies. The major contributions of the field have been to produce counternarratives that document multiple realities and lived experiences, and to expose legal and institutional practices that continue to prevent successful educational outcomes for Mexican Americans, both men and women (see *Harvard Educational Review* 2012). Such research is beginning to launch new approaches to the study of Mexican American educational progress. Contemporary intersectional theorists who study the educational trajectory of Mexican Americans engage in four main analytic tasks (see Zambrana 2011; Zambrana and MacDonald 2009; Espino 2012):

1. Placing the lived experiences and struggles of racial/ethnic minorities and other marginalized groups at the forefront of the development of theory;
2. Exploring the complexities of individual identities and group identity, recognizing that variations within groups are often ignored and essentialized;
3. Unveiling the ways interconnected domains of power organize and structure inequality and oppression, particularly in P–16 educational systems; and
4. Promoting social justice and social change by linking research and practice to create a holistic approach to the eradication of disparities, and to change higher education and other social institutions.

Advancing this kind of understanding of students' educational trajectory—along with multiple other contextual factors, such as lack of a welcoming academic environment, the community-resource education (P–12) environment, and educational institutional policies and practices—has a powerful impact on the life course processes that shape the formation of Mexican American ethnic identity, life choices, and life options. Over the life course, the accumulation of social and psychological disadvantage erodes a sense of self-efficacy and too frequently contributes to depression and a diminished sense of hope and control over one's life. Social and historical determinants of educational achievement, in conjunction with psychological disadvantage, have powerfully affected the real-life educational experiences of Mexican American students in the United States.

Núñez (2014a) reviewed the literature on Latino access and success in higher education to find that very few studies fully employed an intersectional lens in which power dynamics are addressed at the societal and institutional levels, often leading researchers to ascribe unequal outcomes to individuals rather than to institutions or educational practices that perpetuate inequality. She argues that not understanding how power dynamics work makes it more difficult to achieve the task of advancing social change. Further, she indicates that many more studies are beginning to document the lived experiences of Latino P–16 students, graduate students, and faculty with specific social identities (of gender, ethnicity, and class), but very few have focused on varied structures of inequality to understand unique contextual effects. Drawing on intersectionality, Núñez (2014a) applies existing frameworks to the study of Latino access and success in education, so as to take into account: (a) the multiple social identities (of gender, immigrant status, race, phenotype, national origin, religion, sexuality, language, and class); (b) the four domains of power that operate in educational contexts, including the organizational, representational, intersubjective, and experiential; and (c) historicity. In doing so, she advances the study of intersecting identities among Latinos that have been understudied in education and critical race theory. Attending to the structures of opportunity and inequality, and to variation in educational environments, is an important starting point for uncovering the invisible role of the domains of power in different historical eras, and how the force of power relations has shaped complex identity formations.

Perceptions of the dominant society, historical treatment, and institutional practice all play a significant role in processes of (non)integration of marginalized Mexican American groups into a host society. Interestingly, a small number of studies on Latino immigrant college students propose a framework of resiliency as their key to educational success and performance (Perez, Sribney, and Rodríguez 2009; Alva 1991; R. Garza 2009). These researchers have attempted to highlight the resilient strengths of immigrant students, but sometimes such stories speak to the American imagination of individual strength, absent a context of race, history, parental resources, and social capital. As a result, other scholars have sounded urgent calls to move well beyond the well-worn debates on individual achievement outside of a social context (Noguera 2006; Valenzuela 1999).

Although the research on resilience has come a long way in recent years, major considerations have been ignored in its conceptualization. The traditional notion of resilience "tends to place the responsibility of achieving success primarily on the effort of the individual without considering the economic, historical, and political contexts of schooling," thus "leaving the dynamics of power embedded in the schooling systems unexamined" (Campa 2010, 431). Excluding the larger institutional systems of society from the operation of resilience attributes the blame for failure and credit for success primarily to the individual, and relieves educational institutions and society of responsibility, perpetuating the status quo. Another mechanism that veils power dynamics is promotion of the fallacy of Hispanic pan-ethnicity and aggregating all Hispanic native-born and immigrant groups together, regardless of race and racialized identity. This aggregation, both at the Hispanic group level and at the immigrant-status level, belies subgroup differences and masks educational disparities and inequities, particularly for Mexican Americans. Questioning power dynamics within social and socioethnic contexts is crucial in order to have a deeper and complex understanding of resilience. These limitations triggered a reconceptualization of resilience, and the term "critical resilience" evolved as a result of applying a feminist critical perspective (Anzaldúa 1987; Campa 2010; Collins 2000; Delpit 2006; Delgado Bernal, Elenes, Godinez, and Villenas 2006), adding more complexity to the original theory.

This new construction of resilience critiques established power and knowledge in educational practices and therefore can help us examine in greater depth, for instance, how the social systems (peers, teachers, families) in a learning community influence the success of a group of Mexican American English as a Second Language (ESL) students. Critical resilience emphasizes the importance of social, cultural, economic, and historical contexts in understanding the lives of Mexican American ESL students, and therefore allows us to see a more nuanced and multidimensional portrait of their experiences (Campa 2010). For example, community college students in general, and the participants in Campa's study in particular, inhabit multiple intersections; they tend to be older, female, and Latino, and are in the process of learning a second language. Collins (2000) reminds us that oppression cannot be reduced to one cause, since race, gender, class, sexuality, and other social forces intersect to produce injustice. Thus, we move from traditional notions of resiliency to propose that Mexican American men and women (U.S.-born or Mexico-born) have effectively used strategies of resistance as an ethnic group to inform and promote their use of social agency to overcome barriers and pursue avenues of educational opportunity.

Critical Intersectionality in Life Course Pathways to Higher Education for Mexican Americans

Another emerging model that extends a critical intersectional lens is proposed by Zambrana and colleagues (2015), specifying the role of mentoring as a form of intersubjectivity and highlighting the factors that affect Latinos uniquely over the life course. This extends previous intersectional work to include life stages as a form of historicity. Previous studies have focused on different stages of the educational trajectory without integrating an intersectional lens across the stages of the life course when critical decisions are made (e.g., decisions about academic objectives and college enrollment). This neglect is caused primarily by the requirement of the critical intersectional approach of a longitudinal design or in-depth retrospective study of a single and/or multiple cohorts, and an understanding of how the lives of Mexican Americans at different stages interact with the educational system. To be more explicit, as we examine multiple identities and their intersections with history, the accumulation of advantage or disadvantage is viewed as an important dimension, particularly in the educational progress of low-income Mexican Americans.

Central to the life course framework is the notion that events experienced by individuals at every stage of their life inform subsequent ones, and individuals are constantly relearning stages, while progressing forward along a spiraling path. This interrelationship of events starts before birth, and in fact, before conception. There are four central components to a life course framework:

- *Linked lives*: parental choices, behaviors, and biological vulnerabilities affect their children.
- *Life events can be viewed as a trajectory*: influences have a differential impact at various stages of the life course.
- *Personal agency*: individuals make choices influenced by the social worlds in which they live (e.g., family, peers, neighborhood).
- *Historical and social context matters*: a historical perspective provides a context for understanding how current dominant-subordinate group relations and social conditions, including the intersections of multiple dimensions of identity (e.g., race, sexuality, socioeconomic status, gender), impact how systems of inequality are experienced.

This theorizing lens was found to be salient in the study of pioneer respondents and historically underrepresented minority faculty. The respondents reported on the importance of life course (elementary school through college), access to mentors, and social capital, for the purposes of opening doors and providing information. Many of the participants described the importance of mentors during their educational journey, including parents, religious leaders, community kin, and college professors. Mentors served as role models across many settings and set an aspirational bar for respondents in their personal lives and scholarly work. Mentors helped participants during the college years to negotiate institutions, particularly cultural and political norms at Predominantly White Institutions (PWIs): unwritten rules, institutional climate, access to support, and access to opportunity structures (e.g., financial support) (Zambrana et al. 2015).

In summary, the emerging body of critical intersectional life course scholarship has created an important counterdiscourse to disrupt knowledge production practices that reinforce deficit thinking. This new body of work interrogates the attribution of individual and cultural factors as integral to the deficit-driven paradigm that has dominated scholarship on Mexican American educational performance. This corpus of knowledge demonstrates how multiple institutional factors and majoritarian worldviews, particularly the superior/inferior binary, powerfully shape the opportunity structure throughout the life course of Mexican American youth and, unquestionably, other racialized Latinos and African Americans. We draw on this nascent, yet important, scholarship to extend the intersectional lens and its use in education, specifically higher education and its outcomes, with particular focus on integrating multiple identities and multiple institutional contexts.

Climate Research and a Multicontextual Identity-Based Framework

In the last twenty years, more research has extended to and given emphasis to racialized higher education contexts, and has extended to illustrate the phenomenon of underrepresentation across Latinos identity groups (Ruiz Alvarado and Hurtado 2015). The institutional climate for inclusion or exclusion on campus can be considered part of the normative environment, created by both institutional actors and organizational factors. The earliest large-scale, national study on climate focused on perceptions of a hostile campus environment among Chicano students, in comparison to African American and White classmates, in their fourth year of college (S. Hurtado 1992). It also took care to contextualize within the late 1980s the larger social and historical events occurring at the time, including many campus racial incidents. Chicanos who perceived higher racial tension on campus tended to have higher academic self-concepts and attended four-year public universities. Interestingly, Chicanos were least likely to perceive racial tension at Catholic colleges, presumably because these students may have had greater similarities in religious identity. Another study, on Chicano and African American graduate students, using an earlier longitudinal cohort in the late 1970s, found that students maintained high academic self-concepts in graduate school and had perceived a hostile graduate school climate; S. Hurtado (1994a) believed this phenomenon was historically typical of "pioneering" students, who were the first to experience underrepresentation in their exclusive graduate programs. The effects of parental SES on minority students' academic self-concept diminished over time, as students reached graduate school, suggesting the need to reexamine these issues over the life course. As the survivors of a long educational process, they had acquired resistance strategies and new areas for building positive self-concept that superseded class status and the experience of racism in educational environments (S. Hurtado 1994b). Results indicated that student perceptions of a hostile climate had negative effects on all measures of adjustment to college (i.e., academic, social, personal emotional adjustment), and Mexican Americans had substantially lower outcome scores on social adjustment compared to all other Latino groups (Hurtado, Carter, and Spuler 1996). It is important to note that the Latino students in these latter studies were among the most talented undergraduates by standard measures of test scores, having won a national academic scholarship and/or gained access to a four-year institution. These studies show campus racial climate as an institutional force that could negatively affect the most talented Latino students entering higher education during the 1990s. These national studies were further supported by many earlier small-scale studies conducted on other underrepresented groups at specific campuses that show the negative effect of the campus racial climate on a wide range of educational outcomes (Hurtado, Milem, Clayton-Pederson, and Allen 1999). The underlying assumption of this campus climate research is that students are educated in racialized contexts, and therefore, the climate is conceptualized as an institutional phenomenon that has real consequences for college students. This racialized climate is created by the interactions among majority and minority groups, is dynamic, and is shaped by larger social and historical forces.

Studies of campus racial climate continue to illustrate the experiences of Mexican American students in higher education. Participants in K. P. González's (2002) study reported feelings of alienation and marginalization in the "social world" of campus culture, which were exacerbated by a lack of representation of Mexican Americans among the faculty. Further, students acknowledged that their communities and culture were not reflected in the "epistemological world" via the curricula, or the "physical world" of campus spaces and buildings. In courses where there were few Latino students present, they often felt pressure to serve as "spokespersons" for their race (Yosso, Smith, Ceja, and Solórzano 2009). As a result of racial microaggressions on college campuses, students of color experienced self-doubt, and their academic performance was affected (Allen and Solórzano 2001; Solórzano, Allen, and Carroll 2002; Yosso et al. 2009; Solórzano, Ceja, and Yosso 2000). Ramírez (2013) found that such campus climate concerns also shaped graduate school choice for Latino students.

Hurtado and colleagues (Hurtado, Alvarez, et al. 2012) introduced a multicontextual model of diverse learning environments in higher education that includes attention to broader sociohistorical and political contexts, which in turn influence campus climate and the dynamics among actors within institutional contexts (see figure 4.1). The model is unique in that it both incorporates the multiple intersectional social identities of actors (students, faculty, staff) and acknowledges multiple contextual levels that dynamically shift, as do larger social conditions in different time periods. Institutional climates are composed of (a) a campus's historical legacy of inclusion or exclusion; (b) the compositional dimension or underrepresentation of diverse faculty, staff, and students that shapes interpersonal dynamics; (c) the psychological dimension of the climate based on individual perceptions (e.g., subtle forms of discrimination) and standpoints; (d) the behavioral dimension of the climate (e.g., integration, segregation, overt forms of harassment/bias); and (e) the structural dimension of organizational factors that influence the climate (e.g., diversity in the curriculum, policies, budget/resources). Student identity is at the center of the model, which involves attention to multiple social identities (e.g., race, class, gender) in curricular and co-curricular spheres that operate in dynamic relationship with instructor and staff identities that include sense of belonging, academic and interpersonal validation, and socialization. Such processes mediate and directly affect student educational outcomes (e.g., habits of mind for lifelong learning, retention, and achievement). These student outcomes, in turn, influence the transformation of society in the direction of social and economic equity and democratic participation. Dimensions of the model are supported by empirical data (see chapter 8).

The model captures the capacity for institutions to simultaneously house oppression and develop transformative practices, educational programming, and curriculum content that influence student outcomes and are tied to social progress. It captures dimensions and contexts that de-

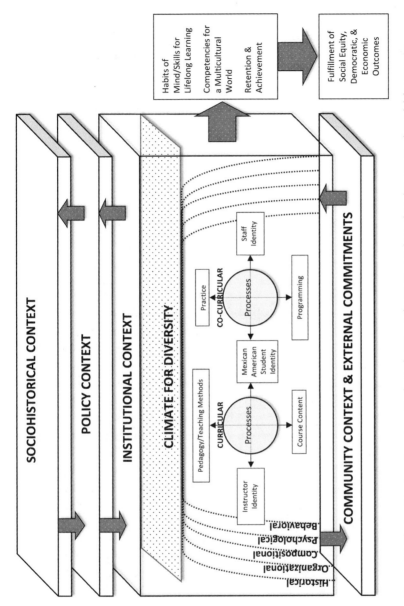

Figure 4.1. Placing Mexican American Student Identity at the Center: Adapted Multicontextual Model for Diverse Learning Environments

Source: Adapted from Hurtado, Alvarez, et al. (2012).

serve the attention of research and practice, and draws from several decades of research on underrepresented-group experiences related to campus climate, social identity theory, critical race theory, and feminist theory. Hurtado and colleagues (Hurtado, Alvarez, et al. 2012) present a coherent relational educational model that advances an intersectional perspective, specifying how the role of institutional actors can be transformed so that they become institutional agents able to improve student success in terms of social equity, democracy, and improved economic outcomes. These institutional actors also have the potential to engage in reflexivity to alter their role in the reproduction of inequality.

Conclusions

We have provided an overview of new and emerging theorizing frameworks that begin to shift the lens through which we view Mexican American educational progress. The debates that have become more visible in the last three decades have sought to disrupt the focus of analysis to combat the deficit perspective and cultural determinist arguments, contest culture-bound myths, and integrate historical and structural forces that continue to shape and will shape the life course and educational journey of Mexican American students. An emerging intersectional scholarly trend has been and continues to be the grounding of lived experiences within emerging conceptual frameworks to guide transformative research and action in the future. A new lens can provide novel insights that result in transformation at the individual and institutional levels so as to affect educational practice. The educational discourse on performance and underperformance has to be decolonized so as to improve the critical quality of educational theory, and provide depth and breadth to the dimensions of the educational trajectory of Mexican Americans.

We have emphasized structure, context, and historicity because contexts matter and students are educated in economically and racially stratified institutions, and these issues have received too little emphasis in intersectionality work (Anthias 2013; Núñez 2014a, 2014b; Espino 2014). An intersectional framework examines patterns of educational attainment, taking into account power relations that shape institutions in which historically underrepresented women and men have participated, and patterns of inequality, which include both hegemonic and disciplinary power (how institutional actors/agents apply school policy—e.g., zero tolerance policies or financial policy for first-generation college students) (see

Zambrana 2011; Ramírez 2013; Covarrubias 2011). We have characterized new developments in intersectional work in higher education in order to encourage scholarship that links research, action, and social change. Chicana/o Studies have typically integrated research with social action, but this has not uniformly been the case for those who study the education of Mexican Americans in different disciplines. Our hope is that veteran scholars will find connections across various theoretical traditions, and younger scholars will be more conscious of how to conduct research that avoids using culture as the default signifier of educational failure. Finally, we hope that our theorizing lens will serve as a catalyst for increasing interdisciplinary connections and social consciousness, so as to move beyond traditional paradigms to build on emerging intersectional analyses of the K–16 pathway to advance critical knowledge production on Mexican American educational progress.

CHAPTER 5

Parental Educational and Gender Expectations: Pushing the Educational Trajectory

RUTH ENID ZAMBRANA AND REBECA BURCIAGA

Researchers have long assumed that poor parents display poor parenting, but we find robust cultural strengths in Mexican American homes when it comes to raising eager and socially mature preschoolers.
BRUCE FULLER, QUOTED IN KATHLEEN MACLAY, "MEXICAN AMERICAN TODDLERS LAG IN PRELITERACY SKILLS, BUT NOT IN THEIR SOCIAL SKILLS, NEW STUDY SHOWS"[1]

The schooling of Mexican Americans has been clouded by a myth that parents do not value education (Valencia and Black 2002). We know, however, that Mexican American families have many strengths and assets that have not been adequately described in traditional education scholarship. Studies have shown that both mother and father are active with their children (A. Hurtado 2003), raise socially agile and mature toddlers and preschoolers (Jung, Fuller, and Galindo 2012), tend to treat male and female children similarly regardless of socioeconomic status (SES as defined by educational level) (Burciaga 2007), and hold high occupational expectations for their children (Velez and Bedolla 2012). The purpose of this chapter is to chronicle the family lived experiences of the first large cohort of Mexican American women who successfully navigated the educational pathways from K–12 through college and beyond, between 1960 and 1978. The major questions guiding this study were: How did parents and other family members' expectations and supports contribute to respondents' aspirations and achievement of a college degree? What were the family messages transmitted to encourage higher education?

In *Outliers: The Story of Success* (2011), Malcolm Gladwell tells the poignant story of how mothers at Bill Gates's private middle school raised money to purchase sophisticated computers to further develop the interests of their children in the school's computer club. We know that the children of college-educated parents are more likely to: attend well-resourced schools, choose from multiple languages for study, choose from an array of extracurricular after-school programs, have higher scores on the SAT, have more books, and have more regular access to high school and college counselors. Thus, for upper-income youth, their life options and opportunities to navigate educational and other institutional spaces and their agents are powerfully shaped by their parents' access to financial resources and social capital.

Although low-income, first-generation Mexican American college youth still face many financial and social obstacles, such as discrimination and racism, family-transmitted strengths have enabled them to overcome and succeed through various educational pathways. While many of the deficit-based studies on Mexican American educational attainment erroneously assert that families are not supportive (Valencia and Black 2002), research shows that structural inequality and limited material resources are critical factors in creating or blocking opportunities, influencing educational careers, and shaping the life course for Mexican American youth (Lareau 2003, 2014; Telles and Ortiz 2008).

A growing body of knowledge depicts myriad roles that families play in the successful academic performance of Mexican American girls (Burciaga 2007; Ceja 2004; Flores Carmona 2010; Villenas 2006; Villenas and Moreno 2001). Less is known, however, about the pioneers—what types of family strengths and social capital did the families of the first Mexican American female cohort transmit to their daughters to help them successfully navigate the educational pipeline, from K–12 through college and beyond (Gándara 1995, 1997)?

Asset-based research challenges overly simplistic studies that often examine delinquent behaviors as a catalyst for why Mexican American girls have left school (Chavez and Oetting 1994)—such deficit-based research seems to assume that we learn best about their lives by examining failure. The major shortcoming of this research is its narrow focus on the individual or cultural aspects of the phenomenon without an understanding of the relationship of ethnic groups, specifically Mexican Americans, to the historical record and existing social structures. To understand these conditions, in the study of persistence and aspirations, one must look beyond traditional conceptualizations of education as mere schooling. Burciaga (2007) found that both education (formal schooling) and *educación* (informal family values based on integrity, respect, and communal responsibility) provide an important foundation for persistence in school and future career aspirations. Inquiry into how family expectations and value transmission make a difference in Mexican American girls' educational performance is central to understanding how to increase their access to higher education.

The Role of Family in Life Course Educational Milestones

Families are the prime motivators in the education of their children (Usher 2012; Brooks-Gunn and Markman 2005; Velez and Bedolla 2012). The role of the family in motivating their children to perform well academically includes emotional and instrumental support—including financial support and information—which can be used to attain one's goals. Goal-setting for the future is a process guided by the parents in middle-class families, and it is related to their own set of educational, financial, and cultural resources. In the social science and family science literature, it is helpful to see how broader conceptualizations of the Latino family, in general, have been depicted in idealistic and non-normative terms. Families are characterized as centers of nurturing and survival (Massey, Zambrana, and Alonzo Bell 1995; Baca Zinn and Wells 2000); locations of support, stability, and coping mechanisms (Velez and Bedolla 2012); and purveyors of values—including *educación*—that influence persistence and aspirations (Burciaga 2007) and gender socialization (A. Hurtado 2003). Among low-income Latino families, the gender socialization of children is deeply shaped by the material conditions of their parents' lives. Child care and parents' presence in the labor force have been linked to less time and emphasis on educational goals (Gándara 1995, 1999a; Zambrana, Dorrington, and Bell 1997).

For Mexican American youth, traditional gender role expectations are more likely to exist in low-income families than in middle-class families. Yet these traditional gender roles have been translated by social science researchers into stereotypes of deviant cultural traits of male dominance and female submissiveness characterizing familial processes, especially with regard to value placed on education and gender role socialization. In many low-income families, children have contributed in instrumental ways to supporting the family, including translating (Faulstich Orellana 2003) and providing care for siblings so parents could earn a living (Burciaga 2007). Empirical work on Mexican American socialization processes has consistently demonstrated variability in gender role attitudes and family processes (Baca Zinn 1995; Cofresi 1999; Toro-Morn

2008). Ethnic differences in family integration among Mexican Americans, Puerto Ricans, and Whites show that social class position matters more than culture (Sarkisian, Gerena, and Gerstel 2006). In a study on gender role attitudes, Latino and White women respondents did not differ in terms of the values they placed on work, marriage, and parenting or in terms of the time allocated to each of these roles. However, differences remain between men and women in their gender-specific behaviors (Franco, Sabattini, and Crosby 2004). Emerging research shows that higher education is a major marker of more egalitarian attitudes and more fluidity in family gender roles, and that the parental transmission of gender role socialization messages varies by SES.[2]

Multiple socialization institutions—namely, family, school, and media—play a central role in the opportunity structure of an individual. Access to power structures through social capital as proffered by family material conditions greatly determines the transmission of social norms and expectations and is a marker of access to the opportunity structure. Denner and colleagues (2001) similarly employ the concept of *social capital* as "parental and kin support, relationship networks that provide collective supervision and resources for youth" (5). Additionally, Bourdieu's construct and theory of multiple capitals suggest that students develop their future aspirations through their accumulation (or lack of accumulation) of economic, informational, social, and other resources (Bourdieu 1986). For example, Marlino and Wilson (2006) identified significant sources of personal influence on the career aspirations of Latinas: mothers, fathers, and the media (in that order); mentors and professional women who give career advice. Recently, research has revealed myriad funds of knowledge (Moll, Amanti, Neff, and Gonzales 1992) and community cultural wealth—the cultural knowledge, skills, and abilities nurtured by families and communities that influence persistence and social mobility, often in the face of significant obstacles (Yosso 2005).

In addition to increasing opportunities for Mexican American girls and women, early pioneering college graduates of the 1980s challenged cultural deficit models and provided a growing intellectual force to advocate for revisionist scholarship. For example, in 1978 the Ford Foundation commissioned the first report about Chicanas in higher education. The report found that the educational barriers Chicanas confronted included (1) the high number of hours of domestic labor they engaged in, (2) less parental support in comparison to their male counterparts, (3) greater stress, and (4) the quality of the institution they attended (Chacón and Cohen 1982; Chacón, Cohen, and Strover 1986). In 1980, participants at the National

Hispanic Feminist Conference articulated an educational agenda for Hispanic women. This agenda, along with the 1982 publication of Patricia Gándara's article "Passing through the Eye of the Needle," advocated a need to understand Chicanas as a heterogeneous group with diverse needs. What is more, conference participants claimed that academic failure must not be blamed on women, but rather must be contextualized.

An interdisciplinary lens with a focus on cultural capital, forms of resistance, and agency would further illuminate the reality of Chicanas. In other words, Mexican American scholars strongly argue for the disruption of "colonizing discourses that distort and erase the relationship between ineffective schooling and the educational experiences of Chicano youth" (Calderón, Delgado Bernal, Pérez Huber, Malagón, and Vélez 2012, 530). Cuádraz (2005) suggests five theorizing lenses that might be applied to understanding and addressing the needs of Chicanas in higher education: (1) Chicana feminist theory, (2) social reproduction literature, (3) post-colonial studies, (4) cultural studies, and (5) critical race theory. The study of Chicanas in higher education can be traced back to the grassroots activism of the Chicano movement and to a push by both feminists and scholars to identify Chicanas as an "invisible minority" (Cuádraz 2005, 218). These social forces have made visible a Chicana educational history that, in some ways, gains critical momentum with the Civil Rights Act in 1964 and the Higher Education Act (HEA) of 1965.[3] Hurtado (see chapter 3) indicates that national data are not available to confirm how quickly Mexican American college students increased in numbers in the 1960s, but data at the Higher Education Research Institute (HERI) demonstrate that although a new door opened for Chicanas/os in the 1970s at four-year colleges, Chicanas remained underrepresented relative to males until the late 1970s/early 1980s. Chicanas who obtained their degrees before this period are considered relative pioneers, and were outnumbered in terms of representation relative to all men and to women from other racial/ethnic groups. Given the era when these pioneers first attended college, they were able to do so because financial aid (due to HEA, 1965) had become widely available, so as to decrease economic barriers and "level the playing field" for historically underrepresented minorities. It was then that colleges and universities began to admit Chicanas in precedent-setting numbers.

This chapter answers Cuádraz's call for the use of critical theories to capture the experiences of Chicanas in higher education. We investigate the associations of Mexican American community cultural wealth with the transmission of family and aspirational capital to their daughters as strategies for success. Further, we highlight critical race theory (CRT), which posits racism's intersections with other forms of marginality. It informs the study of educational inequalities with an asset-based lens of inquiry—as opposed to conventional deficit models of inquiry (Solórzano and Yosso 2000). A community cultural wealth (Yosso 2005) framework informed by CRT is especially useful, as it foregrounds gender, race, ethnicity, and socioeconomic status—among other intersections of marginality—with respect to educational attainment. Community cultural wealth highlights values and capacities nurtured by Mexican American communities—that enable persistence and social mobility in the face of significant challenges. These resources are often overlooked in widely used analyses of cultural capital and social mobility, which tend to frame historically underrepresented minorities as merely deficient with respect to a constructed norm (Bourdieu and Passeron 1977). We apply several of Yosso's community cultural wealth assets (familial, social, resistant, and aspirational) to inform our analyses and understanding of the families and the respondents who overcame many challenges to succeed academically.

We argue that in understanding the role of low-income Mexican American families in the educational performance of their offspring, both the economic context of family resources and access to social capital and community cultural wealth must frame the discourse on educational performance. Therefore, this cohort of women we study represents a unique opportunity to show which family factors, in tandem with other school-related factors discussed in chapter 6, are associated with high educational performance. This study contributes to our theorizing lens on family socialization processes of Mexican American women who successfully completed higher education, an area of inquiry decidedly absent from conventional scholarly discourses.

Methods

The mixed-methods study had a retrospective, cross-sectional design. The study collected data from the first large cohort of three hundred Mexican American women who successfully navigated the educational pathways from K–12 through postsecondary education and into their careers. All data were collected in Los Angeles, California, during the period 1987–1990 (methods are fully described elsewhere; see Zambrana, Dorrington, and Bell 1997).

Sample Selection and Procedures

Respondents were identified through a network sampling technique. Hispanic/Mexican American/Chicana professional organizations of women and Zambrana's professional networks were solicited to assist in the identification of Mexican American women who fulfilled the educational and racial/ethnic criteria. Potential respondents were then contacted by telephone and informed of the referral source and purpose of study. An interview time and place were mutually agreed upon. In addition, all individuals contacted were asked to provide names of three women who fulfilled the criteria. The interviews took, on average, 1.5 hours to complete.

Survey Instrument

Face-to-face interviews were conducted using a 233-item questionnaire that included both closed-ended and open-ended response options. The survey was designed to obtain in-depth quantitative and qualitative retrospective information and drew items from other interview and survey protocols (Allen 1985; Chacón, Cohen, Camarena, and Strover 1983; Higginbotham 1980). The instrument was designed to reconstruct the educational trajectory of the respondents to identify specific familial and institutional factors that contributed to completion of a college degree. In addition, for this chapter, respondents' lived experiences were chronicled through the life course, from childhood to early adulthood, focusing on characteristics of family of origin, residential setting, and family educational and gender expectations.

Characteristics of family of origin, including education level, marital status, work status of parents (when respondents were 0–18 years of age), income, state of residence, residential setting, and relatives in neighborhood, are presented in table 5.1. Perceptions of mothers' and fathers' educational expectations were measured by asking three items concerning each parent (six items total). Initial items were: whether their mother and father expected A's in primary and high school (1 = yes and 2 = no) and how far their parents expected them to progress (ranging from completing high school to college or beyond). Respondents were then asked to rate their parents' involvement in their primary school education. Involvement was recoded as 1 = actively involved and 2 = not actively involved. In addition, they were asked to rank how helpful assistance from parents had been during college in the areas of encouragement, financial and emotional support, help entering college, and practical assistance with domes-

Table 5.1. Characteristics of Family of Origin

Variable	Mother	Father	Both Parents
Reported in percentage			
Education			
< High school	58.6	54.5	
High School plus	41.4	45.5	
Marital Status			
Never married			1.7
Married/living with partner			68.3
Sep/divorced/widowed			30.0
Parents worked			
(respondent 0–18 years of age)			
0–6 years	4.8	64.9	25.1
7–12 years	6.8	44.1	49.1
13–18 years	9.2	32.1	58.7
Parents' income			
(respondent 0–18 years of age)			
0–6 years			
$0–$20,000			96.5
$20,000+			3.5
7–12 years			
$0–$20,000			93.0
$20,000+			7.0
13–18 years			
$0–$20,000			77.3
$20,000+			22.7
State of residence			
California			86.3
Other			13.7
Residential setting (age 0–12)			
Urban			47.4
Rural			22.7
Suburban			29.9
Relatives in neighborhood			
<20 miles			75.9
>20 miles			24.1

tic chores/responsibilities (1 = most helpful to 5 = least helpful). Whether their mother or father saw marriage as a primary life goal was measured by 1 = yes and 2 = no. Last, perceived educational expectations between sons and daughters were measured (1 = expected sons to excel/not daughters, 2 = expected daughters to excel/not sons, 3 = equal expectations).

Six open-ended questions were asked about perceptions of mother/ father attitude toward education, high school experiences such as academic resources and factors that influenced motivation, and decision to enter college (see chart 5.1 for original coding categories and recodes). Open-ended items provided rich qualitative data. These narratives provided rich insight into the early life course stages of this cohort, extended the depth and breadth of the survey results, and illustrated what family messages and behaviors were the driving forces in respondents' decisions to attend college, despite the odds.

Who Are the Respondents?

The study respondents were all of Mexican origin (300) and residents of the state of California, with a mean age of thirty-five years at the time of the interview. Eighty-six percent (86.3 percent) had been reared and had received their baccalaureate degree prior to 1978 in California. Their high school and higher educational careers spanned a period from the 1960s to 1978. All women had completed a minimum of a bachelor's degree, with 43 percent having credits toward a master's (MA) or having received an MA degree, 36 percent having credits toward or having been awarded a doctoral degree, and 91 percent employed. Close to half were married; about 20 percent were separated, divorced, or widowed; and close to one-third of respondents were single. Slightly over half of the respondents had children (51.6 percent). Respondents were predominantly first-generation, "out of the barrio" trailblazers, shattering the dominant-majority structural ceiling in many cases, overcoming what were all too often perceived as insurmountable barriers of low expectations, and achieving the "American dream" (Zambrana, Dorrington, and Bell 1997).

Results

Who Are the Families? Characteristics of Family of Origin

Parents of the respondents were all of Mexican origin, with 40 percent of the mothers and fathers having been born in Mexico. Thus, 36 percent

Chart 5.1. Open-Ended Survey and Items on Parental Involvement

Survey Questions	Response Options
During primary school, did your mother/father expect you to get A's in school?	1=Yes, 2=No
During high school, did your mother/father expect you to get A's in school?	1=Yes, 2=No
When you were growing up, how far did your mother/father expect you to progress in school?	1=High School, 2=Business/Technical School, 3=Four-year College, 4=Graduate/Professional School. Items were then recoded: 1=High School, 2=College and beyond
Throughout your primary school years (K through junior high school), how would you describe your mother's/father's involvement with your schooling?	1=Very Involved (regular visits to school, PTA, helped with homework), 2=Involved (regularly helped with schoolwork, occasional visits to school functions), 3=Interested but not actively involved (encouraged to do well in school but rarely assisted), 4=Not actively involved (did not verbally encourage or actively participate in your schooling). Items were then recoded: 1=Actively involved, 2=Not actively involved
What did your mother/father do to assist you in pursuing a college education?	Rank order of 1=Encouraged me to continue my education, 2=Provided financial support, 3=Provided emotional support, 4=Actively participated in helping me enter college, 5=Relieved me from family/domestic chores
Did your mother/father emphasize that a good marriage should be your primary life goal? In what ways?	1=Yes, 2=No
If you had siblings, were there differences in your mother's/father's educational expectations between sons and daughters?	1=Expected sons to excel/not daughters, 2=Expected daughters to excel/not sons, 3=Equal expectations for sons and daughters, 4=Expected daughters to excel/no sons, 5=no siblings. Items were then recoded: 1=Expected sons to excel/not daughters, 2=Expected daughters to excel/not sons, 3=Equal expectations)

Six Qualitative Questions

(1) In general, how would you characterize your mother's/father's (2 questions) attitude toward your education?
(2) What factors most significantly encouraged your educational performance?
(3) Were there academic resources (that is, specific programs or organizations) that influenced your motivation to succeed in school?
(4) In what ways did high school affect your later educational performance?
And (5) Why did you decide to go to college?

of the sample spoke only Spanish or mainly Spanish in their home during their early years. However, 85 percent were born in the United States, and close to 60 percent had parents that were U.S.-born, which shows that the majority were at least third-generation. The overwhelming majority of the parents of the respondents were married (68.3 percent). With respect to education, close to 60 percent of the mothers and 55 percent of the fathers had not completed high school, and almost 50 percent had less than a ninth-grade education. The majority reported that in 0–6 years only the father worked (64.9 percent); 25.1 percent reported that both parents worked. However, as the respondents grew older, both parents working doubled to 48.8 percent (not shown). Not unexpectedly, 96.5 percent reported family income $0–$20,000 during the early years (0–6 years) of the respondent's life. However, by later in the life course of respondents (13–18 years), family income of over $20,000 was reported by about one-quarter (22.7 percent) of respondents.

Community Characteristics

The community in which the respondents were reared and the types of networks available provide us with a sense of their social environment. Only 22.7 percent of parents reared their children in rural areas; almost half (47.4 percent) were located in urban areas, and one-third in the suburbs. The majority were reared in predominantly Mexican American neighborhoods, although as they got older, the ethnicity of their neighborhoods became somewhat more diversified. For over 70 percent of the respondents (0–18 years of age), the neighborhoods were reported to be lower or working-class. Of interest is that three-quarters (75.9 percent) of respondents reported living within twenty miles of relatives (aunts, uncles, grandparents, and cousins).

Parental Educational Involvement and Expectations

Many insights are proffered about the role of family in the lives of Mexican American women (table 5.2). Questions were asked about parents' expectation of high grades in school, and over 50 percent of both mothers and fathers had a high expectation of grades (A) through age eighteen. Fathers (55.5 percent) were slightly more likely than mothers (51.2 percent) to expect high grades in high school. Although mothers (41.8 percent) were more likely to be involved in school activities than fathers (28.4 percent), mothers were also less likely to work outside the home. The majority of

Table 5.2. Perceived Parental Expectations and Involvement in Grade School

Variable	Mother	Father
Reported in percentage		
Expect high grades (A's) in primary school		
Yes	50.7	55.2
No	49.3	44.8
Expect high grades (A's) in high school		
Yes	51.2	55.5
No	48.8	44.5
How far did your parents expect you to progress?		
High school graduate	43.2	41.9
College or beyond	56.8	58.1
Involvement in primary school		
Actively involved	41.8	28.4
Not actively involved	58.2	71.6
Parents' assistance in pursuing college education		
Encouragement	61.0	68.2
Financial assistance	16.3	29.3
Emotional support	21.7	21.8
Helped me enter college	1.2	5.8
Relieved me of family/domestic chores	22.1	9.1
Emphasize marriage		
Yes	30.1	22.8
No	69.9	77.2
Expectation of siblings		
Expect more of sons	17.9	30.7
Expect more of daughters	4.8	6.1
Same expectations of both	77.4	63.2

respondents (55.5 percent) reported that their mother had a very positive view of education and showed support by providing encouragement (61.0 percent) and viewing education as a vehicle to success. Similarly, fathers were reported to be proud and encouraged their daughters to reach high (68.2 percent). The encouragement and high expectations embody the parents' aspirational capital (Yosso 2005) for their daughters—the women spoke about this support at length in their interviews.

Mothers' Expectations: "Encouragement in humble ways"

There were a number of prototypical themes that provide the context for understanding the strengths and force in the families behind these women, and what motivated the women to persist in education. Interestingly, 56.8 percent of mothers expected their daughters to complete college and go on to graduate school. To understand these data more deeply, respondents were asked, "In general, how would you characterize your mother's attitude toward your education?" Responses revealed the mother as a critical figure—a source of inspiration and of silent approval. They described their mother's support in the following ways: "let me be," "never tried to hold us back," and "didn't try to get in the way." The mothers telling others about their daughter's achievements suggested a vicarious experience. A salient theme was the respondents' perception that education was very important to their mothers, who were living their lives vicariously, or "living their dreams" through their daughters' success. Respondents described the perception of aspirational capital in the following ways:

> She always wanted me to do the best I could with myself and she encouraged me to do that. My education was very important to her because she was living it vicariously.

> She sees it as something very positive that she wasn't able to do.

> She would tell me how fun school was and that I was lucky to have this opportunity. The only way was to make something out of myself— through education.

The mothers supported their daughters' educational attainment in important ways, such as relieving their daughters of domestic responsibility and caring for siblings. A substantial number of women reported that their mothers felt inadequate in providing access to the necessary social capital. One woman stated: "She was extremely supportive, but frustrated because she felt that she didn't have much to offer her daughter. However, she never stood in my way." In general, the respondents perceived their mothers as having an extremely positive attitude toward their education. The role of the mother in providing affective support, encouragement, and high expectations substantiates the findings of other studies (Burciaga 2007; Gándara 1979). An important message transmitted by mothers that inspired and encouraged the participants was the importance of economic success and upward mobility. Respondents described this "push" in the following ways:

> She had high expectations and felt education was a way to economic success.

> She felt education was very important. She didn't want me to work in blue-collar jobs.

These findings further attest to the students' familial capital (Yosso 2005) in their use of *consejos*, or advice, encouraging school persistence. Ceja's (2004) research also asserts that family stories and *consejos* serve as motivation for Chicanas in greater Los Angeles as they complete higher education. Through semistructured interviews, Ceja learned that parents created a "culture of possibility" (357) using family stories, lived experiences, and *consejos* to instill the value of education.

Fathers' Expectations: "He took me to the fields"

Fathers were more likely than mothers to expect A's from primary to high school, and to expect completion of college or beyond (58.1 percent). Although fathers were not as actively involved (28.4 percent) in schools as mothers (41.8 percent), they were nonetheless a strong vehicle of support and encouragement for their daughters. When asked, "How would you characterize your father's attitude toward your education?," respondents reported that their fathers' involvement in their education was almost equally as high as that of mothers. Several themes emerged regarding the fathers' attitude and expectations regarding educational achievement. One overriding theme can be summarized as "proud and supportive." Fathers were reported to be encouraging toward the educational efforts of their daughters, but not emotionally expressive. Nonetheless, respondents perceived support, as described in their own words:

> It was something he could tell his friends that his daughter was going to college.

> Proud. He was never demonstrative about his feelings. He was proud that I was in higher education. He continued to encourage me, give me positive status.

Very proud that all his children had gone to college. He expected me to get a PhD.

A second major theme was the fathers' wanting their daughters to go to college for financial reasons and to achieve more than the parents had. The fathers were more likely than the mothers to continually emphasize the need to get out of poverty, to be different from their parents, and they were the ones who took their daughters "to the fields," or pointed out low-level jobs and told them that was not their future. The following reflect the fathers' desire for the daughters to have a better life:

My father verbalized often that he wanted us to go on. He took us to the fields to show us.

He was hysterical about education. He would say, "You have to finish college. If not, you will be scum."

The majority of fathers encouraged respondents to work hard and to try to be financially independent. Some of the fathers perceived education as a backup in case marriage didn't work. Others encouraged their daughters throughout high school and recognized their intelligence, but perceived "higher education as a luxury" or expressed concern about financing higher education. Yet, one father who had learning disabilities always encouraged his daughter to go on. When he died, he left his life insurance policy for her education.

Equally important, the data reveal that the majority of parents held high expectations for sons and daughters, which supports prior findings on Mexican American families (Burciaga 2007). In response to the question "If you had siblings, were there differences in your mother's and father's expectations between sons and daughters?," respondents reported that 77.4 percent of mothers and 63.2 percent of fathers held equal expectations of male and female siblings. In instances when parents did not have high levels of formal schooling, they often worked as a couple to reinforce informal learning in the home as a foundation for supporting formal schooling. One respondent shared coparenting strategies employed by her family:

My mother took time out to teach me how to read and write in Spanish before entering school. My father tried to help me with my homework. I witnessed my father work hard for me to obtain a degree. He encouraged and motivated me to get a degree. My father stressed that because I was Mexican I would be educated.

In this instance, pedagogies of the home (Delgado Bernal 2001) served as the foundation for persistence in schools.

Role of Other Family Members and Siblings

For three-quarters of the respondents, relatives (grandparents, aunts, or uncles) lived within twenty miles of their residence. The close proximity of extended family members afforded many opportunities for the respondents to call upon their social networks. For close to 60 percent of respondents, siblings were reported to be role models, and about 70 percent of siblings had a degree. When asked about whom they most identified with, respondents reported siblings (29.8 percent), followed by mother (25.2 percent), father (12.2 percent), aunts, uncles, cousins (15 percent), and grandparent (9.2 percent). For 85 percent of respondents, these individuals strongly influenced their education through offering encouragement, supporting their striving for excellence, being a role model, and occasionally helping with schoolwork. The role of extended family members is well illustrated in the following quote. In describing the powerful influence her grandmother had, one respondent stated:

> My maternal grandmother lived with us. She taught herself and me to read in Spanish. She used to read to me a lot. Tell me a lot of stories. Took me to the movies in downtown Los Angeles.

A maternal uncle who was twelve years older was another relative who influenced educational persistence: "He was very bright, read books and quoted Plato and Socrates." Brothers were also a major source of inspiration and were often perceived similarly—as very smart, hardworking, and talented. One respondent shared, "My brother insisted that I go to high school and college." For the overwhelming majority of respondents, siblings and other relatives served a critical role in encouraging their education and serving as role models of hard work, responsibility, and overcoming of barriers.

The findings reveal a consensus around major factors associated with motivation for educational persistence and family transmission of a strong set of values promoting a work ethic, discipline, and independence. Parents "pushed" their daughter with the clear messages that "they [daughters] didn't want to be in the same position as the parents and [parents] did not want them to work in the fields." Thus, combined parental encouragement, high expectations, and the support of extended family were perceived as influencing educational aspirations and career aspirations. The community cultural wealth framework receives support from the finding that immediate and extended families are important resources for the respondents. From parents sharing family stories and lived experiences as a way to communicate hope (familial capital), to siblings insisting that respondents pursue higher education (aspirational capital), these findings demonstrate the intricate ways in which immediate and extended families are a source of social capital that aid pursuit of higher education. As well, these data demonstrate that there are informal values (*educación*) that are cultivated and practiced to influence formal schooling (education).

Gender Role Expectations, Economic Concerns

> For example, the idea that you're not supposed to move out of your home until you get married . . . this limits your academic ambitions and forces you to settle to attend a school close to home that may or may not be the best choice for you. (National Women's Law Center [NWLC] and Mexican American Legal Defense and Educational Fund [MALDEF] 2009, 17)

The data reveal the family fears and material conditions that constitute barriers. We discuss barriers along two interrelated dimensions: fear of reaching too high for financial reasons (material conditions), in conjunction with limited understanding of long-term education options, such as staying in school for higher education (the majority of parents having not completed high school). Although parents (especially mothers) had insight into the necessity of immediate work versus planning for a career, daughters received mixed messages regarding marriage and family expectations. Nonetheless, the majority of parents engaged in parenting practices that motivated and inspired their daughters to overcome the obstacles.

ECONOMIC ASSISTANCE AND CONCERNS: FEAR OF REACHING TOO HIGH

To interrogate the barriers further, we asked questions about educational and marriage expectations, and financial and other sources of support. Only 16.3 percent of the sample reported mother's financial assistance, and 29.3 percent reported father's financial assistance. Parents' emphasis on marriage was lower for fathers (22.8 percent) than mothers (30.1 percent). A small number of respondents (8.5 percent) reported indifference toward education by mothers, and about 15 percent reported the same for fathers. For these respondents, their families made it harder for them to achieve educationally. The reasons were invariably related to both the economic resources of the families and traditional gender expectations and values. Common themes in this small percentage of participants included parents' inability to financially support educational aspirations beyond high school, rigid gender role expectations, and other responsibilities to the family of origin. Two respondents shared the following reasons:

> Our families expect something else. They don't know how to support us and most of our families cannot support us financially. Our own expectations keep getting crushed.

> A lot of time we are stuck in taking care of younger siblings and are not able to participate in school activities. There is a lack of time and money.

These themes illustrate the importance of considering economic conditions in the lives of young, aspiring Mexican American women, as well as the limited opportunities for upward social mobility for their parents. Although in this study these findings on lower educational expectations were the exception, not the norm, these themes have often been interpreted by conventional theorists as a lack of value placed on education by the Mexican American community. Missing from these incomplete theories was an understanding of the economic circumstances of these families. These barriers can be understood within the context of parents' experiences with limited options for upward social mobility, as well as a fear of their daughters reaching too high because of financial concerns.

LIMITED UNDERSTANDING OF LONG-TERM EDUCATION OPTIONS

Respondents also expressed discouragement at their mothers' lack of understanding, because of economic fears, of the importance of college as a path to better opportunities for long-term employment. One respondent reported that her mother opposed her going on to college because "she didn't see the long-range benefit. She felt that I could get a job as a secretary." Another respondent described the economic fears:

I won a scholarship to UC Berkeley. Mom wanted me to become a secretary. As a child she was encouraging; but she felt higher education was not possible unless you were rich.

Several respondents revealed that their mothers did not feel education for women was important "because of domestic obligations." A number of other mothers saw education as a way for their daughters to support themselves until they got married. Yet oftentimes these attitudes were contradicted by their mothers' high expectations of academic performance. This type of maternal support stimulated the young women's sense of self-confidence and increased their desire to learn. Other respondents strove to live different lives than those of their mothers, some of whom were, for example, trapped in cycles of hard labor for little pay, dependent upon men, or battered by their husbands. The attitudes of the mothers were predominantly influenced by their lack of knowledge of what was possible for their daughters and a fear of "losing" them to the "American culture." These families struggled financially and perhaps were hesitant to provide their daughters with dreams they believed could not be fulfilled. Nonetheless, there was a general push by mothers for their daughters to obtain more education than they themselves had had opportunities to pursue. In general, the mothers' encouragement was reinforced by the positive and supportive attitudes of the fathers.

A significant number of fathers were supportive but feared they would be unable to provide financially. One respondent stated:

My father saw education as very important, but beyond high school, my education—as well as that of my brothers and sister—depended on loans and scholarships. He did not have the money to help out.

On the other hand, a few fathers would help out only if the daughters stayed close to home: "He would support us only as long as we lived in his home." Many of these fathers expressed fears or were critical of their daughters "leaving the family and changing lifestyles." Fears prevailed that education would dilute their values and sense of cultural origins. One respondent, reflecting on her father's attitude, stated:

He felt some education was good, but too much would be bad. He felt that you could get absorbed in the system and sell out, forget where you came from. He also felt there were other things in life.

The respondents reported that oftentimes fathers, like mothers, were not aware of the options and discouraged their daughters from reaching too high. Some of the respondents perceived their parents as ambivalent. For example, fathers were not initially supportive—yet parents would show pride and give support after the daughter had reached a major milestone, such as the completion of the bachelor's or master's degree. Overall, parental messages clearly transmitted familial, social, and aspirational capital encouraging their daughters to engage school so as to "have a better life than they did," but parents also wanted their children to remain a part of their life.

Discussion

The educational trajectories of the respondents were greatly influenced by their families' support of persistence in pursuit of higher education. Pedagogies of the home (Delgado Bernal 2001) are not taught in schools, but instead are indicative of the way community cultural wealth is cultivated and practiced. These pedagogies of the home, often referred to as *educación*, are informal transmissions of family values that played an important role in respondents' persistence and aspirations. Major findings demonstrate the following:

1. The majority of parents transmitted the value of education and a strong work ethic as magic keys to success.
2. The majority of parents with low material resources had educational aspirations. For some, there were economic concerns and fears, and for a few, traditional gender role beliefs that conflicted with educational expectations. Furthermore, the parents did not have access to, and therefore could not offer, information on college preparation, applications, or financial resources, but supported their daughters in other ways, including providing relief from family chores. In addition, extended family members (aunts, uncles, grandmothers) were a significant source of support, as bearers of knowledge that parents did not have, and served as an adaptive social group to help buffer the effects of obstacles in the school environment.
3. Mothers' expectations were a powerful source of support and strength. Fathers were equally important, though in different ways, which included "taking them to the fields" to demonstrate how lower levels of education limit occupational opportunities.

These characteristics of the participants' families of origin were similar to those found in other studies (Chacón and Cohen 1982; Ceja 2004; Gándara 1995) of successful Mexican American women. These data support the hypothesis that although families influence educational persistence, for Mexican American families, financial concerns may shadow parents' ability to sustain aspirations in pursuit of educational opportunities for their daughters. Thus, the role of socioeconomic status, not a low value on education, shapes parents' and children's access to material resources to strengthen educational options and achievement. Further, these findings contribute to our understanding of the ways community cultural wealth (Yosso 2005) is developed among siblings and extended family members to support and supplement schooling (Burciaga 2007). The narratives also describe the role of coparenting strategies, with fathers actively involved with their children, and confirm prior scholarship, which reported an active role by fathers among both Mexican American and White lower- and middle-class families (Caldera, Fitzpatrick, and Wampler 2002, 123).

Emerging scholarship contributes to challenging the master narrative of Mexican Americans as not valuing education (see Zambrana 2011 for a review). Among Mexican Americans, the family may serve as a buffer to environmental and institutional stressors, yet the limited material resources of the family may also be a cause of stress as the women attempt to negotiate the demands of higher education. The reality of living in traditionally underresourced communities and in economic poverty often forecloses educational options and reinforces traditional gender role expectations (Gándara and Contreras 2009). These data challenge the ideal and mythical role of the poor family by contextualizing family processes and drawing on intersectional theorizing constructs of history, power, and racialized ethnicity. We provide a clear portrait of what it means for many low-income Mexican Americans to have limited economic options, while also clearly identifying and describing family assets and strategies of resistance.

The findings and prior literature strongly suggest multiple directions for future research and practice. Future studies of Mexican American women need to take into account SES, which is highly associated with financial resources; residence in "neighborhoods of opportunity"; segregation (Acevedo-Garcia 2000); and gender role expectations, all of which influence life chances and options. Differences by gender, parental education, and generational level among Mexican-origin groups are critical variables to be explored in subsequent investigations. Future research and practice with Mexican Americans in K–12 pathways must take into account the diversity of family patterns (Baca Zinn and Wells 2000) and the specific role of the historical legacy of racism and structural inequality. The role of schools in providing resources, information, and options to increase chances of access to college is vital in opening doors to low-income Mexican American youth (see chapter 6).

There is much to learn about how educators and school administrators work with Mexican American families who—because of work hours, the unwelcoming attitude of institutional school agents, and unfamiliarity with or fear of the schooling system—may be unable to fulfill traditional expectations for parental involvement but display a clear investment in their children's *educación*. Because low expectations for Mexican American students are so prevalent (Valencia and Black 2002), much work remains in areas of teacher education, principal certification, and professional development in schools. However, a greater understanding of the socioeconomic challenges confronted by families and a simultaneous cultivation of community cultural wealth by families will disrupt the more conventional interpretations of Mexican American families as deficient and unable to help their children pursue higher education. This study demonstrated tangible ways that families provided magic keys to higher education.

CHAPTER 6

Examining the Influence of K–12 School Experiences on the Higher Education Pathway

RUTH ENID ZAMBRANA, ANTHONY DE JESÚS,
AND BRIANNE A. DÁVILA

*Principals and guidance counselors may provide data about college preparation
courses, applications, and financing for students without access to these data at
home. Guidance counselors may take students on trips to colleges to help them
make informed choices. Education personnel may choose students whom they
believe worthy to "sponsor" and thus enable their educational achievement.*
LETICIA OSEGUERA, GILBERTO CONCHAS, AND EDUARDO MOSQUEDA,
"BEYOND FAMILY AND ETHNIC CULTURE: UNDERSTANDING THE
PRECONDITIONS FOR THE POTENTIAL REALIZATION OF SOCIAL CAPITAL"

While much has changed in K–12 schooling over the past four decades,
dropout rates for Mexican American women and their reasons for exiting
school have not changed significantly. Overall, research analyses attribute
the academic failure of Mexican Americans in transitions to high school
and colleges to the lack of academic preparation received in many schools
today. For example, for every one hundred Chicano children who entered
first grade in 1985, only sixty graduated from high school (Mirande 1985),[1]
and many students are precluded from successfully making the transition
from secondary schools into colleges and universities (Moreno 1999). By
the year 2000, the data show a decrease to forty-six Chicanos graduating from high school for every hundred entering first grade; but more
distressing is that for every hundred first-grade entrants, eight Chicanos
completed a bachelor's degree (Yosso and Solórzano 2006). Mexican
American women attain fewer years of schooling than all other underrepresented racial and ethnic women. Gándara (1982), for example, observed:
"Mexican American women are among the most poorly educated women
in our society. . . . As of 1978, the median years of schooling completed by
all adult women age 25 and over was 12.4, compared with only 8.6 years

for Chicanas of the same age" (167). As a result, "the low educational attainment of Chicanas has important consequences, for in American society education is said to be the key to success and upward social mobility for the poor and racial and ethnic minorities as well" (Mirande and Enriquez 1979, 129). In the last three decades we have observed only modest improvement in high school graduation and college enrollment rates. The persistence of approximately one-quarter of Mexican Americans not graduating high school is powerfully associated with historicity and racialized identities that inform the low socioeconomic status and limited educational progress of Mexican Americans. A review of Chicana/o education history reveals a consistent theme of educational neglect (see chapter 2). Children were forced to attend segregated schools, were prohibited from speaking Spanish, and were subject to inferior instruction (Carter and Segura 1979; Moreno 1999; San Miguel, Jr. 2013). Attitudes of racism and classism prevailed and served to marginalize these students. As Carter and Segura observe: "Educators shared the community's view of them as outsiders who were never expected to participate fully in American life" (1979, 15). The neglect of Mexican Americans over time by the political and educational system is the result of persistent structural inequalities associated with disproportionate academic underperformance. Drawing upon previous studies that examine early schooling with a focus on the high school experiences of Mexican American girls, this chapter analyzes data on the experiences of the pioneering cohort of Mexican American women, the majority of whom were in K–12 during the early 1960s, who successfully completed college prior to 1978.

These data allow for a closer examination of structural factors that facilitate and/or constrain Mexican American women's motivation to complete college. Accordingly, the following questions guide this inquiry: (1) What factors contributed to the successful navigation of early schooling experiences? (2) What institutional and interpersonal practices encouraged them? (3) What factors influenced their decision to attend college? The aim of this chapter is to identify the institutional supports available as well as the strategies of resistance used by the Mexican American cohort to overcome educational, social, and economic barriers.

Our analyses are framed by an intersectional and social capital theorizing lens that interrogates the barriers to academic performance as part of a set of historical and social structural determinants, including discriminatory practices and stereotypic markers that are associated with institutional agents' perceptions of student abilities. The integrative concept of social/cultural capital, jointly with intersectionality, provides a useful lens to interpret what participants reported worked for them (Bourdieu 1986; Coleman-Burns 1989; Lopez and Stack 2001). Social/cultural capital, which manifests in multiple forms, constitutes a key resource in the academic achievement of Mexican American women.

The opportunity for historically underrepresented Mexican American students to form supportive relationships with teachers and other adults with access to insider information about college and careers (or "*hot knowledge*") (Ball and Vincent 1998, 379) is a scarce but potentially transformative resource for Mexican American women, in particular (Stanton-Salazar 1997; De Jesús and Antrop-González 2006). Understanding the transmission of "hot knowledge" by institutional agents and the strategies of resistance invites an in-depth examination of the multiple and intersecting factors that influence the academic performance of Mexican American girls. Recent studies using an intersectional lens focus on institutional factors, such as the poor quality of public educational systems in low-income Latino communities, low teacher expectations, and other forms of racism and discrimination, that undermine Mexican American student success (Zambrana 1987; Maxwell-Jolly and Gándara 2006; Hyams 2006; M. H. Lopez 2009; Reyes 2006; Valencia 2010). We provide a brief overview of the bodies of knowledge that contextualize critical factors in the educational trajectory of Mexican American girls.

The Effects of Gendered Schooling Experiences on the Pathway to College

A large body of research has examined poor educational performance and dropout rates as an individual issue, placing responsibility for student failure with the student and his or her family. This perspective can be labeled *epistemological racism*, as the implicit assumptions driving the framework fail to take into account the central socializing role that schools, particularly public schools, play in the educational trajectories of racially and ethnically distinct low-income groups (Bowles and Gintis 1976; De Jesús 2005). Insufficient family economic resources, combined with inadequate school resources and lack of access to technological resources, is a major contributor to educational underperformance (Livingston, Park, and Fox 2009).

A strong emerging body of knowledge challenges individual attributions of failure and refocuses the educational discourse on structural issues, such as schooling practices and personnel. Several factors have been empirically documented as associated with educational underperformance and dropout rates for Mexican American students; these include academic tracking, teachers' stereotypic perceptions of low ability, attendance in underresourced schools, limited family material resources (compelling children to work), cultural/ethnic stereotypes, and racism (Armendariz 2000; Conchas and Goyette 2001; Pérez Huber, Johnson, and Kohli 2006; Fuligni 2007). A considerable set of empirical findings has documented the role of teacher attitude and expectations of Mexican American students. For example, a U.S. Commission on Civil Rights study (1973) compared teachers' communication patterns with Mexican American and Anglo elementary and secondary students and showed that teachers directed praise or encouragement at the Anglo students 36 percent more often than at the Mexican American students, built on the spoken contributions of Anglo students 40 percent more often, and asked Anglo students 20 percent more questions than they asked Mexican American students. These results weave together language, race, ethnicity, and social class factors and suggest that teachers' negative attitudes and low expectations contribute to a lower-quality classroom experience for the low-income Mexican American/Hispanic student (Ascher 1985; Aguilar 1996).

What we have learned in the last thirty years is that educational achievement is linked with access to social and cultural capital (Bourdieu 1986; Coleman 1988; Putnam 2000). Due to the close interaction between social and cultural capital, they are merged into an integrative concept, *social/cultural capital* (Lopez and Stack 2001). In the social reproduction theories of inequality, social capital generally refers to access to material and intangible resources, obtained through social networks that nurture intellectual and interpersonal development (Bourdieu 1986; Coleman 1988). Cultural capital can be defined as forms of knowledge, dialects, and dispositions that are valued by a society's dominant culture. Within academic and economic markets, cultural capital is converted into academic and occupational rewards for those who are in possession of its most valued form. Bourdieu's (1986) articulation of social capital as "the sum total of the resources, actual or virtual, that accrue to an individual by virtue of being enmeshed in a durable network of more or less institutionalized relationships of mutual acquaintance and recognition" (250) suggests that it is both interactive with and inclusive of cultural capital, and is a dynamic resource that can be acquired, developed, and refined in school settings.

This operationalization of social/cultural capital is especially relevant to our analysis of Mexican American women who are in need of *bridging* forms of social/cultural capital—which provides to individuals information not available within their own communities (Putnam 2000; Camras 2004). Teachers, principals, guidance counselors, school social workers, and other school-based personnel may serve as *bridging agents* who provide access to social networks and broker connections to institutions of higher education (Mehan 1996; Stanton-Salazar 2010). In essence, while playing roles as institutional gatekeepers, these institutional agents can also serve as bridges to information and role models, transmitting to students the skills of negotiating institutions, or using *navigational capital* (Yosso 2005). Further, as Stanton-Salazar (1997) observes, the nature of these relationships may be *instrumental*, or life-trajectory changing, as these adults may provide "regular, personalized, and soundly based evaluative feedback, advice and guidance that incorporate the thoughtful provision of institutional funds of knowledge, as well as genuine emotional and moral support," constituting a critical resource for student academic success (11). If school personnel educating Mexican American girls are ill equipped to generate bridging social capital for their students, they are likely to reproduce inequality in the lives of these students. Often, the decision of institutional agents to provide such support and access to social/cultural capital is a political decision, and can be considered a form of active resistance against the forces that would otherwise maintain inequality in the lives of underserved racial/ethnic students (MacLeod 1995; De Jesús 2005).

Academic performance indicators have not changed significantly over time. Academic disparities between Latina students and other racial/ethnic students begin as early as preschool and remain through age seventeen (for review of the literature, see Zambrana and Zoppi 2002; Zambrana and Morant 2009).

Latinas are underenrolled in gifted and talented education courses, are underrepresented in advanced placement (AP) courses (Ginorio and Huston 2001), are less likely to take the SAT—and those who do score lower, on average, than their White and Asian counterparts (KewalRamani, Gilbertson, Fox, and Provasnik 2007)—and have lower high school grade-point averages (HSGPA) than Black and White girls (Teranishi, Allen, and Solórzano 2004). Disparities in testing scores are often reflective of inadequate schooling experiences rather than actual academic potential (Farkas 2003). In fact, HSGPA is strongly associated with school resources, geographic location, and the attitudes of high school personnel.

Practices that are intertwined in the school setting are important to understanding the multiple ways that young women come to understand themselves as Mexican Americans with limited options. The stereotype that Latinas are less capable and less intelligent is present in the classrooms, where some teachers act on these false assumptions (Bender 2003; Rolón-Dow 2005), contributing to the high rates of high school dropout (Dance 2009; Y. Flores 2006). Further, low-income Latinas are more likely to be tracked into vocational courses (Marlino and Wilson 2006; Bettie 2003) and to experience sexual harassment in schools (Romo, Lefkowitz, Sigman, and Au 2002). Neighborhood effects, jointly with racist schooling practices, produce a trajectory of accumulated disadvantage that begins with inadequate access to early schooling programs, few recreational spaces, and the depletion of psychosocial resources (Timberlake 2007; Acevedo-Garcia, Osypuk, McArdle, and Williams 2008).

Subtractive Schooling and Praxis of Critical Care

Persistent themes in educational performance and the school dropout crisis include parents' low-income status and the attribution of stereotypes by teachers and other school agents that perpetuate low self-esteem and low expectations (Zayas, Lester, Cabassa, and Fortuna 2005; Pérez Huber, Johnson, and Kohli 2006), such as that some students have "low potential" (Marlino and Wilson 2006; National Women's Law Center [NWLC] and Mexican American Legal Defense and Educational Fund [MALDEF] 2009). From elementary to postsecondary education, teachers and other school agents often overlook, ignore, and avoid Latinas in the classroom, while privileging interaction with Anglo males (Solórzano and Delgado Bernal 2001; Ginorio and Huston 2001). Stereotypic attitudes of instructional school agents and limited access to mentors, professional women, and positive role models in the home, school, or community are factors that greatly constrain educational achievement among Mexican American girls.

Chicana sociologist Angela Valenzuela elaborates on how forces of assimilation inform the ways in which non-Latina/o educators interpret the behavior of Mexican American students. In her now classic book *Subtractive Schooling: U.S.-Mexican Youth and the Politics of Caring*, Valenzuela (1999) describes how traditional comprehensive high schools are organized formally and informally to divest Latina/o students of "important social and cultural resources, leaving them progressively vulnerable to academic failure" (3). Based on an ethnography of Mexican American and Mexican immigrant students in a Houston high school, Valenzuela observes that "rather than building on students' cultural and linguistic knowledge and heritage to create bi-culturally and bilingually competent youth, schools subtract these identifications from them to their social and academic detriment" (25). Building on Noddings's (1984) caring framework, Valenzuela (1999) analyzes competing notions of caring (aesthetic versus authentic) among teachers and students that are rooted in fundamentally different cultural and class-based expectations about the nature of schooling. These expectations inevitably clash and, when they do, fuel conflict and power struggles between teachers and students, who see each other as not caring. As Valenzuela (1999) observes:

> The predominantly non-Latino teaching staff sees students as not sufficiently *caring about* school, while students see teachers as not sufficiently *caring for* them. Teachers expect students to demonstrate caring about schooling with an abstract or *aesthetic* commitment to ideas or practices that purportedly lead to achievement. Immigrant and U.S.-born youth, on the other hand, are committed to an *authentic* form of caring that emphasizes relations of reciprocity between teachers and students. (61)

Valenzuela further argues that teachers who subscribe to *aesthetic* forms of caring confront debilitating institutional barriers that impede their abilities to connect effectively with youth. As a result, these teachers are prone to developing negative perceptions, including the disapproval of students' self-representations that prevent them from ever viewing these students as serious learners. Valenzuela (1999) states: "From these adults' perspective, the way youth dress, talk and generally deport themselves 'proves' that they do not care about school" (61). Extending this framework to incorporating an analysis of gender stereotypes held by many dominant-culture teachers also reveals the ways in which school-based adults interpret the representations of Mexican American students. Rolón-Dow (2005), for example, theorizes the optimal relationship between teachers and Latina girls as one to be grounded in *critical care praxis*:

> First, critical care is grounded in a historical and political understanding of the circumstances and conditions faced by minority communities. Second, critical care seeks to expose how racialized beliefs inform ideological standpoints. Finally, critical care translates race-conscious historical and ideological understandings and insights from counter narra-

tives into authentic relationships, pedagogical practices, and institutional structures that benefit Latino/a students. (104)

Building upon these ideas, Antrop-González and De Jesús (2006) advanced an *ethic of critical care*, which is defined by an emphasis on high-quality (supportive and instrumental) relationships between teachers and students coupled with high academic expectations. In their analysis of critical care at two Latino community high schools, authentic caring on the part of teachers is linked to broader school missions that more fully embody the educational interests of Latino communities.

In summary, two-thirds of Latina/o students are enrolled in highly segregated minority school districts, compared to 9 percent of NHW children. One-ninth of Latina/o students attend schools where almost 100 percent of the student body is minority (Pew Hispanic Research Center 2004). The absence of high-quality educational resources negatively affects Mexican American students' academic performance and access to higher education, while factors such as teacher encouragement, participation in extracurricular activities, and role models in the family or community are positive forms of reinforcement. Our data capture the domains of subtractive schooling and the counterforce of the caring ethic, as well as the individual agency of the respondents in the form of resistance strategies as they overcame social and educational obstacles.

Methods

Data collection methods are described elsewhere (see chapter 5; Zambrana, Dorrington, and Bell 1997; Zambrana and MacDonald 2009). For the purposes of this chapter, we employ survey and narrative data that describe the key educational experiences and practices that motivated these women to excel, successfully navigate K–12 schooling, and pursue college. The following survey items elicited retrospective data on respondents' perceptions of high school performance in particular subjects, preparation for college, and teachers' discouragement or encouragement of their college attendance. In addition, information on ethnic background, nativity, ethnic heritage and pride, and academic performance indicators (self-reported high school and college grade-point averages) was included. Four open-ended questions asked respondents the following: (1) What factors most significantly encouraged your educational performance? (2) Were there academic resources (that is, specific programs or organizations) that influenced your motivation to succeed in school? (3) In what ways did high school affect your later educational performance? (4) Why and when did you decide to go to college? Qualitative responses on what factors most influenced their motivation in high school, including persons, events, and programs, provide a rich context for interpreting the survey findings.

Results are organized to describe the following: (1) the demographic and ethnic identity characteristics of the study's participants, followed by a description of their peer characteristics; (2) high schools' characteristics and the role of teachers in encouraging college enrollment; (3) factors associated with high academic performance, specifically early recognition and praise and encouragement from family members and teachers; (4) academic resources provided by high schools that shaped college aspirations, such as scholarly competitions and student government; and (5) the role of academic course work, ethnic studies, and outreach programs in the college decision-making process. Despite all of the factors that facilitated college access and success, our respondents also described the barriers they confronted, such as poor quality of education, a lack of college-readiness preparation, and discriminatory practices in schools.

Results and Discussion

Awareness of Ethnic Identity

As noted in chapter 5, 85 percent of respondents were U.S.-born, and close to 95 percent of the respondents spoke English and Spanish.[2] When asked whether parents taught them about their ethnic background, such as the history of Mexico, about 75 percent reported "yes." Interestingly, about 45 percent reported that they were aware of their ethnic identity from early on, while 8.8 percent reported that their awareness emerged in junior/senior high school and 16.6 percent reported initial awareness in college. In response to two additional questions asked about ethnic identity awareness and pride, close to 80 percent reported being very/somewhat consciously aware and 78 percent reported being extremely proud of their ethnic background. Many of the respondents also reported their participation in academic enrichment programs and organizations that were oriented around ethnic identity (e.g., MEChA, Chicano Club). These students attended school during "*el movimiento*," with activism present in their schools and the media.

Ethnic Characteristics and Academic Aspirations of Peers

Data suggest that respondents grew up in mainly working-class Mexican American neighborhoods (52 percent) and their network from K–12 was mainly within the Mexican American community. Twenty-five percent of respondents lived in neighborhoods that were mostly non-Hispanic White. Respondents were least likely to live in Black and/or White/Black integrated neighborhoods, and 12 percent resided in mixed White/Latino/Asian neighborhoods. When families chose to move, respondents reported that 23.1 percent of parents moved to secure better schools.

For those respondents who reported that their peers were exclusively Latino (48.5 percent) prior to high school, the pattern remained similar through the educational pathway. Almost half of respondents had predominantly Latino peers in high school, and about 20 percent had predominantly White peers or a mix of White/Latino/Asian. Almost 70 percent of high school peers were perceived as lower-/working-/lower-middle-class, almost one-quarter were reported to be middle-income (22.5 percent), and 6.6 percent reported their peers as upper-class.

Questions were also asked about respondents' perception of their high school peers' motivation. Over 50 percent perceived their peers to be highly motivated and college-bound, while close to 40 percent perceived their peers to have moderate/low/no college aspirations. About 60 percent of respondents reported that friends were in the same college-bound tracking group, and 56.3 percent reported that their friends went to college.

High School Characteristics and Role of Teachers

The majority of these Mexican American women attended public schools during elementary (67 percent) and junior high/high school (68 percent). About 30 percent of respondents attended schools that were predominantly Latino, while almost 40 percent attended schools that were predominantly White. About 16 percent attended schools that were a mix (White/Latino/Asian), and only 3 percent attended predominantly Black schools. The majority of respondents (83.4 percent) reported that their school had a tracking system that included college versus lower academic tracks by subjects, coinciding with social class and ethnicity. Further, the majority of respondents (83.1 percent) reported that they were in a college-bound group, and 27.4 percent reported that it was not easy to access the college track.

Overall, 90 percent of respondents perceived teachers to encourage education, but only 67 percent of respondents reported that teachers encouraged them to attend college. Finally, 56.7 percent reported that they were close with teachers in high school, and among them, almost 90 percent stated that these teachers encouraged their education. Data reveal that respondents believed there was a strong link between the quality of relationships developed with teachers and the perception that teachers were encouraging of their academic development and engagement. These data suggest that despite teachers' gatekeeping function, students experienced authentically caring and instrumental relationships with them and benefited from the social/cultural capital provided in these relationships.

Factors Associated with Academic Performance

Approximately 90 percent of respondents reported performing well in school. Interestingly, only about one-quarter (27.4 percent) of respondents reported doing well in all subjects, while 44.5 percent reported doing well in two or more subjects. Students were most likely to excel in English language (20.3 percent), social studies (12.5 percent), math (11.7 percent), and science (9.4 percent), with an average HSGPA of 3.37. The majority of respondents (73 percent) perceived their academic abilities as above average, and about one-quarter perceived average academic ability. Notably, close to 50 percent did not feel well prepared for college, and 77.3 percent reported that inadequate high school preparation affected their later educational achievement.

Eighty percent of respondents reported that they were rewarded for high academic performance and received special achievement awards. Several factors were critically important in nurturing the educational performance of the respondents: recognition by school personnel beginning in the elementary grades, acknowledgment and praise from family, and encouragement from teachers.

Respondents consistently reported that academic recognition and praise by teachers for their achievement played an important role in their development of an achievement orientation. The following statements are illustrative of what the respondents reported helped them to succeed:

Achievements—elementary school, won awards, liked being in the limelight, working on a project and being rewarded; [a] special relationship with fifth grade teacher, single woman, role model.

Yes—family/school recognized academic achievement; elementary school—loved my teachers—first they were sweet and loving toward me.

In first grade I was the first to memorize things to win prizes; I was very motivated by things like that.

These relationships and forms of recognition played important roles for the respondents in their development as confident learners, as well as reinforcing achievement as a goal within their families.

In contrast, a number of respondents indicated that experiences with teacher prejudice or racism also motivated them to demonstrate achievement and go to college. One respondent referred to being called "the smartest Mexican" in her class for several years. Another stated: "I had a fourth grade teacher who put our pictures on a bulletin board with a little saying next to each child; next to my picture she put 'an ordinary girl.' Those stupid nuns didn't understand my culture!" Another respondent observed: "Issues concerning discrimination motivated me to pursue higher education. So I became the top student to show them that we could perform just as well as they." These respondents point to strategies of resistance in their response to racial microaggressions (Sue 2010; Solórzano, Allen, and Carroll 2002). As Nieto (1999) notes, "Negative expectations can prove to be a motivating source to succeed" or "prove them wrong" (43).

While many respondents acknowledge the supportive role of some White teachers in nurturing their academic skills, the scarcity of Mexican and African American teachers led to the few available role models of these ethnicities playing considerable roles in acknowledging respondents' abilities and supporting their achievement. For example, one respondent observed: "I had a good relationship with a Black teacher. She encouraged me to pursue a college education." Another stated: "My first Mexican teacher in the seventh grade told me that I wasn't stupid. I just liked to talk." The role of encouraging and caring teachers was a compelling theme throughout the responses. Perceptions of teacher caring, assistance, and praise were powerful forces in motivating these respondents toward academic excellence. Several illustrative quotes capture the sentiments of the respondents:

Teacher in fifth grade gifted class. She took special interest, encouraged me and other children (Black). I was a gold seal bearer.

During fourth grade my teacher encouraged education. This caused me to fantasize about education.

The sixth grade teacher explained that I needed to improve my grades—it made me feel like he cared and I turned my grades around.

I had a close relationship with principal and teacher in fourth and fifth grade. Sixth grade teacher had high expectations of me and was very encouraging and provided a lot of positive praise.

These statements reveal that many respondents were supported by parents, and engaged in reciprocal and authentically caring relationships with teachers, who were thereby acting as bridging institutional agents (Stanton-Salazar 2010). These were key factors that informed respondents' decisions to prepare for and enter college. Supportive teachers and other school-based agents made a difference in the education of these respondents by forming authentic, reciprocal relationships that conveyed to respondents that they were *cared for* as capable individuals. As Valenzuela (1999) observes, "Their pre-condition to caring about school was that they be engaged in a caring relationship with an adult in school" (79). The role of encouraging and caring teachers was a compelling theme throughout the responses, as such educators are often capable of transmitting social and cultural capital to their students (Espino 2014).

Perceiving teachers as caring, and receiving assistance and praise, helped respondents develop a sense of confidence and possibility, which diminished the impact of discouraging messages. An important implication of this finding is the necessity for educators to be knowledgeable about their students' identities (Hurtado, Alvarez, et al. 2012). While data describing in more detail the nature of these student-teacher relationships are not available, respondents' statements suggest that teachers served as *bridging institutional agents* and provided respondents with access to social/cultural capital that assisted their development of skills and informational networks, and informed their decisions to prepare for and enter college. In these cases, students likely experienced *educational pivotal moments*, which, according to Roberta Espinoza (2011), occur when a college-educated adult "intentionally reaches out to a student to provide the student with guidance and support to reach an educational goal" (33). To be sure, these supportive relationships existed within schools where Mexican American girls also found adults who were hostile toward them and their nascent identities as achievers. These data confirm the importance of adopting a life course perspective on accumulating social and aspirational capital in the K–12 pathway.

Access to Academic Resources: Fuel for College Aspirations

Six items were questions regarding availability and types of academic resources/programs in high school specifically designed to encourage minority participation in higher education. Only 16.4 percent of respondents stated that such programs—including, among others, cultural enrichment programs, special advancement programs, counseling, and recruitment— were available. Only about one-half of respondents who had access to these resources participated, with slightly over one-third (35.7 percent) of respondents reporting participation in Latino student organizations such as MEChA (Movimiento Estudiantil Chicano de Aztlán).[3]

Many of the respondents had a history of active involvement and participation in spelling bees, writing contests, honor roll, and leadership positions in student government. They were then able to seek out and become involved in other programs that recruited for college and/or they formed social clubs. The majority of respondents were able to access academic resources outside of school in programs that recruited and helped to prepare students for entry to college, such as Upward Bound, New Horizons, and Expanded Horizons. These programs provided them with experiences that were not readily available in schools or neighborhoods. Several responses capture the essence of what participation in these programs meant to the respondents:

> MEChA motivated me to go to college by not making the university foreign. One counselor guided me to taking the appropriate classes that would prepare me for college.

> If I wouldn't have belonged to Upward Bound, I wouldn't have known about higher education, for example, summer school on UC Berkeley campus. Special scholarships were available and then one counselor was set aside for Latinos.

Several respondents commented on the importance of ethnic-specific courses and exposure to professional Mexican Americans' lectures/presentations. In addition, many were part of, or helped to form, ethnic-specific clubs, such as Maya Club, Spanish Club, Mexican American Club, Chicano Club, and MEChA:

Chicanos would come in and talk about college requirements.

Special courses were offered for Hispanics and Black Americans.

One course offered an opportunity to view Mexican American women being educated rather than barefoot and pregnant.

[The] outdoor camping program was a motivational program geared toward ethnic students.

I was involved in [the] Maya Club that was very positive and enriching because I met various professionals.

Emphasis on ethnic-identity-based support programs and scholarships speaks to the significance these programs (often founded and staffed by Chicanos) had in generating social/cultural capital, which provided respondents with academic support, role models, and motivation. These programs, while associated with *bonding* forms of social/cultural capital, are also reflective of *bounded solidarity*, which links individual student achievement to a broader goal of community development (Putnam 2000). As Portes (1998) observes, identification with one's own group, sect, or community can be a powerful motivational force. Furthermore, through exposure to role models who were Latino, respondents were supported in developing a *bicultural network orientation*— "a consciousness which facilitates the crossing of cultural borders, the overcoming of institutional barriers, and thereby facilitates entrée into multiple community and institutional settings" (Stanton-Salazar 1997, 25). Recognition by Chicana/o or Mexican American organizations was especially important in that it enabled respondents to link achievement to family and ethnic identity, as respondents were also aware that for most of their teachers, academic success and Mexican identity were not synonymous.

The Role of High School in Decision to Attend College

When respondents were asked how their high school experiences affected their subsequent educational trajectory, they mentioned a number of key academic resources that prepared them for college. These resources included college preparatory courses, such as science and math courses that enabled study participants to perform well in required courses in college. Respondents also spoke of the significance of Mexican American and Black Studies courses, ESL classes, and tutoring for English language learners.

In addition, respondents indicated that exposure to different cultural and social activities—such as museums and other cultural institutions, beaches, boat rides, and restaurants—was an important learning and community-building opportunity. Finally, they identified the provision of caring and critical feedback as very important in the development of their writing and analytical thinking skills. Despite these important academic and social re-sources, most respondents also identified many barriers to their academic success in high school and discussed how they overcame them.

Barriers in College Decision-Making: Strategies of Resistance

While respondents identified many resources that prepared them for college entry and success, they also described numerous barriers they had to overcome in order to succeed and complete college. These responses can be categorized into three major areas: (1) poor quality of education, particularly in major skill-building areas, such as essay writing; (2) lack of college-readiness preparation; and (3) discriminatory practices associated with stereotypic attitudes and beliefs about a particular ethnic group. The following responses present powerful and representative narratives of many of the respondents' experiences:

> I was not in a good school. [The] quality [of schooling] was poor and the result was that I didn't know English grammar enough to write an essay. No college prep classes. Only one college counselor for six hundred students in my class; set ideas for "what kinds" of people go to college while in high school. Counselor tracked me into junior college. Counselor told me that I didn't have high enough grades or SAT scores to go to college. It was all a lie—I found out later.

> [I] never learned how to think. No clue how to study. Expectation was to do homework in [the] hallway—writing papers/research. No sense of independence [in high school] to handle expectations in UC system.

> I was in an Upward Bound program—my close association with one of the counselors got me into AP classes—only the cheerleaders and drill team could get [into AP classes].

[I was] not adequately prepared for college. Advanced courses did not compare to what other high schools in more affluent areas had. Racial remarks also made me doubt myself but I still worked for A's.

English teacher gave me an F or D and told me I didn't know any English. A counselor also saw my SAT scores and told me to forget it and go get married and attend a vocational school.

I had to go through special admissions. Even though I had the grades, I didn't have college-prep classes. I wanted to take an algebra class—they said what are you doing here and put me in a business math class; [I was] judged by my appearance.

Despite these adverse experiences, the respondents exhibited powerful resilience, resistance, and agency, and tremendous motivation to persist and attend college.

College Decision-Making: Strategies of Resistance

Interestingly, 38.6 percent of respondents decided by age fourteen to attend college, while 50.5 percent made their decision during high school (ages fifteen through eighteen). The majority entered college directly after high school. They attributed their decision to attend college to family expectations and parental encouragement (36.1 percent), learning achievement needs (19.3 percent), teachers (8.6 percent) and peers (5.6 percent).

Narrative data provide insight into the fabric and meaning of their reasons for deciding to attend college. As demonstrated by the quotes below, the majority of respondents had compelling aspirations and approaches of resistance. Five major themes emerged: (1) some had a hunger to learn; (2) some to prove themselves; (3) some a desire to achieve upward mobility; (4) others did not want to experience their parents' challenges; and (5) many wanted to follow in the footsteps of siblings or received special encouragement from a sibling.

I wanted an interesting profession and I always loved school.

Didn't want to get married or be a secretary.

I had a yearning to know. I was told about programs and scholarships—which made college accessible to me.

I knew I didn't want to work in the fields.

Desire to better myself as a person and to counter the stereotype that people have of Mexicans.

At age fourteen, [a] key interaction with [my] sister. She told me, "You're really smart, if you study hard, you can get a scholarship and get a PhD." At age fourteen, I decided to get my PhD. My sister mapped out my next twelve years. I want a PhD.

Although respondents achieved a higher level of academic success than their parents (defined as having completed college), most indicated that they accomplished these goals *despite* numerous barriers confronted in their K–12 schooling. Study participants reported enduring many barriers that included limited family material conditions and the low expectations (often informed by stereotypes) of their teachers. These barriers were mediated by caring racial/ethnic and White teachers who made the effort to be instrumental bridging agents activating their social/cultural capital and likely manifesting praxes of critical care. Siblings and extended family members also played a pivotal role in assisting these respondents in overcoming barriers, as observed in chapter 5. Respondents' decision to pursue college was strongly associated with the role of supportive parents, older siblings, and teachers. Notably, some respondents reported a strong desire to learn, having access to information about higher education (likely provided by bridging institutional agents), and being motivated by the desire to counter negative stereotypes of Mexicans. These themes were persistent and speak to a form of resistance by the women, their parents, and school- and community-based institutional agents—all motivated to prove that a generation of Chicanas, previously denied access to higher education, could achieve and make considerable contributions to their communities and the larger society.

Conclusions and Recommendations

The Mexican American study participants represent the first significant cohort of Chicanas to attend college after the civil rights era victories of the 1960s (Zambrana and MacDonald 2009). They entered upon a K–12 pathway that was not designed to see them succeed, but rather maintained unequal racial, ethnic, linguistic, and gender relations by default. Institutional arrangements and structures have not changed significantly over the past several decades, and obtaining the right combination of quality instruction and social support appears to have become more challenging in recent years (e.g., a growing number of states singularly emphasize high-stakes tests as graduation requirements). While there are some promising trends, especially with regard to increased levels of Mexican American enrollment in higher education, these have not resulted in widespread change in the opportunity structure. As a result, U.S. public schools continue to play an important role in reproducing inequality for low-income Mexican American men and women.

The data describe several key factors in the achievement of Chicanas that transcend decades of social and educational policies. Many factors converged to facilitate the achievement of these women. The opportunity to form positive relationships with teachers was a compelling theme across the participants' responses. We theorize that instrumental support provided by bridging institutional agents (Stanton-Salazar 2010) allows for the transmission of social/cultural capital to students and its activation in their lives (Lopez and Stack 2001), developing among them a social network orientation and increased chances of attaining academic and occupational success (De Jesús 2005; Stanton-Salazar 2010). In addition, the support of teachers and other nonfamilial agents assisted them in navigating adverse institutional environments, and developed within them strong motivation to pursue higher education despite discouragement from other teachers and formidable social and economic forces.

Chicanas resisted assumptions by teachers that they did "not care" about academic achievement. Indeed, their resistance strategy was to focus on achievement as a way of overcoming pernicious stereotypes and racialized microaggressions—such as being called "ordinary" or "the smartest Mexican" (implying somehow the status of being the smartest of the nonsmart). This is a reaction similar to college students' desire to *prove them wrong*, as documented in previous research on racial micro-aggressions (Solórzano, Allen, and Carroll 2002; Yosso, Smith, Ceja, and Solórzano 2009). Likewise, our study shows that proving them wrong was a motivating force that ensured participant success.

Strikingly, academic enrichment and support programs external to the respondents' schools, especially those tied to ethnic identity, exposed the respondents to *"hot knowledge"* (Ball and Vincent 1998) about the nature of higher education and the role it could play in transforming their trajectories. Gilda Ochoa (2013) found MEChA to be a transformative space for Mexican American high school students, as it "provides a space for students to systematically understand the differences in course placement, disrupt the assumptions, and change the patterns" of educational inequity (225). The ethnic-identity-oriented programs in particular appear to have been infused with a political clarity expressing an understanding that an individual Chicana's achievement was tied to the broader community's development. This suggests an important form of bounded solidarity, and bonding social/cultural capital also served as bridging capital in what were likely more affirming and protective cultural spaces that supported the academic achievement of these Chicanas. These study findings are instructive to practitioners seeking avenues to promote success and institutional integration for Mexican American students. Respondents strongly suggest that educational pivotal moments (Espinoza 2011) can enable college and professional success.

The findings have yielded important practice recommendations:

- Teachers and other school agents served as bridging institutional agents, activating their social/cultural capital and transmitting it to respondents; they should support their students in developing ethnic pride and social networks.
- While many students confronted barriers in their schools, these high-achieving Chicanas resisted stereotypic assumptions. Educators must recognize the persistent stereotypes that Chicanas face in their educational pursuits and incorporate efforts in their work to dismantle such pervasive attitudes in schools.
- Chicano and ethnic identity academic enrichment programs provided considerable support to respondents and linked the success of individual students to broader goals of community and ethnic group progress. Schools should increase the number of such programs and integrate them into the curriculum.
- Parents who lacked sufficient knowledge of course work subject content nonetheless supported and transmitted an achievement orientation and supported respondents' decisions to attend college in the form of *familial and aspirational capital*. Educators should engage in outreach to parents (and siblings) to provide intergenerational family education regarding college and career opportunities.

Although a number of successful and high-profile Chicanas (e.g., Susana Martinez, Lucille Roybal-Allard, Loretta Sanchez, and Janet Murguía) have emerged on the national landscape and have disrupted the stereotypical narrative regarding Chicana academic and professional achievement, the first generation of college-educated Chicanas, represented by our sample, were *pioneras*. They confronted and overcame a U.S. school system oriented toward their failure rather than their success. The adverse conditions that these *pioneras* confronted have scarcely improved in the intervening decades. In fact, they have worsened as a result of educational policies characterized by standardization and diminished autonomy for educators, who might otherwise be able to form instrumental relationships that engage marginalized students. Nevertheless, committed teachers, parents, social workers, tutors, and countless other institutional agents continue to advocate for improved educational outcomes for Chicanas on micro and macro levels, ensuring a future cohort who will overcome institutional and interpersonal obstacles and continue to "prove them wrong."

PART III

CONTEMPORARY COLLEGE EXPERIENCES

CHAPTER 7

The Ivory Tower Is Still White: Chicana/o-Latina/o College Students' Views on Racism, Ethnic Organizations, and Campus Racial Segregation

NOLAN L. CABRERA AND SYLVIA HURTADO

We have to give up part of ourselves to be with, to hang out with, White people.
DIVERSE DEMOCRACY PROJECT PARTICIPANT FROM THE
UNIVERSITY OF NEW MEXICO

Conversations about college diversity encompass not only which students get into college, but also what happens to them once they enroll. This is an especially salient issue for racial and ethnic minorities, who tend to have dramatically different perceptions of the campus racial climate relative to their racially privileged counterparts (Hurtado, Alvarez, Guillermo-Wann, Cuellar, and Arellano 2012; Rankin and Reason 2005). Few issues are as contentious as race and racism on campus, and perceptions of racial hostility vary across racial lines. This tension is exacerbated, in part, because White students are outwardly skeptical of minority claims of campus racism (Cabrera 2012; Gloria and Castellanos 2003; Johnson 2003; Rankin and Reason 2005). This view has become so entrenched that White people now believe that anti-White bias is more prevalent than anti-Black bias (Norton and Sommers 2011).

The expectation of students of color[1] at a Predominantly White Institution (PWI) is frequently to assimilate and lose native culture (Feagin, Vera, and Imani 1996; Jones, Castellanos, and Cole 2002; Tierney 1992). Studies have indicated that to both preserve culture and carve out a safe space for their development and learning, Chicana/o and other Latina/o[2] students frequently seek out racial/ethnic-specific organizations and centers as a means of support (Cabrera and Padilla 2004; K. P. González 2002; V. Orozco 2003; Patton 2010). "Safe space initiatives" are environments on campus where social identities are validated and supported

(Hurtado, Griffin, Arellano, and Cuellar 2008). Within PWIs, these environments frequently are ethnic-specific centers and programs (Patton 2010), and many are student-initiated and student-run organizations. Education scholars in the Latina/o critical race literature sometimes refer to these ethnic-specific environments as "counterspaces" (Núñez 2011; Yosso, Smith, Ceja, and Solórzano 2009), where students counter the predominantly White racial norms and affirm their ethnic identity.

This chapter explores college experiences with race and racism among a sample of Mexican-origin university students, and their methods of resistance, with a specific focus on their utilization of Latina/o-specific campus organizations. In doing so, we contribute to the literature on ethnic identity and student views of the university racial climate. We also address students' perceptions of campus racial segregation and what this means in terms of debates about campus *balkanization* (i.e., self-segregation). Specifically, some identify these organizations as reinforcing group antagonisms on campus (e.g., D'Souza 1991; Malkin 2003), and Arizona's state superintendent of public instruction equated ethnic studies with sedition (Horne 2010), fueling the misconception that Mexican American Studies creates anti-American sentiment. In contrast to this negative portrayal of culture-specific spaces for learning, recent research has shown how participation in racial/ethnic student organizations and taking ethnic studies classes contribute to a wide range of civic learning outcomes (e.g., social agency, political engagement, and civic engagement in public forums), across all racial groups in college (Hurtado, Ruiz, and Whang 2012).

Background

Most of the campus climate literature refers to Latina/os; only a few studies specifically focus on Mexican-origin students, or identify when these students constitute the majority of their study samples (S. Hurtado 1992; S. Hurtado, Carter, and Spuler 1996). While all of the students were of Mexican origin in this study and most referred to themselves as Mexican American or Hispanic (based on biographic information on participants gathered prior to each focus group and on the participants' narratives), the terms students used in their own narratives varied across the country, including the use of "Mexican," "Chicano," "Latino," and "Hispanic." In this section, however, we review literature using the terminology the authors use to most accurately reflect their studies on Chicana/o-Latina/o students' perceptions of the campus racial climate and their scholarship on Latina/o-specific campus organizations, dorms, and centers. We specifically focus on how these locations can help students carve out a safe space to develop cultural identity on college campuses. We conclude this background section with a review of the frequently contentious debates regarding campus racial and ethnic segregation.

The Campus Racial Climate

Hurtado, Milem, Clayton-Pederson, and Allen (1998) define a campus racial climate as composed of four interrelated dimensions based upon their critical review of existing empirical literature: (1) the institution's historical legacy of minority student inclusion/exclusion, (2) the numeric representation of students of color on campus (i.e., structural diversity or compositional diversity), (3) the quantity and quality of interactions across racial groups, and (4) student perceptions of the environment. Colleagues have introduced a fifth dimension to the campus climate that includes the organizational structures and processes that serve to embrace diversity or reinforce exclusivity in higher education (e.g., tenure processes, curriculum, and budget allocation) (Milem, Chang, and antonio 2005).

Scholars extended these previous campus climate models with additional literature, resulting in the Multicontextual Model for Diverse Learning Environments (MMDLE), which includes all these elements of the campus climate, places student identity at the center of practice in the classroom and within co-curricular activity, and links the climate with outcomes for students (S. Hurtado, Alvarez, et al. 2012). Within these features of the college campus, minorities in general, and Latinas/os specifically, tend to experience more hostility and marginality than their White counterparts (S. Hurtado 1992; Johnson 2003; Nora and Cabrera 1996; Rankin and Reason 2005). This is in large part because White space, or those parts of the campus environment where Whiteness is the cultural norm (Harper and Hurtado 2007), can create a tension for students of color whereby they can face cultural isolation and pressure to assimilate, and lose their native culture, or deny their ethnic origins (Feagin, Vera, and Imani 1996; Tierney 1992; Jones, Castellanos, and Cole 2002).

As a function of these White normative environments, Latina/o students are frequently the target of microaggressions (Yosso et al. 2009). Microaggressions are defined as "subtle insults (verbal, nonverbal, and/ or visual) directed toward people of color, often automatically or unconsciously" (Solórzano, Ceja, and Yosso 2000, 60). Within this context, Latina/o students can feel both attacked and isolated (Cabrera and Padilla 2004; Yosso et al. 2009). However, a hostile campus climate and marginalization do not have to manifest themselves as directly as through microaggressions. They can, for example, take the institutional form of representation where only a few Latinas/os in the student body, minimal representation of Latinas/os in the curriculum, or few professors of color on campus (K. P. González 2002). Thus, multiple avenues for student marginalization along racial/ethnic lines exist, and Latina/o students can experience many at the same time.

A hostile racial campus climate has adverse effects on Latina/o student collegiate success. Hurtado, Carter, and Spuler (1996) highlight that Latino perceptions of a hostile campus reduce their cognitive and affective well-being in colleges across institutional types, with Chicano students experiencing more social adjustment difficulty compared to other Latino ethnic groups. In addition, perceptions of a hostile campus racial climate have been shown to adversely affect Latino students' sense of belonging on campus (Hurtado and Carter 1997). This is troubling, because retention theorists argue that students are at increased risk of dropping out of college if they are not both academically and socially integrated into the campus environment (Tinto 1975, 1993; see Nora's 2003 integration model for Hispanic student retention). Identity-based groups that serve as mechanisms of affirmation and social support can contribute to integration into campus environments.

Ethnic-Based Groups and Organizations

Given the marginalization of Mexican American students on college campuses, it is not surprising that many turn to racial/ethnic-specific groups and organizations within the college campus. Joining racial/ethnic-specific groups is frequently a means of finding a safe space on campus (Cabrera and Padilla 2004; Cabrera and Valencia 2012; K. P. González 2002), but it is also controversial. There has been a great deal of negative publicity surrounding racial/ethnic-specific organizations, centers, dorms, and events (see, for example, D'Souza 1991, 1995; Malkin 2003; Thernstrom and Thernstrom 1997). Those attacking race-conscious campus organizations and centers tend to argue that campus administrators would not allow a "White Club," but it is acceptable to have the Chicano organization Movimiento Estudiantil Chicano de Aztlán (MEChA). Yet the long-established White fraternities on campuses that tend to restrict membership and racial/ethnic attendance at social events often go unquestioned because they are part of an exclusive normative environment (Hurtado, Gasiewski, and Alvarez 2014).

MEChA was founded in response to a lack of meaningful inclusion of Chicanas/os in the campus environment (C. Muñoz 1989). It served as an adaptive strategy, as students who are more likely to become involved in ethnic activities are found to have a stronger sense of self through ethnic identity (Saylor and Aries 1999). S. Hurtado (1994b) argues, "Hispanic clubs and organizations, and students who frequently discuss racial issues[,] perceive their campus to be more racially tense. It may be that these behaviors are adaptive strategies used by students to cope with inhospitable climates" (37). That is, greater awareness of one's ethnic identity and unequal status leads to more critiques of the college environment. Other examples of students carving out a niche in higher education include the development of Chicana/o Studies Departments, as well as Latina/o Greek organizations (V. Orozco 2003). Conversely, others claim that high degrees of same-race affiliations in college lead to an increased sense of ethnic victimization for students of all racial backgrounds (Levin, van Laar, and Sidanius 2003). Despite the benefits of these adaptive strategies for Chicana/o Latina/o college students, they are frequently disparaged for promoting campus racial segregation.

"Self-Segregation" on Campus

Self-segregation on campus, or *racial balkanization*, is a key criticism of multicultural education (D'Souza 1991, 1995). Ideally, multiculturalism is supposed to promote racial harmony through interracial interaction; however, this is frequently not the case. Instead, Duster (1993) argued, students at UC Berkeley continued to cluster by race despite the compositional diversity of the campus. What some refer to as campus self-segregation, Villalpando (2003) sees as self-preservation. He argues that racial/ethnic-specific organizations, centers, and dormitories only become necessary when racial/ethnic students are first marginalized on campus. Within this context, they represent an adaptive strategy to increase sense of belonging (Villalpando 2003). Those who label ethnic-specific organizations as self-segregating frequently overlook a simple fact within U.S. higher education: Students of color do not typically have the critical mass to self-segregate. antonio (2001) argued in his study of college students that it is actually White students who have the most racially homogenous friendship groups, "although this result is not surprising, since

White students constitute by far the most numerous of all nine groups on the UCLA campus" (75).

Thus, campus racial segregation is largely a perceptual issue depending on positionality within the context. It is not, as Tatum (2003) asks, "Why are all the black kids sitting together in the cafeteria?" Instead the question should be "Why *don't we notice* when White kids sit together in the cafeteria?" Duster (1993) highlights the frequently ideological nature of critiques of campus racial segregation in a contemporary context by taking a historical perspective: "Over the years, some mild hand wringing occurred about discrimination, but no national campaign was launched against the 'self-segregation' of the all-white, all-Anglo fraternities" (p. 235). Regardless, debates about campus segregation continue, as racial/ethnic-specific campus structures are frequently labeled as promoting campus segregation and ethnic antagonism (e.g., D'Souza 1991; Sabia 2002). This is critically important, because it means that one of the privileges of Whiteness involves seeing White racial segregation as happenstance and not structured. Thus, improving the quality and quantity of cross-racial interactions on campus involves not only pushing students out of their racial comfort zones, but also challenging their perceptions regarding who is actually doing the segregating.

Fifty Shades of Brown: Latina/o Racial Identity Development

Racial identity is not a static, essentialized feature of a person's being. Rather, it is a developmental process that is continually renegotiated and redefined. College becomes one of the arenas of change in the lives of young adults, when they forge their own identities and renegotiate interdependencies with their families (Chickering and Reisser 1993; Wijeyesinghe and Jackson 2001). One important development that occurs during college is that students frequently explore and redefine their racial identity (Wijeyesinghe and Jackson 2001). However, racial identity tends to be studied along the Black/White dichotomy (e.g., Cross 1971; Hardiman 2001; Helms 1990; Jackson 2001), and there are few explorations into how Latina/o students develop their racial identities.

This lack of research is complicated by the fact that Latinas/os can be from any racial groups, and this can influence their racial identity development. Ferdman and Gallegos (2001), instead of offering a series of progressive stages of identity development, developed a range of orientations that describe how Latinas/os experience their racial selves. The orientations range from internalized racism/preference for Whites ("White-identified") to an extreme preference for the in-group ("Latino-identified, racial/*raza*"). The authors additionally offer: Latinas/os accepting dominant norms without a preference for Whites ("Undifferentiated"), Latinas/os seeing themselves as the other without a clear sense of what this means ("Latino as Other"), Latinas/os identifying with their ethnic subgroup such as Salvadorian ("Subgroup-Identified"), and finally a positive Latina/o self that concurrently does not demean White people ("Latino-integrated") (Ferdman and Gallegos 2001, 49).

While Ferdman and Gallegos (2001) offer a theoretical perspective, Torres (1999) advanced an empirically based model of Latina/o identity that focuses on students' cultural orientations as they navigate between their native Latina/o heritage and the dominant White culture. She posited four Latino identity orientations: Bicultural, Latino/Hispanic, Anglo, and Marginal. Each of the orientations represents the level of comfort Latina/o students experience with the two cultures, ranging from comfort in both (Bicultural) to comfort in neither (Marginal). The two other orientations, Latino/Hispanic and Anglo, represent those students who have stronger ties with either their native/ethnic culture (Latino/Hispanic) or the majority (Anglo).

Some commonalities are observed across these two Latina/o identity models. Both argue that Latina/o students occupy different orientations, as opposed to the stages previously advanced in theories of racial identity development (Cross 1971; Helms 1990). These orientations are based upon levels of conflict between the students' native culture and the dominant White culture. Variation in ethnic identity and cultural orientation is largely a function of the interaction of three factors: (1) how much their family transmits the native culture to them, (2) the diversity of their lived environments, and (3) their awareness of societal racism. Racial identity development is an important, frequently missing, issue when discussing perceptions of the campus racial climate. Depending on a person's orientation in this developmental process, the campus can appear more or less hostile. This is not to say that the campus racial climate is purely perceptual, but rather, how students experience it is related to their racial/ethnic identity and positionality. Conversely, the campus climate can also affect how students develop a sense of their racial/ethnic self.

Method

Data for this project were derived from the qualitative component of the Diverse Democracy Project (S. Hurtado 2003). Within this multi-institutional study of public universities, there were seven focus groups composed exclusively of students from different Latina/o communities held in the wake of 9/11 in 2001. Timing of data collection on some campuses was delayed to allow a few months to pass before asking questions about diversity and campus climate. Participants were recruited through their university as a result of being identified as active, engaged students and through self-identification as some form of Latina/o (e.g., Chicano, Peruvian, Hispanic, or Puerto Rican). For the purposes of this analysis, we limited the sample to thirty-eight of the forty-seven students in the focus groups who identified as Mexican-origin (e.g., Chicano, Chicana, Mexican, Mexican American, or Hispanic but of Mexican origin). A semistructured protocol was utilized for the focus groups, consisting of eight grand tour questions. A central concern of the study was understanding how and what students from diverse racial/ethnic groups learn from each other on university campuses, but conversations quickly turned to the campus climate and barriers to intergroup relations. Focus groups were conducted at each of the following campuses: the University of Michigan (UM), University of Washington (UW), University of Massachusetts (UMass), Arizona State University (ASU), University of New Mexico (UNM), University of Maryland (UMD), and University of California, Los Angeles (UCLA). Three different Latina/o facilitators conducted the seven focus groups to ensure comfort when discussing issues of race and diversity.

All focus groups were digitally recorded, the record transcribed verbatim by a professional transcription company, and the transcripts checked for accuracy. In order to develop the coding architecture utilized in NVivo, a qualitative data analysis computer software package, each transcript was open coded by examining the raw data and identifying salient themes supported by the text. This constant comparative approach follows an inductive process of narrowing from particular themes (text segments) to larger themes that allows the researcher to attempt to "saturate" the categories— to look for instances that represent the category and to continue looking until the new information does not provide further insight into the category. Once saturation was reached in generating themes, several iterations of coding schemes were developed wherein codes were created, expanded, defined, and refined. Once the coding structure was finalized, the data were coded and stored under the relevant node, and the link to the full transcript was maintained. Commonalities and differences in student experiences were identified across campuses to understand similarity of experience, as well as issues voiced specifically by Mexican-origin students present in focus groups with other Latina/o students. A pattern-matching analytic technique was employed (Yin 1994) to see how major themes from the interviews reinforced and/or differed from existing literature on campus racial climate, engagement with Latina/o-specific organizations/centers/areas of study, and perceptions of racial segregation in higher education.

Student Voices on the Campus Climate

Three major themes emerged from the analyses of student narratives, each with several illustrative examples detailed here. Students voiced issues related to the first theme, characterized as an isolating and hostile racial climate, which was largely a function of underrepresentation in predominantly White university environments. However, it is important to note that along with these hostile climates were student strategies and responses that illustrated how they maintained resilience in a second major theme: students tended to rely on Latina/o-specific organizations to find a sense of belonging in what Núñez (2011) refers to as racial counter-spaces at PWIs. Along dimensions of the third theme, we captured perceptions of campus racial segregation. Almost all students believed that campus racial segregation was a problem, but some tended to frame it as an issue of minority students clustering together. They almost never mentioned White students as having responsibility for the balkanization (Duster 1993) of their respective campuses. Together, these themes illustrate racial climate dynamics hypothesized in racial climate models in the literature, providing insight into how they work to shape perceptions associated with Chicana/o-Latina/o identity development. Specific illustrations of each of these major themes follow, resulting in a complex portrait of Chicanas/os-Latinas/os with varying forms of identity and awareness of White racial privilege in their campus environments.

Isolating and Hostile Campus Racial Climate

Several components of an isolating and hostile campus racial climate emerged in the students' lived experiences on college campuses. Specifically, students discussed a lack of compositional diversity leading to *racial isolation*, indicating low representation of Mexican American and other Latina/o groups. When they did interact across race, they frequently encountered situations where they were asked to be a type of *racial teacher* to their peers and sometimes professors. Additionally, they encountered *microaggressions* (Yosso et al. 2009) in these cross-racial interactions. There was, however, a heterogeneity of narratives, as the minority of students felt that campus racial discrimination actually was directed at them by fellow Latina/o students as opposed to Whites. A related consequence in White normative environments is that some students felt challenged regarding their identity, blaming other "Hispanics," which we coded as *Latina/o versus Latina/o*, or intragroup, conflict regarding identity.

Racial/Ethnic Isolation. The first area many students highlighted about the campus racial climate was the minimal compositional diversity, especially as it pertained to Latinas/os. The students at UMD were generally unhappy with the disconnect between expectations of campus diversity through university advertisements and actual campus diversity. As two female students explained:

> R: Yeah, I was expecting a little more [diversity]. Like, my friends would tell me, you're going to Maryland, you're going to find a Latino everywhere.
> S: Yeah, that's what they told me, but that's not gonna happen, especially in my dorm, which is just like all White or like Asian.
> R: I'm probably the only Hispanic on my floor.

This was a common experience across campuses, and, as one UCLA male student recalled, "I was kind of like in a culture shock almost because I couldn't see any minorities [on campus]. . . . I felt like . . . I was like lost in a way." It is important to note that the proportion of Chicana/o and Latina/o students in California declined dramatically as a result of Proposition 209 in 1996, which banned affirmative action (Santos, Cabrera, and Fosnacht 2010). This is still evident years later, and will remain so as long as the change to the California Constitution remains in effect.

This lack of representation made many students feel marginalized on campus. A female student at UMass related her experience during her first year in campus housing:

> I lived in [dorm name], . . . it's an honors program there and I happened to be living in the one dorm that was like an honors college, like all students that were honors students, predominantly White. I didn't like it.

This academically talented student had difficulty taking full advantage of the campus academic opportunities through being racially isolated.

The social and psychological burden of being a "racial teacher." The difficulty of becoming socially engaged in the campus culture was further enhanced by the demands placed upon her as a minority student having to consistently provide a "minority perspective" in class. Being singled out to be the representative of all Latinas/os occurred for other students as well. As one UMass female student explained, "Like in lecture hall, if you're the one Hispanic within the lecture hall, they'll ask you just to get the Hispanic's view of like what's going on, you know?" In addition, students received demands made by their peers to educate the rest of the campus on their culture. A female student at ASU, recalling a White student at her institution who had never attended school with people of color, stated, "It would be like my job to teach her about people of color."

Being a representative of all Latina/o people and a teacher of White people took a psychological toll on students. A frustrated UM female student explained how she was constantly correcting misperceptions about Latinas/os among her non-Latina/o peers:

> Like the friends I've had and the people I've talked to that aren't used to Latinos or people of color in general. I've told them time and time again and sometimes it's kind of annoying to constantly say, "That's not true."

A Latino male student within this same focus group simply declared, "But I'm tired." The constant, unspoken requirement to educate his peers and even campus administrators about the "Latina/o point of view" caused him to cease his advocacy work and focus exclusively on his studies. Similarly, Griffin and Reddick (2011) refer to "paying the Black tax" among Black professoriate, but in this instance, the students paid the "Brown tax."

Others faced similar psychological drain and frustration from having to constantly educate White people; however, not everyone had an adverse reaction. One female student explained how she worked through the same issue at UNM:

> I'm trying to get to a point where my goal is to eventually get through this stage and get to a point where I can actually feel comfortable sitting in a room with a bunch of White people and educating them.

She was still tired from the extra effort necessary to educate White students but, she was willing to make personal sacrifices in the hopes of both improving campus racial climate and growing as a person.

Microaggressions and Racial Marginalization. Even though students were not asked during the course of the focus groups directly about tense interracial interactions, this issue continually arose when discussing peer interactions. For example, a Chicana female student from ASU recalled this episode in class:

> When it came to me and I said I was from Mexico, like everybody turned around like oh my God. . . . I was leaving and this guy goes over to me and says, "Oh my God, you are so cool." He's like "How did you learn to speak English" and I'm like what? And he's like yeah, he's like "Oh my God, are you illegal here?"

This type of campus microaggression (Yosso et al. 2009) also occurred within students' living spaces. A male student from UM was cooking, and the following occurred: "Like I'll be making *chorizo con huevos* (sausage and eggs) in the morning and I get a comment from upstairs, 'Why does it smell like Mexico in here?'"

This frustration at racial marginalization was echoed by a male UM student when he said simply, "White is right. White is right." It made facilitating cross-racial interactions increasingly difficult because, as one UNM male stated, "We have to give up part of ourselves to be with, to hang out with, White people." Fostering an inclusive environment frequently meant a one-way street of minority assimilation whereby Latinas/os on campus were the ones expected to lose their culture. Given the numerous examples of campus microaggressions articulated within the focus groups, it is not surprising that many felt rejected by the dominant, White campus racial culture.

This marginalization did not always take the form of direct conflict. As one UNM female student explained, "But we, like African Americans, Hispanics, American Indians, we associate with each other. You know what I mean and it's like I don't know maybe like the White race doesn't really want anything to do with it." The White students frequently did not want anything to do with diversity efforts, thereby locating the onus of improving campus racial climate within communities of color.

Latina/o versus Latina/o: Intragroup Conflict Consequences for Identity. While the sense of campus marginalization was generally present in the focus groups, there were some who, conversely, felt attacked by the Latinas/os on campus. A UW female student explained, "And so I totally feel that if there's any discrimination, it would come from the people being, 'You're half-White,' or 'You're not Mexican.'" Another female participant in this focus group concurred: "So I think that, for the most part, outside of the classroom I face discrimination by Hispanics." As an offshoot of these feelings, one participant went so far as to claim that Latinas/os were "unwilling to work with Whites." These differing attributions make theoretical sense because, in racial identity theory, once individuals realize the unequal status of their racial/ethnic identity group, they can choose to redefine the value of their group or choose to dissociate from being identified with the racial/ethnic group (Cross 1971; Helms 1990; Torres 2003).

Resilient Responses: Participation in Latina/o-Specific Organizations and Sense of Belonging

Given the campus microaggressions and marginalization many students experienced, in redefining and discovering the value of their own ethnic identity group, many turned to Latina/o-themed organizations for support during their college years. Interestingly, few students were associated with MEChA or other political organizations; however, they frequently spent time carving out counterspaces (Núñez 2011) within the university. We found examples of participation in multicultural Greek organizations, academic peer organizations, cultural centers and dorms (when available), artistic collectives, and conferences; self-exploration through academic course work; and co-opting of predominantly White student organizations (e.g., student government). Students spoke about each of these areas.

White Privilege in the Greek System versus Multicultural Greek. One means of creating a counterspace was through the Greek system. On one campus many students were tired of having the Inter-Fraternity Council (IFC) ignore issues pertinent to Latinas/os on campus. As a UM male student remarked, "But the thing is, why am I going to join and pay dues for something that doesn't have anything to do with me or my community?" Another described the IFC's function for minorities as "taxation without representation." Despite encountering a lot of resistance from the largely White members of the IFC, ethnic-specific fraternities broke off to form the Multicultural Greek Council (MGC).

IFC leaders took offense because they considered themselves multicultural even if many students of color did not. As one UM male student explained, "We called [the Council] 'Multicultural' and I heard the argument that was assuming the quote/unquote White Greek wasn't multicultural." The MGC was established as one means of racial minorities establishing a safe space on campus. A similar experience occurred at UCLA, where a male student commented, "Anglo fraternities by far outnumber that of minority fraternities and sororities, and so . . . you go with what you're most comfortable with." The lack of comfort led many to pursue the Latina/o-specific Greek affiliation.

Once the Latina/o-specific Greek organizations were established, cross-racial interactions were difficult to foster, as the primarily White fraternities and sororities did not want to interact with the minority ones. This was also prevalent at ASU, where one student actually worked at Greek Life. She explained, "You know, we have pushed for four years now to try to do . . . to interact with [White sororities and fraternities], to do other things and they just, they're not stupid, they're just . . . okay they're stupid." Another female student from ASU felt marginalized when attending Anglo Greek parties: "I just felt excluded away from the way they party. . . . I can relate more to African-American Greek life than the mainstream sororities." While the primarily White Greek system could not support the needs of these students, minority sororities and fraternities helped foster a sense of comfort on campus.

Other methods of seeking counterspaces. Greek life was the preferred path for many focus group participants; however, there were also a number of other Latina/o-specific campus organizations students gravitated toward. One female engineer found her place in the Society for Hispanic Professional Engineers (SHPE), while concurrently working within the Latino Student Union. One group of students were involved in the Comprehensive Studies Program, which functioned as a campus-wide academic support system. However, it became a de facto Latina/o-focused center, as this student population clustered in this area. Sometimes students were drawn to ethnic-specific dorms or floors within dorms. Students at UMass discussed the draw to the multicultural dorm, and one female student explained:

> It's very diverse, and you know, no one there will make you feel out of place, you know, you go in and a lot of people there, they want to learn more about other cultures. They want to know about where you're from and you know different religions and stuff like that.

This respect for cultural differences did not occur by happenstance, as students wanting to live in this housing arrangement had to sign a contract stating they would try to gain a better understanding of different cultures through the experience. This respect for difference was echoed by others in the group, with one student wanting more: "Why is there only one multicultural dorm?"

Focus group participants sometimes had the benefit of a cultural center on campus that functioned as a "safe space." A UNM female student explained:

I like to be in places where I feel free to express myself in however it is that I need to and whatever I say and so when I hang out like at El Centro which is where I am usually at, I feel like I can voice my opinion on whatever I want at any time.

This was an unexpected statement, given that this university is a Hispanic-Serving Institution (HSI), but even within this context, the participant found a strong need to establish a racially/ethnically safe space to voice opinions. This was not to say that El Centro was an arena free from conflict. "But," she elaborated, "I feel safe that the criticism that is going to come back to me is good-hearted." She valued a dialogic process of learning and personal development, not one that was destructive to her identity and perspectives.

Self-Exploration and Classwork. Students also gravitated toward areas of study and classes that incorporated diversity into the curriculum. This fostered not only an increased sense of belonging, but also the development of self-understanding. As one male UCLA student taking a Latin American music class explained, "I'm learning some of the issues of my culture and at the same time music." One male ASU student made a similar comment about his increasing self-understanding through the university's Chicano Studies program: "But you can't forget that you're still evolving in this country, and I think it helps a lot to learn about [the Chicano] ethnic background, especially with such a good program as this one."

Not all students found sanctuary within Chicano Studies. A UNM woman explained, "Then I took a Chicano Studies class and I figured that it will help me identify myself with the rest of the Hispanic community." It did not have the desired effect, as she never felt part of this campus Latina/o community, although it was not clear from her narrative how the class failed to meet her expectations. Regardless, she expressed her frustration: "I don't know why I decided that's what I needed in order to become more aware of where I'm from." This coincided with her belief that discrimination on campus stemmed from Latina/o students on campus as opposed to Whites.

Agency in creating counterspaces. In addition to finding fulfillment in classes, some students carved out their niche on campus by joining Latina/o-specific artist collectives. One female student worked with an off-campus group called *La Casa de Arte*, where Latina/o artists came together to promote their work. When groups were not established, sometimes students created them. As a female ASU student explained:

> We're trying to start an organization for Chicano artists, and then the organization has Chicano in it, and people ask me well, you know, is this an exclusive just for Chicanos and I say, "No, it's an organization created by conscious Chicanos, conscious about being Chicanos and conscious about other people as well."

Another group even held a Latina/o-specific literature conference. All of these efforts were spawned by students wanting to establish a racial/ethnic comfort zone and opportunity to learn more about their own culture. These Latina/o-specific organizations helped some students gain a sense of belonging on campus. As one male UM student stated, "Because with the Latino, at least you already know you have something in common. . . . You feel a little more comfortable." In addition to this level of comfort, a UCLA male student emphasized, "As far as race and ethnicity, you definitely want to join clubs and organizations that teach you more about your own culture and ethnicity."

Co-opting Traditionally White Organizations. Not all Chicanas/os-Latinas/os had to create separate organizations to create a Latina/o student voice. A UCLA student described how students of color came together to run for office in the student body elections under the banner "Student Empowerment." This slate highlighted how students of color had been excluded previously from university electoral politics, but "Student Empowerment mainly consisted of minority students, and when they read off the results, I was right there, and it's weird cause this whole side was all minorities, this whole side was like basically a couple of minorities." The many victories of the Student Empowerment slate highlighted that through concerted organizing, students of color could have a meaningful voice within existing campus structures.

Rejection of Latina/o-specific organizations. However, not all students had the same perception of Latina/o-specific groups and organizations. These very organizations served to alienate some Chicanas/os-Latinas/os on campus, as there were Latina/o students who proactively avoided Latina/o-specific groups. One female UW student said, "I didn't join the Latino organizations because I felt like I was segregating myself from the other organizations that were not Latino-based." As previously noted, this was also one of the students who felt that most campus discrimination originated from Latinas/os. The framings of campus racial discrimination, interestingly, were apparently independent in students' minds from perceptions of campus racial segregation. Participants failed to make this connection and tended to perceive the races as homogeneous clusters.

Perceptions of Campus Racial Segregation

In a third major theme, we found that students in the study across all campuses generally concurred that racial segregation occurred on campus. As a female student at UMASS declared:

> Latinos sit with Latinos, well Latinos tend to mix in with Blacks a little, but then Whites, mostly they sit together and there's, and then there's the athletes that they all sit together. They don't want to intermingle with anybody else.

These visions of the multicultural, integrated university sometimes turned fatalistic as a UM female student explained, "In the long run, everybody's going to stick to their own people." One male UW participant expressed particular disdain for campus racial segregation. Speaking as an outsider to the campus Latina/o community, he said, "I mean, you do see the mingling of students of different races, but it seems to me with minorities that you end up just kind of sticking with your own." He specifically targeted the minority communities as the ones creating campus racial segregation. This made sense, as he had been able to integrate into the dominant, White campus culture, and if he had the ability to assimilate, he believed, then so should others. To the extent that they did not, it was their choice rather than the racial dynamics of exclusion in relation to White privilege.

The narratives regarding campus racial segregation tended to echo similar experiences, and appear almost nihilistic in tone. As a UCLA male student articulated, "Yes there are like self-segregating groups, but what is the university going to do? You know? Send out the police squad and force us to you know, hold hands and be happy, happy, joy, joy?" Students generally accepted that campus racial segregation existed; it was seen as a natural part of the environment, and it was primarily discussed as a function of racial minorities sticking together. These comments were informative based upon not only what they said, but what they did not say: there was little discussion of White students segregating on campus and more institutionalized versions of normative exclusion (e.g., White fraternities).

Placing the onus of self-segregation on campus communities of color ignores the basic issue that minorities do not usually have the representational numbers to truly self-segregate at PWIs. This is a key, unquestioned tension within the focus group participant narratives because, on the one hand, they perceived a lack of compositional diversity, yet there were high levels of same-group activity. One male student expressed it clearly when he said, "You don't have a choice because there are so few Latinos here and so much majority are White, that you really don't have much of a choice but to interact in class." A male UCLA student offered a similar viewpoint: "What we've learned is the ability to interact."

Discussion

The students on these university campuses tended to be, at best, marginalized and, at worst, treated with hostility, and this generally held true across all institutions. We found that the three major themes from students' narratives were interrelated. Experiencing racial/ethnic isolation and a hostile climate may cause students to either reject identity or respond with resilience, seeking counterspaces that reaffirm racial/ethnic identity and allow them to explore it with others in college. Such culturally affirming learning activities lead to widespread notions of campus segregation, but the root of the problem goes unacknowledged—White privilege in the campus climate shapes students' experiences and consequent orientations related to Chicana/o-Latina/o identity.

Returning to the campus racial climate framework (Hurtado, Alvarez, et al. 2012; Hurtado et al. 1998; Milem, Chang, and antonio 2005), one of the first issues students discussed was a lack of representation, or compositional diversity. There tended to be relatively few students of color on campus, even at HSIs. This led to a sense of cultural isolation, whereby students had difficulty constructing a sense of belonging to their campus. The finding supports recent scholarship that highlights how Latinas/os in low-diversity institutions experience the most discrimination and stereotyping compared with moderately or highly diverse institutions (Hurtado and Ruiz 2012).

Within this context, the Chicana/o-Latina/o students had difficulties in intergroup relations for a number of reasons. First, they were consistently required to be "racial teachers" to their White peers and professors. This tended to take a psychological toll on the students, as they were asked to be the representative of their race/ethnicity, providing the "Hispanic point of view" on a subject. Second, students were also racially targeted via microaggressions (Yosso et al. 2009). Their peers would use terms like "illegal," and the truly insidious impact of these racial slights is cumulative. Students can generally deal with one microaggression, but multiple microaggressions over the course of time are what lead students to feel like second-class citizens of a university, and they also have the potential to adversely affect academic performance and health (Solórzano, Ceja, and Yosso 2000; Yosso et al. 2009).

Within the context of campus racial climate, the participant responses highlighted the organizational context for diversity, which encompasses curricular/pedagogical diversity (Milem, Chang, and antonio 2005). As some of the participants noted, class content can serve as a method of racial inclusion or exclusion. This is consistent with numerous studies citing both the cognitive and affective growth that occurs from taking ethnic studies courses (Sleeter 2011) and the association of such courses with civic learning outcomes (Hurtado, Ruiz, and Whang 2012).

In terms of navigating the hostile campus racial climate, the respondents frequently sought to create organizations, events, and activities where people of their own racial/ethnic background could celebrate their culture without fear of racial persecution. These counterspaces included organizations and centers that were created to be Latina/o-specific, and in some instances, they were de facto Latina/o spaces (Patton 2010). Additionally, students frequently found a sense of belonging by joining Latina/o or multicultural fraternities and sororities, as the traditional Greek system was ostensibly White. Sometimes, the construction of the safe space included co-opting campus structures that were traditionally White, as demonstrated by the takeover of the UCLA student government in 2009. Regardless, the consistent theme throughout the student narratives was the need to find a sense of belonging via counterspaces within PWIs.

There was some heterogeneity in the responses, as there were participants who felt marginalized primarily by fellow Latinas/os on campus for not being "Latina/o enough." For these students, Latinas/os and Latina/o-specific organizations were the ones primarily responsible for campus racial antagonism. Racial/ethnic identity development theory hypothesizes that the early orientation of students is marked by a lack of racial awareness and by White identification, followed by Latina/o self-awareness, which is frequently marked by equating all features of Whiteness with oppression (Ferdman and Gallegos 2001). This functionally alienated those Latina/o students who were not going through the process of racial/ethnic identity formation, especially those who were already questioning "how Latina/o" they were. The involvement in racially specific organizations did not, however, mean the students were able to self-segregate. The students consistently talked about the university being a space where they had to learn to interact across races and, therefore, develop an orientation as a bridge builder. If they did not interact across races (or "self-segregate"), the potential would not have existed for them to experience the level of microaggressions they did or report having to be cultural educators for their White peers and professors. This is consistent with antonio's findings (2001), where White students were primarily the ones who had the ability to self-segregate on campus. Within this context, it was surprising to learn that some of the students unquestioningly recited the dominant paradigm attributing primary responsibility for campus racial segregation to racial minorities. By blaming the racially isolated communities, they tended to leave the following question unaddressed: How do White students self-segregate? Without this analysis, it locates the onus for campus integration within communities of color. It additionally assumes that majority White areas are welcoming to Chicana/o-Latina/o students, and therefore students not assimilating into the dominant norm are percieved as fueling racial antagonism or, worse, acting racist.

The general consensus among the focus group participants was that self-segregation existed on campus; however, some tended to locate the problem within themselves, thereby internalizing this racist view. Bivens (1995) identifies one part of internalized racism. She argues, "There is a system in place that misnames the problem of racism as a problem of or caused by people of color and blames the disease—emotional, economic, political, etc.—on people of color" (p. 2). Thus, racism does not have to be explicitly enacted upon students of color by majority students in order for it to have power. Students of color themselves—in this case, Chicana/o-Latina/o students—unconsciously forgo their power of definition by unquestioningly accepting the dominant discourse. Many Latina/o students have to work through internalized racism as part of their identity formation process (Ferdman and Gallegos 2001; Torres 1999, 2003). Thus, it was not surprising that even some very racially conscious students failed to make the connection between a lack of representation (compositional diversity) and the numerical improbability that Chicana/o-Latina/o students can self-segregate. They tended to decry the lack of campus compositional diversity, while frequently highlighting microaggressions (Solórzano, Ceja, and Yosso 2000). However, rather than seeing their creation/ utilization of safe spaces through Latina/o-themed activities, organizations, and living spaces, the students pejoratively referred to their own activities as self-segregation instead of a self-preserving response to a hostile climate (Villalpando 2003).

Thus, the students' narratives in this study added nuance to the intersection of the campus racial climate and racial/ethnic identity. The more White-identified the students, the more likely they were to mislabel color-consciousness as a form of racism. Conversely, the students who were more Latina/o-identified tended to be the ones who sought out same-race and same-culture connections. Thus, the same components of the campus racial climate that served to signal inclusion to some Chicanas/os-Latinas/os signaled exclusion to others. This highlights a key missing component of climate research. While the current climate framework illustrates the importance of student perceptions of the environment as a central dimension, there is little examination of how these perceptions are informed by a student's individual development. This study chronicled Chicana/o-Latina/o students' lived experiences of inclusion and exclusion in the campus climate, and some students' resilience responses linked with their racial/ethnic identity development and simultaneous growing awareness of racism and White privilege in their environments. Criticism of culturally affirming programs and student organizations will not abate until we acknowledge and respond to exclusionary practices in higher education and the complexity of Chicana/o-Latina/o student responses.

Implications and Conclusions

As a consequence of these findings, a central issue becomes: What can faculty, administrators, policymakers, and practitioners within institutions of higher education learn from these students' narratives? There are many possible lessons. From a policy perspective, minimal compositional diversity can have an isolating effect on students while also subjecting them to the increased likelihood of racial harassment and discrimination (Hurtado and Ruiz 2012). Thus, policymakers and higher education administrators need to be prepared to defend policies such as affirmative action to enhance compositional diversity. In environments where this is not possible (e.g., California due to Proposition 209), there need to be inventive strategies for creating and maintaining a racially diverse student body (e.g., altering administrative policies to include holistic review of students' personal and academic accomplishments). However, compositional diversity by itself is insufficient to promote a healthy and inclusive campus racial climate (Hurtado, Alvarez, et al. 2012; Milem, Chang, and antonio 2005). Once students enter the university environment, it becomes imperative that faculty and student affairs practitioners understand and offer them the following. First, there needs to be education regarding the fact that students of color are not responsible for educating White people (students and faculty alike). If White people want to learn about minority cultures, it is their personal obligation to do so. Students of color owe White privileged individuals nothing, and this is a particularly important lesson for professors to learn. There is a power imbalance between professors and students, and therefore, their demands that students "provide a Hispanic perspective" carry more weight than those from peers (i.e., the consequences are greater if a student refuses). How can we expect students to educate others if they are just learning about their own Chicana/o-Latina/o histories in college? This suggests that more faculty and staff should learn more about the backgrounds of their students to transform their course content, pedagogy, programs, and practices so that they become institutional agents who help students succeed and who encourage multicultural competencies among all students (Hurtado, Alvarez, et al. 2012).

Second, there needs to be greater education about the nature and impact of microaggressions and racism. A common misconception is that in order for an act to be racist, it has to be *intentionally* racist (Cabrera 2012). Rather, student affairs practitioners need to reframe racism in terms of impact as opposed to intent. This is especially important in the context of racial joking, which frequently becomes the source of campus racial incidents and is easily framed as "just a joke" and therefore harmless (i.e., *not* racist) (Cabrera 2014; Picca and Feagin 2007). The aggressors cannot accept responsibility for change if they are not aware of what sorts of incidents may affect the climate for Chicana/o-Latina/o students. Climate assessments on campuses should be linked with action to increase awareness on campus and promote discussions of race and racism.

Finally, there needs to be support (both vocally and in terms of resource allocation) for institutionalizing ethnic-specific spaces for exploring Latina/o identity and multicultural education. This can include race-/ethnicity-themed dorms, cultural centers, and diversity course requirements. These are important for a number of reasons. When the institution takes responsibility for educating about diversity, it removes some of the burden on Latina/o students to be "racial teachers" to their White peers. Also, it can signal that the institution sees diversity as a core value. Additionally, the creation of counterspaces can help Latina/o students find refuge when the campus climate becomes hostile, while also offering a place for cultural affirmation.

The support of multicultural programs can be perceived as promoting campus racial segregation (Duster 1993). When the issue of campus segregation arises, student affairs practitioners and higher education administrators need to be prepared to address it. One possible way of doing this is highlighting areas where de facto segregation already existed in the campus environment (e.g., in traditional Greek organizations), well before the creation of multicultural organizations. This can be the basis for a dialogue on campus racial segregation by interrogating a double standard: When White students segregate, it is invisible and framed as normal. When students of color create counterspaces, it is framed as racial segregation.

This segregation awareness needs to be tempered with an understanding by practitioners and administrators that there is heterogeneity of perspectives within the pan-ethnic Latina/o identity. While there were some general trends in student narratives (e.g., experiencing microaggressions), there was a minority of participants who located issues of racial discrimination among Latinas/os as opposed to White students. Thus, the narratives of the Chicana/o-Latina/o students in this chapter highlight the complexities of engaging diversity in higher education, indicating how piecemeal approaches frequently fail. Until diversity is engaged in a holistic way, the ivory tower will continue to be White in both composition and as a normative culture that shapes daily campus life.

CHAPTER 8

Campus Climate, Intersecting Identities, and Institutional Support among Mexican American College Students

ADRIANA RUIZ ALVARADO AND SYLVIA HURTADO

Our separate struggles are really one — a struggle for freedom, dignity, and humanity.

DR. MARTIN LUTHER KING, JR., TELEGRAM TO
CESAR CHAVEZ, SEPTEMBER 1966

In the last decade, Latinos contributed more than half of the general population growth in the country (U.S. Census Bureau 2010), and have correspondingly increased their presence in higher education institutions. For the first time, Latinos account for a 15 percent share of all college student enrollments (Fry 2011). Although more than half of this enrollment is at two-year institutions, the raw number of Latino students in all segments of higher education is increasing, which signals progress but is also accompanied by challenges. Prior research on Latino and Mexican American students attending college in earlier eras documented discrimination and perceptions of a hostile climate where representation of Latinos was low (S. Hurtado 1992, 1994b; McKenna and Ortiz 1987; Zambrana and MacDonald 2009). One challenge of particular concern is that students at four-year colleges and universities continue to experience acts of discrimination, even at *highly* diverse institutions, and often at higher rates than for all other underrepresented racial/ethnic student populations (Hurtado and Ruiz 2012).

The purpose of this chapter is to expand previous research on the campus climate for Latino college students (Hurtado and Ponjuan 2005; Yosso, Smith, Ceja, and Solórzano 2009) by examining variation in the perceptions and experiences of Mexican American college students across multiple dimensions of the campus climate. Research that includes Mexican Americans in campus climate studies tends to group them with either all students of color or all other Latino subgroups, resulting in limited information about their unique experiences with discrimination and unwelcoming environments. Building on an intersectionality lens, this chapter affords a unique opportunity to understand intersecting identities, campus climate, and sources of institutional support in different campus contexts for Mexican American students in the contemporary era.

The Campus Climate

Scholars have aptly documented that racialized minority students experience a more hostile campus climate at higher education institutions than White students (Ancis, Mohr, and Sedlacek 2000; Cabrera and Nora 1994; Fischer 2007; S. Hurtado 1992; Locks, Hurtado, Bowman, and Oseguera 2008; Museus, Nichols, and Lambert 2008; Nora and Cabrera 1996; Pewewardy and Frey 2002; Rankin and Reason 2005). Prior studies have also demonstrated that experiencing a hostile climate has different effects on students from different racial groups (Fischer 2007; Museus, Nichols, and Lambert 2008). For Latino students in particular, experiences of discrimination, often in the form of racial microaggressions, have been linked to high levels of race-related stress and other negative outcomes (Solórzano, Allen, and Carroll 2002; Yosso et al. 2009). Though these qualitative studies did not specify the ethnic composition of their Latino sample, the quotes used to support the findings suggest that many of the microaggressions pertained to being from a Mexican background. The review of quantitative studies on the following pages will note when studies specified results or implications as directly pertaining to Mexican American students. Otherwise, the term "Latino" will be used to reflect the aggregate group that likely includes Mexican Americans but is not specified in the literature.

Latinos who perceive discrimination or racial tension have more difficulty in transition and adjustment to college. Hurtado, Carter, and Spuler (1996) found that high-achieving Latino students in the second year of college who reported perceptions of racial tension had significantly lower scores on scales measuring academic, social, and emotional adjustment to college. Controlling for all other background factors, Mexican Americans showed lower levels of social integration compared to other Latino groups. Other research has found that Latinos who perceive greater levels of discrimination and hostility have lower levels of academic and intellectual development (Nora and Cabrera 1996), as well as a lower sense of belonging to their institutions (Hurtado and Carter 1997; Levin, Van Laar, and Foote 2006; Locks et al. 2008; Núñez 2009). In contrast, satisfaction with the campus racial climate has positive indirect effects on both grade-point average and degree completion for Latino students (Museus, Nichols, and Lambert 2008; Nora and Cabrera 1996). In their examination of the effect of campus racial climate on the persistence and degree completion of Latino, Asian, Black, and White students, Museus, Nichols, and Lambert (2008) found noteworthy evidence that climate affected the outcomes differently for each group, indicating the importance of conducting separate group analyses to understand unique effects for specific racial/ethnic groups whenever possible.

One contradictory finding in the literature on the campus climate for Latino students involves social integration. Some of the earlier studies on Latino climate have shown that perceptions of discrimination lead to lower levels of social involvement on campus (Hurtado, Carter, and Spuler 1996; Nora and Cabrera 1996), while some of the more recent work demonstrates the opposite—that greater satisfaction with racial climate is associated with lower levels of student involvement with on-campus activities (Mayhew, Grunwald, and Dey 2005; Museus, Nichols, and Lambert 2008). This relationship deserves further investigation with a larger sample of students to explore the variation in Mexican American students attending different types of colleges. This is especially important because particular intersections of identity are more vulnerable to different forms of discrimination in contexts of underrepresentation (Ruiz Alvarado and Hurtado 2015), and such intersections may also influence both students' social involvements and their perceptions of discrimination on campus.

Although the outcomes associated with experiencing racial tension and discrimination on campus for Latino students are unfavorable, only limited research has examined the individual and institutional characteristics that shape the perceptions of those experiences. Perceptions of the climate are usually included in studies as environmental contexts that students experience rather than as outcomes in and of themselves. The few studies that have explored this area for Latinos have found only two student background characteristics to be associated with perceiving greater racial tension: not being a native English speaker or speaking Spanish on campus, and being of the first generation born in the United States (K. P. González 2002; Hurtado and Ponjuan 2005; Núñez 2009). In a study of "talented Latino students" who were the top scorers on the PSAT, S. Hurtado (1994b) found that one-quarter of these students reported a great deal of campus racial conflict as college sophomores and juniors. The students in the study with higher academic self-concepts (self-rated academic ability) perceived less racial tension on campus. However, students who frequently discussed racial issues with peers reported both greater racial tension and higher levels of discrimination regardless of academic self-concept. This suggests that contextual differences are associated with students' self-perceptions and behaviors that may shape interpersonal and intergroup relations on campus.

Other studies have found that both positive cross-racial interactions and participation in co-curricular diversity programs are associated with perceptions of a more hostile climate for diversity (Hurtado and Ponjuan 2005; Núñez 2009). That is, the more students interact with diverse peers in positive ways and engage in diversity programs, the more negatively they perceive the institutional environment when it comes to racial issues. Though these relationships may appear counterintuitive, scholars have suggested that more familiarity with diversity might allow students to recognize and be critical of treatment that is based on group identities (Hurtado and Ponjuan 2005; Mayhew, Grunwald, and Dey 2005). From a theoretical perspective, students may be demonstrating resistant capital (Yosso 2005), challenging inequality and/or subordination and working toward positive ends. Further, diversity programs may be an indication of climate problems on campus if these are developed in reaction to racial incidents. Likewise, membership in Latino student organizations has been associated with higher perceived levels of racial tension (S. Hurtado 1994b), which might accurately reflect greater levels of prejudice from majority group members on campus. It is likely that students experiencing significant racial isolation or conflict are more likely to join such organizations for comfort and/or to combat racism on campus in the absence of campus ethnic-specific "safe space" initiatives (Hurtado, Griffin, Arellano, and Cuellar 2008). Furthermore, White students are more likely to negatively judge Latino students whom they perceive as having high ethnic identification, as determined by membership in Latino or ethnic-specific student associations, or who phenotypically look more Latino than those who signal less ethnic identification (Kaiser and Pratt-Hyatt 2009; Kaiser and Wilkins 2010). These findings suggest that strongly identified minorities might indeed experience more prejudice and discrimination on campus.

At the institutional level, increased Latino representation in the student body has been associated with students feeling less racial tension and experiencing less discrimination, while lower Latino undergraduate enrollment has been associated with increased marginalization and alienation (K. P. González 2002; S. Hurtado 1994b). Similarly, students at more selective campuses perceive greater racial tension (S. Hurtado 1992, 1994b), which makes sense given that more selective institutions are typically less compositionally diverse. Two additional factors that can be within an institution's control, curricular diversity and faculty concern for students, have been previously tied to perceptions of a positive climate for diversity. Though not attending specifically to Mexican American or Latino students, Mayhew, Grunwald, and Dey (2005) found that students of color who perceived the curriculum to be diverse had more positive perceptions of the climate than White students who perceived the curriculum to be diverse. Likewise, K. P. González (2002) found that cultural representation in courses made Latino students feel less marginalized. Students who felt that faculty cared about them and were accessible outside of class also perceived less racial tension and reported fewer experiences of discrimination (S. Hurtado 1992, 1994b), demonstrating the capacity for faculty and other institutional agents to shape the climate on campus. These studies, however, did not tease out the effect of institutional agents on the different dimensions of the climate to determine how their role may differ in helping students deal with perceptions compared to more overt experiences of discrimination.

Prior studies have narrowed in on high-achieving or "talented" Latino students, on traditional college-going samples, on first- and second-year students, or on a limited number of selective institutions. The current study builds on this research by utilizing a more inclusive sample that incorporates both nontraditional students and broad-access institutions (two- and four-year colleges) where Latino college students are concentrated (Fry 2011). Mexican American students are the group of interest, since understanding within-group variability is important and very little is currently known about what influences climate outcomes specifically for Mexican American college students. Previous research has included Mexican American college students in general climate models for Latino students, but has not found significant ethnic differences in students' experiences and perceptions. In fact, very few differences have been found among students at public universities based on student identities and background (Hurtado and Ponjuan 2005), but these studies have operationalized the campus climate as strictly one experienced through a lens of racial identity. In examining influences on the behavioral, psychological, and organizational dimensions of the climate, this study broadens the definition of the campus climate regarding diversity to include hostile experiences and perceptions related to a range of social identities in addition to race and ethnicity, including gender, socioeconomic status (SES), generational status, and sexual orientation. This intersectional approach is a central piece of the study and is further discussed in the following section.

Conceptual Framework

The Multicontextual Model for Diverse Learning Environments (MMDLE) (Hurtado, Alvarez, Guillermo-Wann, Cuellar, and Arellano 2012) provides a framework for understanding the various contexts in which diverse students learn and how these contexts are linked to educational practices and student outcomes. The model situates diverse students and their multiple social identities at the center of interacting sociohistorical, community, policy, and institutional contexts. In situating multiple social identities at the center, the model is informed by an intersectional approach that lends itself to understanding the climate and outcomes for students. "Intersectionality" involves an examination of the unique experiences created by the integration of multiple social identities, which are embedded and exist within structures of inequality (Bowleg 2008; Dill, McLaughlin, and Nieves 2012). In other words, intersectional analysis operates at two levels: the individual and the structural (L. Weber 2010). At the individual level, it creates an opportunity for the expression and performance of interlocking identities, and at the structural level, it helps to reveal how power is implicated. This is important in examining the campus climate for Latino students, since the intersections of race with certain social identities, such as sexual orientation, have been largely unaddressed in past research, even though it is known that LGBTQ Latinos often face additional challenges in reconciling their sexual identity with cultural expectations (Akerlund and Cheung 2000; Almaguer 1993; Ryan, Huebner, Díaz, and Sanchez 2009; Trujillo 1991), which likely affects how they experience college.

Permeating the institutional context are the five dimensions (historical, organizational, compositional, psychological, and behavioral) of the campus climate for diversity, as documented by prior research (Hurtado, Milem, Clayton-Pederson, and Allen 1998, 1999; Milem, Chang, and antonio 2005). For the purposes of this study, we determine how Mexican American students experience oppression or institutional support along psychological, behavioral, and organizational dimensions of the climate. The climate of an institution is influenced by larger social forces (historicity), but is also shaped by the dynamics among individuals on campus (intersubjectivity), much of which takes place in the formal curricular and co-curricular spheres, but some of which also occurs through informal experiences students have with each other (experiential). When negative, the climate can be seen as a form of oppression experienced by individuals, through both subtle forms of discrimination and bias and also more overt instances of harassment punishable as "hate crimes." We distinguish between these two to understand how they are experienced differently by Mexican American college students, depending on the intersections of ethnicity with other social group identities.

Along with student identity, within the core of the institutional context are curricular and co-curricular spheres that demonstrate the parallel role of instructors and staff in advancing student outcomes through course content, pedagogy, programs, and practices. These spheres highlight the importance of intentional educational practices that are often neglected in assessments that focus on students and their individual actions (Outcalt and Skewes-Cox 2002). Further, institutions have the capacity to alter students' experiences with the climate by providing evidence of commitment to diversity; structures that support diversity, such as offering a college curriculum that is inclusive of diverse populations; and interactions in the classroom that affirm students as empowered learners. Individual educators also have the power to alter student experiences through their interactions with them. For instance, faculty and staff can provide students with a sense of both general interpersonal and academic validation, which have been previously tied to student success, particularly for underrepresented and nontraditional students in community colleges (Barnett 2011; Rendón 2002). A sense of validation can come through interactions in which students feel that staff and faculty are serving as institutional agents who transmit knowledge that fosters their development and helps them navigate the college environment (Rendón 1994).

Outside of the institutional context, it is important to also acknowledge the sociohistorical and political contexts in which Mexican American students live. Just as the pan-ethnic term "Latino" varies in meaning based on the social context and on the different political meanings associated with its use (Dill and Zambrana 2009), Mexican Americans experience the world through both marginalization and privilege, depending on their other social categories and on their relationship to the conditions experienced by others within the environment and historical era they inhabit. In situating the sociohistorical and political era in the MMDLE framework for the students in our sample, several important facts are observed that uniquely characterize these students in college and their environments. First, they are the first to witness the election of a two-term Black president of the United States, and many are attending colleges with unprecedented numbers of Latino students. However, the media are also covering heated debates regarding undocumented students and the right of same-sex couples to marry, and racial profiling is prevalent in public spaces in the hypersecurity of a post-9/11 epoch. Moreover, most of these students were admitted to college during an era in which "race neutral" policies were implemented in admissions, as affirmative action has been overturned for ten years in most of the states where they are currently being educated. This may be less of an issue when selectivity of the college is low, but in contexts where selectivity is high, Mexican Americans are once again finding themselves as "one of the few" in their classrooms. Therefore, differences across college contexts and within organizational dimensions of the campus climate are key in assessing the experiences of Mexican Americans from different social identity groups during this historical era.

Prior studies have demonstrated a connection between experiencing a hostile campus climate and multiple aspects of a student's social identity, including gender (Kelly and Torres 2006), sexual orientation (Evans and Broido 2002; Rankin 2004), and socioeconomic status (Langhout, Rosselli, and Feinstein 2007). In this sense, we extend research on intersectionality by clarifying the historical context and aim to measure the four domains of power—organizational, representational, intersubjective, and experiential (Anthias 2013; Núñez 2014a)—as they relate to the campus climate. In this way we "unveil the ways the interconnected domains of power organize and structure inequality and oppression" (Dill and Zambrana 2009, 5) via the climate in relation to multiple social identities, experiences on campus, and dynamic student interactions with others.

Methods

Data Source and Sample

The data for this study were derived from a combination of the 2010 pilot administration and the 2011 national administration of the Diverse Learning Environments (DLE) survey conducted by the Higher Education Research Institute (HERI) at UCLA. The DLE measures institutional practices, the campus climate, and student outcomes, and also assesses student experiences across multiple social identities, inclusive beyond race and ethnicity.

The DLE was administered at thirty-four campuses that included broad-access and compositionally diverse selective institutions, community colleges and four-year schools, and public and private universities. Two private institutions were lost when the sample was filtered to include only students who identified as Mexican American. The final sample size was 2,753 Mexican American students, and was composed of 17.9 percent freshmen, 27.2 percent sophomores, 30.6 percent juniors, and 24.4 percent seniors. One-fourth of the students entered their institutions as transfer students, and 14.9 percent were still enrolled in community colleges. The majority of respondents (67.5 percent) were female, and more than half (52.4 percent) of the sample was composed of first-generation college students.

Analysis

Frequencies on all variables of interest were conducted to examine missing data. Since our variables all had less than 5 percent missing values, the expectation maximization (EM) algorithm was used to impute values for missing cases on all continuous variables with the exception of the dependent variables. EM uses maximum likelihood techniques to provide a more robust method than other missing-value techniques, such as listwise deletion or mean replacement (McLachlan and Krishnan 1997). For our analysis, we utilized hierarchical linear modeling (HLM) to examine the individual and institutional characteristics related to the three outcomes of interest, using the same analytical model in a separate analysis for each outcome. HLM is appropriate when data have a nested structure, as in this case, where students were nested within institutions. By accounting for the nested structure of the data and the homogeneity of errors within groups, HLM helps to avoid Type I statistical error. HLM also simultaneously estimates equations for both the individual and the institutional effects, allowing the variance to be partitioned at each level of the data (Raudenbush and Bryk 2002).

Outcomes

Table 8.1 provides a list of the items comprising all of the factors in the model, including the three that serve as the dependent variables representing the psychological, behavioral, and organizational dimensions of the campus climate for diversity. Outcomes in this study can be generally

Table 8.1. Psychological, Behavioral, and Organizational Factors of the Campus Climate

Factor	Reliability and Factor Loading
Dependent variables	
Discrimination and bias	α = .889
Verbal comments	.792
Written comments (e.g., e-mails, texts, writing on walls)	.762
Witnessed discrimination	.750
Exclusion (e.g., from gatherings, events)	.746
Offensive visual images or items	.733
Heard insensitive or disparaging racial remarks from faculty	.677
Heard insensitive or disparaging racial remarks from staff	.664
Heard insensitive or disparaging racial remarks from students	.644
Harassment	α = .917
Physical assaults or injuries	.935
Threats of physical violence	.912
Anonymous phone calls	.844
Damage to personal property	.794
Reported an incident of discrimination to a campus authority	.685
Institutional commitment to diversity	α = .857
Has campus administrators who regularly speak about the value of diversity	.724
Appreciates differences in sexual orientation	.711
Promotes the appreciation of cultural difference	.698
Rewards staff and faculty for their participation in diversity efforts	.666
Promotes the understanding of gender differences	.665
Has a long-standing commitment to diversity	.651
Accurately reflects the diversity of the student body in publications (e.g., brochures, website)	.631
Independent variables	
Co-curricular diversity activities	α = .903
Participated in ongoing campus-organized discussions on racial/ethnic issues (e.g., intergroup dialogue)	.866
Participated in racial/ethnic or cultural center activities	.848
Attended debates or panels about diversity issues	.810
Participated in the women's/men's center activities	.782
Participated in the LGBTQ center activities	.729

(continued)

Table 8.1. Continued

Factor	Reliability and Factor Loading
Attended presentations, performances, and art exhibits on diversity	.649
Curriculum of inclusion	α = .854
Material/readings on race and ethnicity issues	.824
Materials/readings on gender issues	.715
Materials/readings on issues of privilege	.705
Opportunities for intensive dialogue between students with different backgrounds and beliefs	.635
Serving communities in need (e.g., service learning)	.578
Academic validation in the classroom	α = .863
Instructors provided me with feedback that helped me judge my progress	.842
I feel like my contributions were valued in class	.811
Instructors were able to determine my level of understanding of course material	.776
Instructors encouraged me to ask questions and participate in discussions	.673

applied to understand inequality for all identity groups and do not focus solely on experiences based on race or ethnicity. Each factor score has been rescaled to have a mean of 50 and standard deviation of 10. Discrimination and bias ($\alpha = 0.89$), a factor measuring the frequency of students' experiences with more subtle forms of discrimination, represents the psychological dimension of the campus climate. Harassment ($\alpha = 0.92$), a factor measuring the frequency that students experience more overt threats, represents the behavioral dimension of the campus climate. Institutional commitment to diversity ($\alpha = 0.86$), a factor measuring students' perceptions of their campus's commitment to diversity, represents students' perceptions of the normative organizational dimension of the climate. The compositional dimension is included in each model as an independent measure to understand the relationship between Mexican American representation (one of the domains of power) and the other dimensions of climate. The other domains of power (organizational, experiential, and intersubjective) are also captured through independent variables in relation to the outcomes and are described in the next section.

Independent Variables

Guided by our conceptual framework and prior research, the model includes variables representing student identity, as well as measures of inter-subjectivity (relations between individuals), experiential measures shaped by college and peer structures, and institutional/organizational structures and contexts that shape inequality. To examine heterogeneity in the Mexican American student population, this study incorporates three student identities in the model (gender, class, and sexual orientation), in addition to a dichotomous measure indicating whether students were born in the country (generation status). Measures of student background that control for enrollment status are pathway into the institution (first-time freshman or transfer) and class standing (freshman, sophomore, junior, or senior). Other student characteristics that differentiate psychological concerns, self-concept, and commitment among students and serve as important controls are level of concern about ability to pay for college measured on a three-point scale (1 = None to 3 = Major), self-rated academic ability measured on a five-point scale (1 = Lowest 10 percent to 5 = Highest 10 percent), and importance placed on the goal of helping to promote racial understanding measured on a four-point scale (1 = Not Important to 4 = Essential).

Formal college experiences that occur in the curricular (classroom) and co-curricular spheres of the MMDLE model include participation in academic support services, and factors capturing the amount of exposure to campus-facilitated co-curricular diversity activities ($\alpha = 0.90$) and a curriculum of inclusion ($\alpha = 0.85$). Informal college experiences include participation in racial, political, and religious student organizations, hours per week working on and off campus, and amount of positive cross-racial interactions ($\alpha = 0.88$). To capture the role of faculty dynamics in relation to individual Mexican American students within the curricular sphere of the MMDLE model, a factor measuring amount of academic validation students receive in the classroom ($\alpha = 0.86$) is included. At the level of institutional structures, we include selectivity, which previous research has shown to lead to more hostile climates (S. Hurtado 1992), as measured by the mean SAT score of the student body; aggregated peer level of participation in a curriculum of inclusion; and percentage of the full-time-equivalent student body that is Latino, as the representational domain of power that coincides with the compositional dimension of the climate.

Results

Table 8.2 shows the results of the three HLM models. Confirming the importance of considering multiple aspects of students' identities in examining their experiences with various dimensions of the campus climate, results show that gender, income, sexual orientation, and generation in the United States are all significant in at least one of the three models. Compared to males, Mexican American females are less likely to perceive discrimination and bias (b = −.75, p < .05) and experience harassment (b = −.79, p < .01). Low-income students with parental income below $50,000 are more likely than upper-middle-income students with parental income between $75,000 and $150,000 to experience harassment (b = .53, p < .05). Students who identify as homosexual, bisexual, or other sexual orientation compared to heterosexual are more likely to perceive discrimination and bias (b = 2.28, p < .01) and experience harassment (b = 1.42, p < .05), and they are less likely to believe that their institutions are committed to diversity (b = −2.13, p < .01). Finally, students who were not born in the United States perceive less discrimination and bias (b = −.89, p < .05) than Mexican Americans who were U.S.-born. Interestingly, there is no significant difference in the behavioral dimension between U.S.-born and non-U.S.-born students. Given that few studies have examined differences in Latino college experiences based on generation status (Hurtado and Ponjuan 2005; Núñez 2009; Stebleton, Huesman, and Kuzhabekova 2010), this study extends previous work, indicating that recent immigrants maintain a less critical outlook on discrimination than later generations, even though they actually tend to have more limited access to opportunities (Pérez, Fortuna, and Alegría 2008; Viruell-Fuentes 2011). Collectively, these findings demonstrate, even when controlling for experiential domains, within-group variability in how Mexican American students experience different dimensions of the campus climate for diversity.

Other student statuses that are significant are pathway into the institution, class standing, having concern about ability to pay for college, and placing importance on the goal of helping to promote racial understanding. Mexican American students who transferred into their college or university perceive less discrimination and bias than students who began there as freshmen (b = −.98, p < .01), but as students advance in class standing they also perceive more discrimination and bias (b = 1.03, p < .001) and less institutional commitment to diversity (b = −1.09,

Table 8.2. Final Models for Discrimination and Bias, Harassment, and Institutional Commitment to Diversity

Variable	Discrimination and Bias *b*	Harassment *b*	Institutional Commitment to Diversity *b*
Gender (female)	−0.748*	−0.789**	−0.814
LGBTQ	2.280**	1.418*	−2.132**
Low income (less than $49,999)	−0.270	0.530*	0.228
Lower-middle income ($50,000 to $74,999)	−0.314	0.301	−0.295
High income (more than $150,000)	0.039	−0.071	1.074
First generation in country	−0.885*	−0.199	0.079
Transfer student	−0.977**	−0.478	−0.465
Class standing	1.033***	0.224	−1.091***
Financial concerns	1.655***	0.812***	−0.649
Self-rating: academic ability	0.360	0.232	0.217
Helping to promote racial understanding	0.279	−0.884***	0.183
Academic support services	0.090	0.062	−0.057
Co-curricular diversity activities factor	0.369***	0.325***	−0.145***
Curriculum of inclusion factor	0.033	−0.071***	−0.007
Joined Latino student organization	1.192*	−0.803	−1.021
Joined political student organization	2.369**	1.234	−1.525*
Joined religious student organization	0.604	0.658	0.802
Positive cross-racial interaction factor	0.001	−0.011	0.204***
Academic validation factor	−1.866***	−0.483***	3.793***
Hours per week working on campus	0.111	−0.030	−0.127
Hours per week working off campus	−0.034	0.080	0.027
Institutional selectivity	0.100	0.169	−1.016
Aggregate curriculum of inclusion	0.029	0.031	0.484
Percent of student body that is Latino	−0.695	0.665	2.685*

*p < .05, **p < .01, ***p < .001

$p < .001$). This suggests that familiarity can breed disillusionment, as students who spend more time on campus have more opportunities to encounter oppression and lose their idealized view of the institution. Possibly also reflecting consciousness of inequality in the economic climate of the era, the more concerned Mexican American students are about their ability to pay for college, the more they perceive discrimination and bias (b = 1.66, p < .001) and report experiencing harassment (b = .81, p < .001). Students who place greater importance on the goal of helping to promote racial understanding experience less harassment than students who place less importance on the goal (b = −.88, p < .001).

A number of informal college experiences are significantly related to the different climate dimensions. Students who are members of a racial or ethnic student organization reflecting their own background perceive more discrimination (b = 1.19, p < .05) than students who are not members of such organizations, supporting previous research indicating that such organizations serve as counterspaces where students seek support and self-preservation in the face of perceived discrimination (Villalpando 2003). It is not possible to tell from the survey data, however, whether the organization a student joined was a pan-ethnic Latino group or one catering specifically to Mexican Americans. Students who are members of political student organizations also perceive more discrimination and bias than nonmembers (b = 2.37, p < .01) and less institutional commitment to diversity (b = −1.53, p < .05). Contradicting prior research (Hurtado and Ponjuan 2005; Núñez 2009), higher levels of positive cross-racial interactions are not significantly related to perceptions of discrimination and bias; rather, these results show that intersubjectivity is related to students perceiving their institutions as committed to diversity (b = 0.20, p < .001). Relations that include cross-racial interactions may be facilitated by institutional efforts that recognize the development of students' multiple identities. Further research is needed to determine how variation in Mexican American ethnic identity, which can be due to region of residence, phenotype, social class, and differences in socialization, relates to cross-racial interactions and participation in racial/ethnic student organizations that can preserve identity and culture.

Other findings highlight the critical role of the experiential domain in shaping perceptions of the climate. Higher levels of participation in campus-facilitated co-curricular diversity activities are significant in all three models and are associated with higher levels of perceived discrimination and bias (b = .37, p < .001), more reports of harassment (b = .33, p < .001), and less belief that the institution is committed to diversity (b = −.15, p < .001). Although the cross-sectional nature of the data does not imply causality, these findings confirm previous research indicating that having an increased awareness of diversity issues allows students to be more critical of intergroup interactions (Hurtado and Ponjuan 2005; Núñez 2009) and demonstrate resistant capital (Yosso 2005). On the other hand, students who take more courses that are part of a curriculum of inclusion report fewer experiences of harassment (b = −.07, p < .001), which might be related to diversity classes being a welcoming space on campus for Mexican Americans who might be experiencing isolation in other areas of the institution (Solórzano, Ceja, and Yosso 2000). Higher levels of academic validation in the classroom are associated with lower levels of perceived discrimination and bias (b = −1.87, p < .001), fewer experiences with harassment (b = −0.48, p < .001), and higher levels of perceived institutional commitment to diversity (b = 3.79, p < .001). Finally, Mexican American students at institutions where there is a higher percentage of Latino undergraduates perceive their institutions to be more committed to diversity (b = 2.69, p < .05). This suggests that the representational domain of power is a dimension of inequality that can be addressed by institutional leaders to challenge oppression, but as part of a system with multiple dimensions, representation cannot be the only dimension if real change is expected.

Because only one of the institutional-level structure variables is significant in the three climate models, while academic validation is a significant intersubjective measure in all of them, we ran additional analyses to determine whether there were significant differences in the levels of academic validation in the classroom by the different types of institutional contexts included in the study. In terms of institutional type, the results suggest that Mexican American students across the thirty-two institutions felt most validated at community colleges, followed by four-year colleges, and finally universities (see figure 8.1). Dunnett's T3 post hoc tests demonstrate that though the mean academic validation factor score was lower at four-year colleges than community colleges, the difference is not significant. However, the post hoc tests do confirm that mean scores on the academic validation factor are significantly lower at universities compared to the other two institution types (p < .001). This finding might be a function of the smaller class sizes at four-year and community colleges versus the larger university classrooms, where it can be more difficult for professors to know students individually. It can potentially also be connected to the historical dimension of the campus climate, since the more selective universities have a historical legacy of exclusion that might still permeate classroom environments, whereas community colleges were established for the very purpose of expanding higher education to the masses. Additional post hoc tests demonstrating that the mean factor score on academic validation decreases as selectivity increases (see figure 8.2) lend support to this hypothesis. Mexican American students attending institutions of the highest selectivity report significantly lower levels of academic validation (p < .001) compared to Mexican American students at institutions of lower selectivity.

In summary, the findings reveal that the climate is perceived and experienced differently among Mexican American college students based on the different intersections of their multiple identities, as gender, sexual orientation, income, and generation status are all associated with at least one of the climate dimensions. Additionally, participation in campus-facilitated curricular and co-curricular activities, as well as informal interactions with peers and Latino representation in the student body, has distinct and significant relationships to the different climate dimensions. This confirms that the experiential, intersubjective, and representational domains of power also play an important role in shaping experiences with the campus climate for diversity.

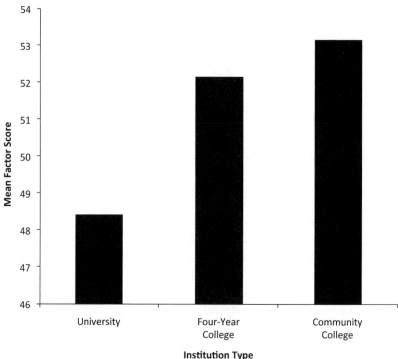

Figure 8.1. Level of Academic Validation by Institutional Type

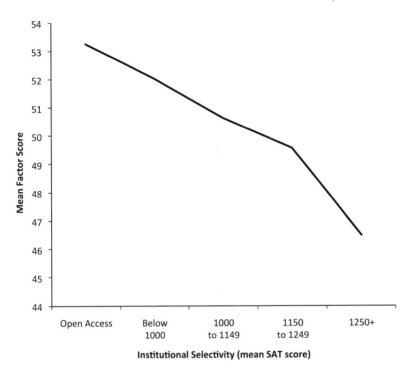

Figure 8.2. Level of Academic Validation by Institutional Selectivity

Discussion and Implications for Research and Practice

Experiences with Climate and Intersecting Identities

This study extends previous research to more broadly define the campus climate for diversity as one that is perceived and experienced through the lens of not just race and ethnicity, but also other social identities, including gender, sexual orientation, generation status, and socioeconomic status. The use of a broader campus climate for diversity definition is important because recent work reports that Mexican Americans think about their race less than other Latino ethnic groups (Ruiz Alvarado and Hurtado 2015), a finding based on the same sample of Latinos attending broad-access and selective institutions used in this study. In the contemporary era, on campuses where there is a larger Latino presence, Mexican Americans may perceive less threat due to their race and ethnicity and be more aware of discrimination in other dimensions of their social identity.

In general, members of stigmatized groups vary considerably in their reports of being targets of prejudice (Kaiser and Wilkins 2010). This may be due to the heterogeneity within these stigmatized groups, as the intersectionality lens suggests that Mexican Americans cannot and do not experience the world through race and ethnicity alone, but rather through a combination of those and the other social identities coconstructed through dimensions of difference, making it problematic to homogenize all students into one category and overlook the effect of various intersections of these identities (Bowleg 2008; Dill, Nettles, and Weber 2001; Dill and Zambrana 2009). Under that premise, it is the specific intersection of ethnicity and gender that may be contributing to Mexican American male students perceiving more discrimination and experiencing more harassment on campus than Mexican American women, since Latino males face unique challenges due to their underrepresentation in higher education (Sáenz and Ponjuan 2009).

Likewise, the results show that individuals inhabiting intersections of ethnicity with other identities that are underrepresented or targeted in society may also face more discrimination on campus, such as those identifying as LGBTQ, which was associated with more negative experiences and perceptions in the behavioral, psychological, and organizational dimensions of the climate. Sexual orientation is often an invisible identity, which can carry with it obstacles such as isolation, lack of resources, stereotyping, lack of role models, and inauthentic personal relationships (Bieschke, Hardy, Fassinger, and Croteau 2008). Moreover, the intersection of LGBTQ status and Mexican American ethnicity can create an additional fear of being rejected at home, or "abandoned by the mother, the culture, *la Raza*" (Anzaldúa 1987, 20). This suggests that LGBTQ Mexican Americans may need different types of support services to deal with these tensions than LGBTQ students from other racial and ethnic backgrounds, who may find it easier to be open in their lifestyle (Nero 2005).

In terms of class identity, low-income Mexican American students experienced levels of discrimination and perceptions of institutional commitment to diversity similar to those of Mexican American students from higher income levels, but were somewhat more likely to report overt forms of harassment, suggesting that climate is not experienced similarly across class. Finances play a role even when controlling for students' income backgrounds, as students' concerns regarding their ability to finance college were positively associated with higher perceptions of discrimination and bias and more experiences with harassment. This finding may be uniquely reflective of the recent economic downturn, as reports have indicated Latinos were more likely than non-Latino Whites to be adversely affected (DeNavas-Walt, Proctor, and Smith 2011). It is also a reflection of structures of inequality that leave those marginalized populations with fewer resources feeling more vulnerable. Our data show that particular Mexican American students are feeling such vulnerability on campus regarding their ability to manage college financing, which may lead them to consider leaving the institution and inadvertently perpetuate the cycle of inequality. Overall, affirming a commitment to diversity means educators must also provide sufficient support (financial, academic, and social) to address Mexican American students' needs, challenge oppression, and enable their success.

The Important Role of Institutional Agents

For those thinking about what institutions can do to create a more positive climate for diversity, the results indicate that receiving academic validation in the classroom is one of the few college experiences contributing to all three outcomes for the Mexican American students included in this study. Higher levels of validation from faculty are associated with more positive perceptions and experiences in the psychological, behavioral, and organizational dimensions of the campus climate. Unfortunately, research on validation has demonstrated that racial/ethnic students tend to feel less validated than White students (Hurtado, Cuellar, and Guillermo-Wann 2011). Moreover, in a longitudinal study of second-year students at nine public universities, Hurtado and Ponjuan (2005) found that Latino students were more likely than White students to hear faculty express stereotypes, report being singled out because of their backgrounds, and generally sense discrimination in the classroom. Such experiences disempower students as learners. They can be made to feel "silenced, subordinate, and/ or mistrusted" (Rendón 1994, 44) in the classroom, which contributes to more negative perceptions of the campus climate in general, especially if the classroom is their primary experience and point of contact with campus. If academic validation in the classroom can serve to curb feelings of a hostile climate for Mexican American students, as the findings indicate, it is critical that faculty members engage in activities that help students develop ways to resist this hostility by fostering recognition, promoting talent development, and empowering students in the classroom.

When instructors take the initiative to create a validating environment, the classroom itself can become one of the safe spaces on campus for students who perceive a negative campus climate elsewhere (Núñez 2009). In addition to faculty showing concern by providing students with feedback and making them feel that their contributions are valued, reflecting their background in the curriculum can serve as a validating experience for students (Rendón Linares and Muñoz 2011). That is, changes in the college curriculum and creating an expectation that all students will learn about identity, power, privilege, and oppression are critical for creating more equitable and inclusive learning environments. Accordingly, our findings demonstrate that being exposed to a curriculum that includes diverse content about different social identities and offers opportunities to have dialogue with other students or serve communities in need (engaging students with diversity) is associated with fewer reports of harassment among Mexican American students.

Staff members also have an important role outside of the classroom in shaping the climate, as Mexican American student participation in campus-facilitated co-curricular diversity activities was a significant predictor in all three models. Campus co-curricular diversity activities included participation in discussions on race and in events sponsored by racial/ethnic, gender, and LGBTQ centers. This measure of students' level of participation in all these activities was positively associated with perceptions of discrimination and harassment, and negatively associated with perceptions of institutional commitment to diversity, lending support to prior research suggesting that such activities provide students with a new critical awareness of campus dynamics (Hurtado and Ponjuan 2005; Núñez 2009). Alternatively, it is possible that students who are already critical of the campus climate may purposefully seek more activities or centers where diversity is openly discussed. Moreover, co-curricular diversity programs are often a reaction to a negative incident, indicating that the students who are participating may be experiencing a hostile campus climate for diversity. In any scenario, it is important that the staff members involved with racial/ethnic, LGBTQ, men's and women's centers, and other campus offices that host presentations or discussions about diversity issues are equipped to help Mexican American students process their critical awareness and are not just symbolic tokens. Given that the co-curricular activities highlighted in this study are sponsored by identity-specific centers, it is important for the institutional agents involved to also keep in mind that no single identity exists in isolation from others (Bowleg 2008).

Overall, student participation in co-curricular diversity activities can predict positive cross-racial interaction for Latinos (Sáenz, Ngai, and

Hurtado 2007), and also positive outcomes in terms of preparation for a diverse workplace (Engberg and Hurtado 2011). However, such co-curricular activities need to provide opportunities for sustained dialogue across differences and create opportunities for students to build coalitions to help resolve climate issues on campus. Both faculty and staff can create more opportunities to learn about diversity and, at the same time, assist Mexican American students in navigating college and reaching their educational goals.

Conclusions

Overall, our findings offer important contributions to the study of the campus climate as experienced by Mexican American college students, using new intersectionality frameworks. At a time when ethnic diversity within the Latino population is steadily increasing, and current political debates, such as immigration and marriage rights, are shaping the perspective of their peers, Mexican American students continue to face unique challenges in college that we have yet to probe further using an intersectional lens. The results highlight the importance of examining within-group differences in order to better recognize some of these unique challenges, and suggest strategies for institutions to consider in order to better serve this growing population on college campuses. The fact that specific intersections of identity among Mexican Americans are more likely to perceive a hostile climate (e.g., males), while others directly experience violence and harassment (e.g., LGBTQ and low-income students) in college, helps educators to use this and similar research to target coordinated efforts in developing a more comprehensive "safety net" (programs and services, identity-specific and otherwise) for students to ensure their success. It is worrisome that Mexican Americans at the most selective institutions experience the least validation in college classrooms compared to their counterparts at other institutions. Improving the climate for Mexican Americans at universities and selective institutions remains a key challenge, as is preparing those who begin as community college students for new challenges they will encounter at four-year institutions—not the least of which are different levels of support in the classroom and a more intense set of power and identity dynamics that characterize the climate for diversity.

PART IV

IMPLICATIONS FOR EDUCATIONAL POLICY AND FUTURE PRACTICES IN P-16 PATHWAYS AND BEYOND

CHAPTER 9

Mexican American Males' Pathways to Higher Education: Awareness to Achievement

LUIS PONJUÁN AND VICTOR B. SÁENZ

The future of our nation's Latino male student population is in peril.
Education stakeholders must develop effective policies and employ promising
practices to encourage Latino males' successful academic transitions into
postsecondary institutions, followed by increased degree completion rates and
promising workforce outcomes.
VICTOR SÁENZ AND LUIS PONJUÁN, "THE VANISHING LATINO
MALE IN HIGHER EDUCATION"

There is a growing concern among educational shareholders that Latino[1] males, the fastest-growing racial/ethnic group, are not enrolling and participating in American higher education at rates comparable to their Latino female peers and other racial/ethnic male ethnic groups. While the number of Latinos attending college[2] and attaining degrees has increased steadily over the last few decades, the proportional representation of Latino males continues to decline relative to their female peers (Fry and Taylor 2013; Sáenz and Ponjuán 2009). Steady gains in college enrollment and degree completion have not been uniform for every Latino male ethnic subgroup.[3] For instance, among twenty-five-year-old Latino males, 21.4 percent of those of Cuban descent (highest among all male ethnic subgroups) earned a bachelor's degree compared to only 6.5 percent of males of Mexican descent (lowest among all male subgroups) (U.S. Census Bureau 2012b).

Mexican American males compared to their Latino male peers have not kept pace in key educational milestones (e.g., high school graduation rates) (Brown and Patten 2013; U.S. Census Bureau 2012b). The large disparity in postsecondary participation and degree attainment among Latino male subgroups warrants a critical examination of the educational outcomes for Mexican American males. The college participation and degree completion gaps for Mexican American males can be described from a variety of sobering perspectives. The purposes of this chapter are to: highlight key differences between Latino subgroups—with particular focus on Mexican American males—at critical life course educational junctures in primary and secondary school experiences, which may account for differences in Latino males' educational achievement; examine the alternative pathways that college-age Latino males take, which divert them from higher education into low-salaried or low-skilled occupations; present some promising outreach programs that target Latino males to provide strategies for increasing their educational success; and present a set of research and policy recommendations to shape future progress on the growing gender gap in educational attainment and improve the educational experiences and outcomes of Mexican American males at the high school and postsecondary levels.

This chapter draws from multiple national data sources. However, we encountered limitations in obtaining data on Mexican American males. When organizations report Latinos as a racial/ethnic group, subgroup differences based on country of origin are often not reported. When data sets are disaggregated by gender and Latino subgroup, we highlight how Mexican American males face unique challenges in college participation and degree completion.

Mexican American Males: The Intersection of Ethnicity, Nationality, and Gender

The challenges confronted by Mexican American males warrant an acknowledgment of the complexity of Mexican American identity. Mexican American male identity is shaped by the intersection of race, ethnicity, nativity, gender, SES, and other socially and coconstituted identities (see chapter 4). Zambrana (2011) suggests that an intersectional lens highlights how power-based relations, Mexican American historical incorporation, and the social construction of Latinos in American society inhibit and distort how we understand their plight. Using this intersectional lens provides insight on how Mexican American males may experience unique challenges to successfully navigating their educational pathway, beginning in the K–12 system and continuing through postsecondary institutions. Several important factors are associated with the lived experiences of Mexican Americans, including residence in low-income segregated neighborhoods, parents with low levels of education, and attendance at low-resource schools with underprepared teachers. Latino males and other boys of color are more likely than their female peers to experience stereotyping and detrimental consequences of zero-tolerance policies (Sáenz and Ponjuán 2009).

Furthermore, for many low-income native-born and foreign-born Mexican immigrants, expectations that they will work, contribute to the family, and assume traditional gender roles often supersede their opportunity to attain a higher education. Moreover, foreign-born males may be at an additional disadvantage, depending on their age of arrival in the United States. Fry (2005a) notes that school dropout rates of the foreign-born are strongly linked to the age of migration. Foreign-born teens that arrive in the United States in early childhood have a better chance of matriculating in school. Those who arrive in late adolescence or who had education difficulties before immigrating have a high school dropout rate greater than 70 percent and are more likely to be labor migrants. In effect, they come to the United States to work and not to attend college (Fry 2005a). Ultimately, the social, familial, and socioeconomic expectations faced by young low-income Latino males (foreign-born or native-born) may manifest themselves in the decision to join the workforce earlier than their peers, indefinitely passing up the opportunity to seek a postsecondary education.

A guiding framework for understanding the educational trajectory of Mexican American males draws from the Multicontextual Model for Diverse Learning Environments (MMDLE) to illustrate the different contexts that affect student learning outcomes (Hurtado, Alvarez, et al. 2012) (see chapter 4). The application of the MMDLE model jointly with an intersectional lens acknowledges that the intersection of different domains (e.g., community context, material conditions of the family, institutional context, educational policy context, and sociohistorical context) influences the life course of Mexican American males, which in turn has an impact on their educational experiences. In addition, language barriers, and oftentimes being the first in their family to attend college, coupled with inadequate information-sharing by high schools and colleges, are common challenges facing Mexican American males and other Latino male students and their families (Gándara and Contreras 2009; Zambrana 2011). What follows is a discussion of the unique challenges that Hispanic students, especially Mexican American males, face in earning educational credentials in high school and college.

The Educational Context: A Growing Concern
for Hispanic Males' Academic Achievement

The broader discourse about Latino males and the gender gap in educational achievement informs the educational experiences of Mexican American males (Sáenz and Ponjuán 2009). Still, the public discussion of a growing gender gap is sometimes met with skepticism, particularly around reframing the gender equity debate within education. Historically, gender inequity was addressed through policy initiatives, such as Title VII of the 1964 Civil Rights Act and Title IX of the Equal Opportunity in Education Act.

These pioneering social policies led the way in increasing the success of women at all levels of education while also providing for more nurturing environments for women in schools, workplaces, and cultural arenas. Today, girls outperform boys on almost every academic indicator in elementary and secondary schools (Crosnoe, Riegle-Crumb, Field, Frank, and Muller 2008; DiPrete and Buchmann 2013). Still, some deem it unconstructive at best or cynical at worst to engage in a discussion of the schooling challenges facing our young boys. Many worry that too much attention to these challenges may detract from the advances made by girls within our educational systems (Crosnoe et al. 2008), or may distract us from the progress that remains to be made on multiple fronts (such as the persistent wage gap) (Corbett and Hill 2012). Nonetheless, when we conjoin the growing gender gap with the persistent educational attainment gap between Hispanic students, the stark reality facing Mexican American males in particular is cause for great concern. Until recently, few researchers have closely examined Latino male achievement despite the pervasive growth in Latino students' P-12 school enrollment, and the potentially grave economic consequences it could portend for our future if they do not complete a postsecondary credential. The larger crisis—in our view—is that there are few meaningful discussions taking place about Latino males in education.

The Experiences of Latino Males in Early,
Primary, and Secondary Schools

The Latino educational achievement gap manifests at multiple points along the educational pathway. In general, most boys are struggling academically relative to their female peers, and their problems are increas-

Table 9.1. Percentage of the Population Who Are 3- and 4-Year-Old Children Enrolled in School by Race and Ethnicity: 1980–2011

	Male			Female		
Year	White	Black	Latino	White	Black	Latino
1980	39.2	36.4	30.1	35.5	40.0	26.6
1990	47.9	38.1	28.0	46.6	45.5	33.6
2000	54.1	58.0	31.9	55.2	61.8	40.0
2009	54.9	58.1	39.4	56.2	58.8	44.4
2011	56.4	53.4	43.6	56.1	57.1	39.6

Source: U.S. Department of Commerce, Census Bureau (2013).
Note: Includes enrollment in any type of graded public, parochial, or other private schools. Includes nursery schools, kindergartens, and elementary schools. Attendance may be on either a full-time or part-time basis and during the day or night.

ingly evident during the impressionable early schooling years (Snyder 2012). For example, observable differences in enrollment rates persist between male and female students in early childhood education, especially among Latino and Black children. In 1990, 33.6 percent of Latino females under the age of five were enrolled in school on a full-time or part-time basis compared to 28 percent of Latino male peers (National Center for Education Statistics 2010). Although by 2000 the gender disparity had increased, by 2011 the gender enrollment gap, while narrowing, was reversed (43.6 percent enrollment for Latino boys and 39.6 percent for Latino girls) (see table 9.1) (Aud et al. 2013).

While these enrollment increases represent a promising trend, Latino students still lag behind their White and Black peers on this early indicator of school enrollment. Other gender gaps in early childhood education milestones (e.g., reading achievement) are particularly troubling, given the importance of the development of emerging social skills, early reading, math literacy, and beginning verbal skills in students' smooth transitions into primary education levels.

The levels of participation in early childhood education can significantly affect early academic success for all students (Zambrana and Morant 2009). Alexander and Entwisle (1988) noted that by the third grade, a child has established a pattern of learning that shapes the course of his or her entire school career. Gurian and Stevens (2005) suggest that boys are being educated within a system that is unaware of the potential mismatch

Table 9.2. Percentage of Public School Students Who Have Repeated a Grade, Been Suspended, or Been Expelled by Race/Ethnicity and Gender, 2007

Race/Ethnicity	Total	Male	Female
Percentage in K–12 who have repeated a grade			
Total[1]	11.5	13.9	8.9
White	8.7	11.2	6.1
Black	20.9	25.6	15.3
Hispanic	11.8	12.4	11.1
Asian	3.5	6.5	0.0
Percentage in grades 6–12 who have ever been suspended			
Total[1]	21.6	27.9	14.9
White	15.6	21.3	9.7
Black	42.8	49.5	34.7
Hispanic	21.9	29.6	14.1
Asian	10.8	14.9	‡
Percentage in grades 6–12 who have ever been expelled			
Total[1]	3.4	4.5	2.3
White	1.0	1.3	0.7
Black	12.8	16.6	8.2
Hispanic	3.0	3.1	2.9
Asian	‡	‡	‡

Source: U.S. Department of Education, National Center for Education Statistics, *Parent and Family Involvement in Education*, Survey of the National Household Education Surveys Program (NHES), 2007.
Note: All data are based on parent reports. Race categories exclude persons of Hispanic ethnicity.
[1] Total includes other race/ethnicity categories not separately shown.
‡ Reporting standards not met.

of the male learning style with current educational practices. They note that boys are on average a year to a year and a half behind girls in reading and writing skills. Consequently, most boys in grades four through eight are twice as likely as girls to be held back a grade, and the rate is even higher for boys of color (Shaffer and Gordon 2006). Other data show that 12.4 percent of Hispanic males and 25.6 percent of Black males have repeated at least one grade (see table 9.2). Serious concerns with boys' grade promotion challenges are exacerbated by differential rates of suspension and expulsion for male students of color (Aud, Fox, and KewalRamani 2010; Gregory, Skiba, and Noguera 2010; Milner 2013).

Overrepresentation in Special Education and the School Discipline Pipeline

Since the late 1960s, the U.S. Office of Civil Rights (OCR) has reported the pervasive problem of overrepresentation of minority children in certain disability categories (Artiles, Harry, Reschly, and Chinn 2002; Dunn 1968; Ferri and Connor 2005), and the disparities are even more pronounced for minority male students. Differing learning styles between boys and girls in the early schooling years can have consequences that may serve to redirect boys away from higher education pathways. For example, boys are twice as likely as girls to be labeled "learning disabled" and are seven times more likely to be diagnosed with ADD or ADHD. Boys constitute up to 67 percent of the special education population and in some school systems are up to ten times more likely to be diagnosed with serious emotional and behavioral disorders (Gurian and Stevens 2005; Pollack 1998). T. Parrish (2002) noted that Latino students are more likely to be overrepresented in special education, and tend to be especially overidentified during their secondary years, sometimes related to their status as English language learners (Artiles, Rueda, Salazar, and Higareda 2002), making their college pathways that much more difficult to navigate. These unsettling trends reflect one of the most long-standing critiques of special education practice, namely, the disproportionate placement of students of color in special education programs, referred to in the education literature as "overrepresentation" (Diaz and Zambrana 2011; Ferri and Connor 2005; Harry and Klingner 2006; Losen and Orfield 2002).

Disparities in grade promotion and school suspension rates can be associated with other forms of unhealthy behavior or misdiagnoses that may lead to missed educational opportunities. For example, Latino and African American males are overrepresented in special education tracks (Losen and Orfield 2002), referrals to juvenile justice agencies (Justice Center 2011), and high school dropout rates (Sáenz and Ponjuán 2009). Some of these trends are an artifact of zero-tolerance discipline policies that have taken root in many schools, especially in urban areas (Skiba 2000). In a recent study of school discipline policies in Texas, 83 percent of African American males and 74 percent of Hispanic males were reported for at least one discretionary school violation between seventh and twelfth grade, rates significantly higher than those of their female or White male counterparts (Justice Center 2011). The same study also reported that suspended or expelled students are almost three times more likely to be involved in the juvenile justice system the following year.

Public School Structures and Potential Obstacles

In his 1991 book *Savage Inequalities*, Jonathan Kozol exposed America's public school systems as having divergent extremes of wealth, opportunity, and segregation that form structural barriers which can discourage the academic success of poor and minority youth. Indeed, Latino students are among the most segregated minority groups in schools, separated out along racial, socioeconomic, and even immigrant characteristics (Orfield and Gordon 2001). Such extremes translate into gross inequalities that result from unequal distribution of school funding, underprepared teachers, high teacher turnover, poor administrative leadership, and an underrepresentation of Latino male teachers.

A structural issue affecting Latinos on their pathway to college is the lack of Latino males in the teaching workforce. In 2013, less than 10 percent of all elementary and middle school (9.8) and secondary school teachers (7.1) were Latino (Bureau of Labor Statistics 2014). Of the over four million teachers employed in K–12, only about a quarter were male, indicating that the proportion of Latino male teachers is much lower than that of all female teachers at all grade levels. Zapata (1988) argues that teachers of color are critical because they can be better equipped to meet the learning and mentoring needs of an increasingly diverse school population. In addition, male teachers of color can serve as role models for Latino students.

Identity and Family Socialization Processes

Further complicating the growing Latino gender gap are the pervasive psychological constructs around masculinity. Prevailing constructs of Latino masculinity tend to focus on the archetypes of *machismo* and *caballerismo*. "Machismo" refers to masculinity traits, such as assertiveness, power, control, aggression, and obsession with achieving status (see, for example, De la Cancela 1993; Rodriguez and Gonzales 1997; Torres, Solberg, and Carlstrom 2002). "Caballerismo," partly in reaction to the negative connotations of machismo, focuses on positive instantiations of masculinity, such as chivalrousness, family-centeredness, nurturing stances, and approaching of problems from a more emotionally connected perspective (Arciniega, Anderson, Tovar-Blank, and Tracey 2008). The concept of a "boy code," which shapes the identity development of all boys at an early age, includes the set of behaviors and rules of conduct that are inculcated into boys by our society. Such gendered norms of behavior include being strong, tough, and independent, and not showing weakness (Pollack 1998). For low-income Latino males, the analogous boy code "machismo" archetype can serve to reinforce gendered behavior expectations through a culturally infused lens, and many young boys can retreat further away from education.

Perhaps feeling ashamed of vulnerabilities, boys tend to mask their emotions, causing a sociopsychological disconnection that can lead to feelings of failure, helplessness, and even depression. Pollack (1998) notes that the rate of depression among boys is surprisingly high, and adolescent boys are three times more likely to commit suicide than adolescent girls (Snyder and Swahn 2004). Overall, Latino youth are at greater risk for attempting suicide, and at increased risk for nonfatal suicidal behavior, when compared with youths of other minority groups (Canino and Roberts 2001). In short, Latino males are more likely to endure disciplinary problems, exhibit suicidal and depressive tendencies, be suspended from classes, and drop out from school.

Emerging theoretical work on Latino masculinity appears headed in a more critical and perhaps purposeful direction. Extant work examines the intersection of race and class, and their simultaneous influence on men's ability to access social and financial capital; when young men are denied access or confront failure within educational spaces, they often revert to nonproductive resistance stances and/or hypermasculinity behaviors (e.g., Ramírez and Casper 1999; Torres, Solberg, and Carlstrom 2002). Such may be the case for low-income Mexican American males, some of whom struggle along their educational pathways and ultimately choose to enact their identities through resistive action in the classroom, or through leaving school to contribute to family economic stability and well-being.

One of the more important and enduring cultural values is *familismo*, which involves the strong identification and attachment to immediate and extended family. In many respects, the *familismo* orientation among Latino families serves to structure gender roles and expectations for family members. For example, Morales (1996) observes that the Latino male's responsibility is to "provide for, protect, and defend his family" (274). Young Latino males are raised with expectations that they are to be family-oriented, strong, brave, and hardworking, and to be family contributors.

Nonetheless, the notion of *familismo* among Latino families should not be seen as a negative or deficit force working to perpetuate gaps in educational attainment between males and females. *Familismo* can serve as a strong source of social support and as a form of social capital and a family asset in educational success (Suarez-Orozco and Suarez-Orozco 1995; Valenzuela 1999; Zambrana and Zoppi 2002). For Latino males, *familismo* can be a valuable asset because of its correlation with strong social and family networks, which can ultimately be accessed to support their academic achievement (Valenzuela and Dornbusch 1994).

A Demographic Profile of Latino Males in the U.S. Education System

In recent years, educational attainment data show significant differences in success rates between male and female Latino students (Aud et al. 2013). For example, in 2011, 31.4 percent of Latino males who were twenty-five years and older were high school graduates compared to 28.2 percent of Latino females. A closer review of these data reveals that Mexican American males have the second-highest high school completion rate (31.7 percent) compared to other Latino male subgroups (i.e., Puerto Rican [34.4 percent], Cuban [30.8 percent], Central American [28.7 percent], South American [30.9 percent], and Other Hispanics [30.2 percent]) (U.S. Census Bureau 2012b).

Latino Males and High School Dropout Status

The high school dropout issue has been a major source of contention among policymakers and educational practitioners, partly as a result of the varied metrics used to define a dropout. We utilize the metric of high school completion. In 2010, the percentage of eighteen- to twenty-four-year-old Latino males who had not completed high school or its equivalent was 34.2, compared to 27.1 percent for Latino females. The rates for not completing high school among Latino males and females were substantially higher than the overall rates for all males and females (Aud et al. 2013).

Despite a decade's worth of campaigns to enhance school accountability and high school completion, these data indicate that much work remains to be done. Further, a national educational report shows that the higher dropout status is also related to a student's immigrant status. "A higher dropout rate among Hispanics who were foreign born (31 percent) versus those who were native born (10 percent) partially accounts for the relatively high overall Hispanic dropout rate (16 percent)" (Aud et al. 2013, 130).

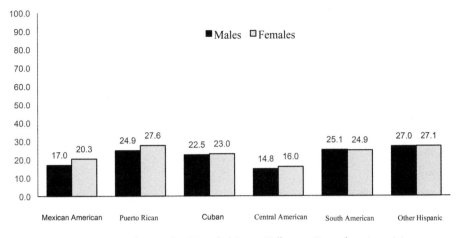

Figure 9.1. Latino Students Who Attended Some College or Earned an Associate Degree by Gender and Hispanic Origin Group (%) (2011)
Source: U.S. Census Bureau (2012b).

Degree Attainment Patterns at Two-Year and Four-Year Institutions

Less than twenty years ago there was little difference in degree attainment between male and female Latino students. However, the gender gap has widened. In 2012 females continued to outpace their male counterparts and earned approximately 60 percent of all baccalaureate, associate of arts, and associate of sciences degrees awarded to Hispanic students (twenty-five years of age and older) in the United States (U.S. Department of Education 2013).

Despite having relatively successful high school completion rates compared to their peers, figure 9.1 shows that Mexican American males are the second-least likely (17 percent) to attend some college or complete an associate degree compared to other Hispanic male ethnic subgroups (27 percent) (U.S. Census Bureau 2012b). These data warrant additional investigation, with some caution to account for the other dimensions of accumulated social, cultural, and structural challenges that accompany males along their educational pathways.

Over the fifteen years from 1995 to 2010, Latino students trailed the overall population in college degree attainment. Furthermore, in 2010, Latino males compared to females earned a smaller percentage of postsecondary degrees—12.9 percent and 14.9 percent, respectively (see figure 9.2). Mexican American males compared to their Latino male peers had

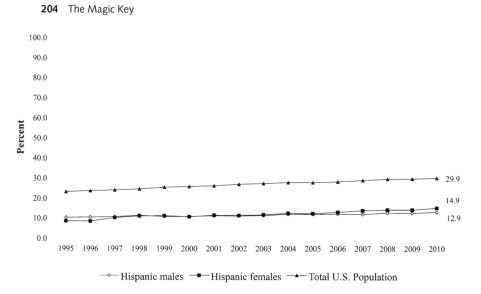

Figure 9.2. Bachelor's or Higher Degree Attainment by Ethnicity and Gender (1995 to 2010)
Source: U.S. Census Bureau, *Current Population Survey, 2011 Annual Social and Economic Supplement.*

the lowest percentage (9 percent) to have earned a bachelor's degree or greater (U.S. Census Bureau 2011).

Since many Mexican American males are not enrolled in college or completing a college degree, the majority are in the labor force.[4] An overview of employment, occupational, and income patterns is provided for Latino males. When data are available, we focus on Mexican American males.

Overview of Employment, Occupational, and Income Patterns by Nativity

Significant disparities exist in employment and occupational patterns by Latino male subgroup. Mexican Americans have historically had among the highest participation rates in the U.S. labor force, but they tend to work in occupations that pay low wages, provide low economic mobility, provide little or no health insurance, are less stable, and are more hazardous to their health (Maldonado and Farmer 2006). Their low occupational positions are associated with lower educational attainment, limited English language proficiency, and lack of work experience, training, and/or other employability skills ("'Deadly Trend'" 2002). In 2011, 82.2 percent of the 11.5 million Latino males ages sixteen and older were employed full-time, compared to 72.3 percent of their 8.14 million Latina counterparts. It is worth noting that Mexican American males were in the bottom third of Hispanic males working with full-time status (81.6 percent), compared to Cuban (86.2 percent) and South American (85.9 percent) males, who constituted the top third of Hispanic workers (U.S. Census Bureau 2012e). The unemployment rate for Latino males sixteen years and older, and in the civilian population, was 12.9 percent. Mexican American males had the second-highest unemployment rate (13.2 percent), compared to South American males (10.7 percent), who had one of the lowest rates (U.S. Census Bureau 2012e). More important, the data indicate urgent concerns about the long-term employment stability for males in unskilled occupations.

Occupational data show that college-age Latino males have a lower representation in management, professional, and related occupations (15.5 percent) compared to the general population (38.7 percent) (U.S. Census Bureau 2012f). Once again, Mexican American males are the least likely to hold management positions (12.9 percent) compared to other Latino male groups (e.g., Cuban males, 31.5 percent) (U.S. Census Bureau 2012g). Latino males represent a lower proportion of white-collar positions in sales and office occupations (15.1 percent) compared to the general U.S. population (17.0 percent). Following a similar pattern, Mexican American males (6.5 percent) and Central American males (4.0 percent) represent the bottom third of these professional and related white-collar positions (U.S. Census Bureau 2012f, 2012g).

Conversely, Latino males occupy blue-collar employment positions (i.e., manual labor positions) in greater proportions compared to the general population: 22.6 percent of the Latino male workforce (sixteen years and older) occupies positions in construction, maintenance, or repair, compared to 14.1 percent of the general male population (U.S. Census Bureau 2012f). Mexican American males (24.7 percent) and Central American males (27.8 percent) represent the largest percentages (U.S. Census Bureau 2012g). In terms of income, Latino male workers have the highest percentage (21.2 percent) of those earning $25,000 to $34,999 compared to the general male population (14.1 percent) (U.S. Census Bureau 2012h). Mexican American males had the highest percentage of men earning less than $34,999 (22.1 percent) compared to other Latino males (U.S. Census Bureau 2012i). In this same category, 20.6 percent of Mexican American males live below the poverty level, a much higher percentage than among their South American peers (13.0 percent). At the upper range of earnings, only 5.2 percent of Latino males earned a salary of $100,000 or greater, compared to the general male population (14.1 percent). As expected, only 3.8 percent of Mexican American males earned in this salary range, compared to South American males (11.9 percent) (U.S. Census Bureau 2012i). This enormous wage disparity reveals the effects of limited workforce opportunities for Latino males, especially Mexican American males, who are less likely to have a postsecondary credential.

Latinos constitute the majority of the foreign-born workforce population, with a significant number categorized as unauthorized workers or undocumented immigrants (Passel 2006). Undocumented Latino males often live below the poverty level. Of Latino males aged eighteen to sixty-four years, 19.5 percent live below the poverty level, compared to the general male population (10.5 percent) (U.S. Census Bureau 2012j). Approximately 26.5 percent of Latino males in the United States do not have citizenship, compared to 3.5 percent of non-Hispanic immigrant populations (U.S. Census Bureau 2012c). Among Latino male subgroups, only 27.1 percent of Mexican Americans do not have U.S. citizenship, compared to nearly half of Central Americans (49.7 percent) who are without citizenship. However, Mexican American males are the largest ethnic group, so there are still four times more Mexican American males (4.5 million) than Central American males (1.1 million) without U.S. citizenship (U.S. Census Bureau 2012d). Within the workforce, these undocumented Latino males are largely concentrated in blue-collar positions, most frequently construction, which rank low in potential earnings and educational requirements and are less conducive to upward social mobility (Kochhar 2005).

Despite the many challenges that Hispanic males face along their educational and career pathways, there is growing interest in meaningfully addressing these challenges at the school, community, state, and national levels. Similar to the ongoing, well-established efforts to improve the educational outcomes of African American/Black males in higher education, there is a nascent and focused national movement to develop outreach initiatives and policies that help Latino males achieve educational and occupational success.

At the Crossroads of Practice, Research, and Policy: Recommendations to Improve Mexican American Males' Educational Achievement

Education shareholders must develop effective policies, along with innovative, promising programs, and seek out unique research approaches to enact more successful academic transitions for Latino males into postsecondary institutions and favorable occupational careers. We argue that translational research benefits all low-income Latino males, and especially first-generation Mexican American males. In a recent article we identified several outreach programs focused on Latino males across the country (Sáenz and Ponjuán 2012). These programs, developed in predominantly Mexican American areas of concentration, represent a starting point for efforts that can be used to improve Mexican American male educational success, especially as momentum builds toward proactive interventions and services. We leverage the research literature to frame (Hurtado, Alvarez, et al. 2012) and support our recommendations (e.g., Gándara and Contreras 2009; Núñez and Crisp 2012).

Recommendations for High Schools

Local school boards are essential change agents for addressing the challenges Mexican American males face in completing high school. We suggest that school districts and high schools enact several recommendations focused on community outreach (e.g., family education seminars), revision of high school curriculum policies (e.g., advanced placement [AP] and dual enrollment course availability, teacher professional development), and programs (e.g., interpersonal, financial aid–related) empowering Mexican American males to attend college.

Family Engagement

Mexican American parents who are supportive of their child help that child to maintain high educational aspirations, regardless of the number of peers who are achievement-oriented (Espinoza, Gillen-O'Neel, Gonzales, and Fuligni 2013; see chapter 5). Given the important role that family plays in the lives of young Mexican American males, particularly those from low-income families and low-resource communities, it is imperative that schools develop policies and practices that encourage Mexican

Chart 9.1. Promising Outreach Programs Focused on Hispanic Males

Programs	Description
Fathers Active in Communities and Education (FACE)	Funded by a GEAR UP grant, this collaborative program engages fathers with information and opportunities to support their students' academic success. Working primarily with Mexican American communities in South Texas and in partnership with K–12, higher education, and local business partners, the program promotes intervention and support for academics through essay contests, hands-on activities, college tours, and many community and family-focused events throughout the year. www.fathersactive.com
Encuentros Leadership	This program, located in northern San Diego County, was formed to address the critical educational, social, and economic issues affecting the quality of education and life opportunities for Latino boys within the community. Encuentros hosts an annual summer leadership academy and an annual career and education conference for male Latino students. It also developed a textbook that it incorporated into its classroom program targeting the educational needs of male Latino adolescents. www.encuentrosleadership.org
XY-Zone	Built within the expansive network of Communities in Schools (CIS), the XY-Zone program actively works with male students in high schools to help them navigate the challenges associated with school issues, healthy personal relationships, and their academic futures. Similar to other K–12 educational programs, this program offers a small-scale, community-based approach to an educational problem that is approaching epidemic levels. The initial XY-Zone chapter was started in Austin, Texas, in 2000, and it has since expanded throughout the CIS network to other sites across the country. www.cisaustin.org/page-xy-zone.cfm
Puente Project	Located in California, the Puente (English translation: "bridge") Project is specifically designed to "increase the number of educationally underserved students who enroll in four-year colleges and universities, earn degrees and return to the community as leaders and mentors for future generations." For over 25 years, the Puente Project has been shown to improve college-readiness and college-going rates for Latino students (Gándara 1998). While not focused solely on Latino males, the Puente Project provides a strong academic, counseling, and mentoring model that has been proven to help facilitate college pathways for underrepresented students. www.puente.ucop.edu

American families to become more actively involved in the educational experience of their young men. Educational leaders at the school and school district levels need to recognize that Mexican American families are a crucial component in creating and instilling a college-going culture (Gándara and Contreras 2009; Núñez and Crisp 2012).

High school administrators need to engage family members (e.g., parents, grandparents) with language-appropriate materials and presentations during nonworking hours (evenings and weekends) about how they can help their son complete high school. Ultimately, schools need to collaborate with Mexican American families to create and nurture a school climate and culture that encourage high school completion, application for college and financial aid, and college enrollment for their young males.

There are several community-led programs, which work with schools, focused on creating innovative outreach efforts for Hispanic families. These partnerships are designed to assist Mexican American males as they navigate the high school pathway, and work with schools and families to impress upon their students the knowledge, skills, and behaviors needed to improve educational outcomes and achieve high school degree completion. Chart 9.1 provides examples of these programs.

Improve Access to a College-Ready Curriculum

At a time when the alignment between high schools and higher education for a seamless college-track curriculum has never been more important, local school districts are wise to develop policies that provide equitable access to precollege curricula to prepare Mexican American males for college and career success. High school administrators must increase equitable access to courses designed to prepare students for the rigors of college and career, including advanced placement (AP), honors courses, dual- and concurrent-enrollment courses, the International Baccalaureate curriculum, and rigorous career and technical education courses. A disproportionate distribution of AP courses in high schools can be traced along racial, ethnic, gender, and income lines (Allen, Kimura-Walsh, and Griffin 2009). Greater access to this type of curriculum enhances Mexican American students' chances to attend higher education. High school administrators must also pay particular attention to the gender gap in enrollment in AP and dual-enrollment courses, since Mexican American males lag significantly behind their female peers in participation.

Empower and Educate

Although there has been progress in developing rigorous academic standards and assessments (i.e., state-mandated exit exams) to prepare high school students for college and careers, high school teachers and counselors need to give more attention to the academic and social developmental supports needed for the most at-risk students to navigate successfully those academic benchmarks. High school counselors who help Mexican American high school students develop problem-solving skills enhance those students' ability to succeed beyond high school (Huang and Flores 2011). High schools need to develop programmatic initiatives focused on proactive career exploration and planning workshops, peer-to-peer mentoring, and study skills for Mexican American males. Such linked programs help to ensure that these most at-risk male students have developed the academic and social capital, behaviors, and capabilities needed to successfully transition into two- and four-year institutions.

Financing College

Policymakers and practitioners must recognize that low-income Latino students and families, during the high school years, face difficult hurdles in financing and paying for higher education (Núñez and Kim 2012). A well-known disconnect exists between the knowledge that families have about the financial aid process and the opportunities that are available to them. Greater transparency on the part of postsecondary institutions and the higher education community is necessary in order to provide students and families with accurate data on the financial costs of attending college, and on what aid, if any, is available. We recommend that high schools work with colleges to develop individualized information packets on financial costs that include not only tuition, but the costs that students from different backgrounds pay to attend the institution, including net price — defined as the full cost of attendance minus any scholarships or grants. Students often lack key information about the relationship between inadequate financial aid and college enrollment (Gándara and Contreras 2009; Núñez and Kim 2012).

In addition to maintaining greater transparency on the financing of college, postsecondary institutions should publish clear and reliable data on average time to degree completion, and graduation rates disaggregated by race/Hispanic ethnic subgroup, gender, income level, job placement, and graduate school admission rates. While it may be cost-prohibitive to create these individualized reports for all students, we argue that these reports should be a priority for certain underrepresented student groups (e.g., Mexican American, first-generation college-bound students).

Recommendations at the College Level

Latino students face challenges when navigating the college climate (Hurtado and Ponjuán 2005). Given the breadth and depth of expertise that exist on college campuses—from faculty to student affairs staff (e.g., financial aid officers, admissions counselors) to students themselves—individuals and departments have much to offer Mexican American males to help them succeed academically and socially. Higher education institutions can address the unique needs of Mexican American males in three major areas: community college enrollment, academic success programs, financial aid, and loan forgiveness policies for Mexican American male teachers.

Earning a Postsecondary Credential

Mexican American males are more likely to enroll at community colleges instead of four-year institutions (Núñez and Crisp 2012). Unlike traditional academic four-year degrees, a community college credential (e.g., in welding, culinary arts, etc.) represents a viable educational option for many Hispanic males, as there are long-term economic and health benefits for males who complete a community college credential (Belfield and Bailey 2011). Community colleges need to proactively help Mexican American males in their efforts to earn a college credential.

Community colleges can also develop programs in the juvenile justice system to assist those remanded to it in transitioning back into society. GED and vocational education programs provide options for continued education. These types of proactive outreach programs illustrate the spirit of nonpunitive forms of rehabilitation for at-risk Mexican American males that are necessary approaches for this student population (Rios 2011). Creating opportunities via this educational route may improve their employment opportunities.

Targeting Programs for Academic Success

Despite the low representation of Mexican American males in four-year institutions, administrators, faculty members, and student affairs professionals need to create special programs and policies tailored to these young men's academic needs, such as curricular and co-curricular initiatives to ensure higher rates of recruitment and retention (Sáenz and Ponjuán 2011).

Implementation of academic policies that require Mexican American males to complete mandatory academic advising sessions (or proactive academic advising sessions for students on academic probation) and career exploration workshops for students who are undecided about their academic major could enhance their academic experiences. Co-curricular programs, such as academic-living learning communities (e.g., engineering, business), tutoring for gateway academic courses, and first-year experience programs, should be offered to complement more traditional learning experiences. Finally, to ensure the availability of role models and mentors throughout these students' college careers, colleges and universities must promote policies that focus on the recruitment, hiring, and retention of U.S.-born Mexican American males, and other men of color, as faculty members (Ponjuán 2011). Linking academic and nonacademic initiatives addresses Mexican American male students' retention beyond the first year of enrollment and increases their odds of college graduation and a successful transition into the workforce.

Tools for Financial Aid Literacy

Financial aid literacy and the long-term implications of financing a college education remain a critical component of the college process. Post-secondary institutions should develop programs and policies that contribute to the development of behaviors and skills needed to make informed and financially secure decisions, particularly for traditionally underrepresented Mexican American student populations. These students and their families are less likely to borrow to pay for college, especially if they have unmet financial need after grant aid has been taken into account (Cunningham and Santiago 2008). Four-year institutions must be transparent about the distinction between grants/scholarships and student loans, as well as types of private company and government-supported student loans. For example, students should have information on the average financial aid package disaggregated by type of aid (Pell grants, institutional aid, state grants, etc.), average student loan debt, average delinquency and default rates disaggregated by student characteristics, and information on unpublished costs, including how financial aid packages may change from year to year. Armed with accurate and user-friendly information, institutional agents can help Mexican American families compare the value of different financial aid packages across many institutional types, which may help these families make informed college application and choice decisions.

Loan Forgiveness Policies for Mexican American Male Teachers

Inasmuch as Hispanic male teachers can serve as role models, mentors, and support systems to male students, incentives such as loan forgiveness, to draw more men into the field of education, should be developed. For example, loan forgiveness for the top 10 percent of new, Mexican American male teacher education graduates from public four-year teaching programs could encourage students to consider teaching careers. Loan forgiveness and other incentivized policies are innovative ways to encourage educational success by capitalizing on a problem area and refashioning it into a sustainable solution.

Conclusions

The sobering and disproportionate underachievements of Mexican American males highlight social and economic disadvantage and a critical need for educational leaders to take action. This chapter raises specific awareness of the bleak portrait of Mexican American males' participation in P–12 schools and barriers to engagement in higher education. The disparity in educational and employment outcomes for Mexican Americans males compared to other Hispanic ethnic subgroups and racial/ethnic males highlights an invisible educational and social crisis, although it remains ambiguous, undefined, and unnoticed in many policy contexts and discussions.

The dearth of disaggregated data for Latino subgroups made it challenging to provide an accurate portrait of key educational and employment outcomes. We encourage governmental and educational agencies to design future data sets so as to provide accurate portraits of this emerging, complex Hispanic ethnic group, with particular attention to Mexican Americans. This unique spotlight on Mexican American males is critical, since they are the largest subgroup and yet remain an untapped resource in our professional, government, military, private, and public workforces.

Finally, from a societal perspective, the critical role of Mexican American males as spouses, fathers, community leaders, and role models for the burgeoning Mexican American population could be in jeopardy due to continual educational struggles and increased incarceration rates. Ultimately, these barriers will inhibit their ability to fulfill the critical economic and social roles essential to securing upwardly mobile and economically stable Latino families and communities. Ongoing demographic shifts show an increasingly young Mexican American male labor supply as the fastest-growing employment pool, and yet the most underutilized talent base. Furthermore, America's human capital capacity and global competitiveness will be increasingly dependent on this growing segment of the population. Therefore, educational leaders should heed this call, take into account the unique educational needs of Mexican American males, and develop and implement programs and policies across the pre-K–college continuum to capitalize on their full potential and in turn ensure the long-term viability of Mexican American communities.

CHAPTER 10

The Role of Educational Policy in Mexican American College Transition and Completion

FRANCES CONTRERAS

Unless solutions are created to assess and repair educational pathways at individual, institutional, and societal levels, countless Mexican Americans will continue to drop out of high school, leave college before completion, and depart from doctoral programs.
FRANCES CONTRERAS, *ACHIEVING EQUITY FOR LATINO STUDENTS*

Educational policy plays a critical role in the experiences and services available to Mexican American/Chicano students in the United States (Gándara and Contreras 2009; Contreras 2011). State and federal policy sectors therefore have the potential to be an avenue for addressing the needs of this consistently expanding, yet underserved, segment of the student population. In my previous work, *Achieving Equity for Latino Students* (2011),[1] I proffer nine policy recommendations for moving an education policy agenda forward for Latinos, among whom Mexican Americans require the most significant attention. These recommendations were designed to introduce and expand upon policy approaches to raise student achievement, engagement, and ultimately college completion among Mexican American and other underrepresented, underserved, low-income, first-generation students. These recommendations are:

- Address the cracks in the pipeline that inhibit successful transition to college
- Develop a college-for-all policy at the federal level
- Reframe the discussion around testing and accountability
- Establish accurate state-level longitudinal data systems that inform practice

- Address college affordability
- Increase financial aid availability
- Revisit the need to pass the DREAM Act
- Prioritize the unfinished business of the stated objectives of affirmative action
- Utilize P-16 councils to address educational inequity and uneven postsecondary access

This chapter draws on prior evidence-based policy analyses to describe key policy frameworks that continue to influence opportunities to learn in the K–12 system, the transition to college/intervention programs and policies, the rising costs of attending college and financial aid, and the potential for higher education to move beyond affirmative action policies to an equity framework. It highlights select public policies that serve to support or hinder the progression of Mexican American/Chicano students through the P-16 pathways. In particular, discussions of accountability policies such as exit exams, inequitable curricular access, rising tuition costs, affirmative action policy, and shifts in financial aid policies are included to assess the role public policies had, and continue to have, on Mexican American/Chicano student transition to, and success in, college. These key policy issues and levers serve as a foundation for viable policy approaches and are essential to promoting Mexican American college completion. I conclude with a specific set of policy recommendations to move the Mexican American educational agenda forward and increase student preparedness and college completion.

My collection of data emphasizes policies related to college readiness, transition, and persistence. Sources include: state-level data from longitudinal systems, census data from the Pew Hispanic Research Center and the American Community Survey, federal financial aid data from the NPSAS (National Postsecondary Student Aid Study), Office of Civil Rights data, and state public higher education data. When possible, I use disaggregated data on Mexican American students. However, many state and national data sources aggregate data pertaining to "Hispanic Origin," making it difficult to assess accurately the plight of Mexican Americans, the largest subgroup, with their long-standing history of facing educational inequity, discrimination, and anti-immigrant public policies (Ortiz and Telles 2012; Donato 1997; Menchaca 1995).

Table 10.1. Educational Attainment (Age 25 Years and Older), Mexican Americans, 2011 (thousands)

	Mexican American (N)	Mexican American Percentage
Less than a high school diploma	7,280	42.3
High school diploma or equivalent	4,638	27.0
Some college	3,630	21.1
Bachelor's degree or more	1,659	9.6

Source: Gonzalez-Barrera and Lopez (2013).
Note: Author calculations of percentage within each category.

Background

Educational policy has the potential to shape opportunity for youth at every stage in the educational pathways as children transition to adulthood and postsecondary options. For Latino students, now 23.3 percent of the K–12 population in the United States (U.S. Census Bureau 2013), the policy arena plays a unique role in mandating reform. However, reforms such as No Child Left Behind have not resulted in measurable gains in access to rigorous curricula, test score achievement, or college readiness and transition for Mexican American students. In fact, Mexican American students are far less likely than their peers to be enrolled in Gifted and Talented Education (GATE), an honors curriculum, or advanced placement (AP) courses, and less than half of those who transition to college immediately following high school begin their higher education journey in four-year postsecondary institutions.

Mexican Americans have lower levels of education compared to other Latino subgroups. For example, only 9.6 percent of Mexican Americans twenty-five years of age and older have earned at least a bachelor's degree or higher, while 13 percent of all Latinos earned a bachelor's degree or higher (Gonzalez-Barrera and Lopez 2013). In addition, 42.3 percent of Mexican Americans have earned less than a high school diploma compared to other educational attainment levels (table 10.1). Tremendous challenges exist for Mexican American youth in achieving greater educational equity, access, and success throughout the P–16 pathway.

Policy Context

The historical interaction between Mexican American students and formal public education systems has been an ongoing struggle for equality (Donato 1997; Menchaca 1995; MacDonald 2004). Mexican American youth have experienced limited access to highly qualified teachers, under-resourced schools, and segregation and discrimination in schools (Gándara and Contreras 2009; Contreras 2011). This trend is ever present, as evidenced by anti-immigrant sentiment over the past fifty years. Figure 10.1 displays a chronology of anti-immigrant public policies from 1994 to 2013 that adversely impacted Mexican American and Latino youth in K–16 settings. Such policies have negatively targeted bilingual and/or Mexican immigrant students and have occurred at a time when our nation is witnessing unprecedented growth in the Mexican American population. These policies can be viewed as a direct response, manifesting as demographic denial, blindness, and fear, to the perceived "browning" of the United States. The changing demographic landscape of the nation is fueling such policies, which are directly targeting Mexican Americans in states like California, where Latinos constitute well over half of the K–12 population and represent a growing portion of the electorate.

Such policy efforts have exacerbated persistent inequities in the public schooling system, legitimizing institutional racism, and continuing to perpetuate a deficit-model paradigm and a culture of low academic expectations for Mexican American students. As a result of experiencing an inferior public educational infrastructure, few Mexican American students transition to college immediately following high school and even fewer complete a college degree. Figure 10.2 shows that since 1975, Hispanic students have lagged behind their White peers in the immediate transition to college. These rates do not reflect the already sizable dropout rates among Mexican American students during their high school years.

Persistent Inequitable Opportunities to Learn for Mexican American Students

Low transition rates to college enrollment are in large part due to persistent inequities that exist throughout the educational system. Mexican American students, particularly those who have parents with less than high school education, have very different educational experiences and largely attend segregated, low-resource schools. Telles and Ortiz (2008) conducted a longitudinal study of the educational progress of Mexican

Figure 10.1. Key Anti-Mexican Proposed Immigrant Policies Affecting Student Progress in K–12 and Higher Education, 1994–2013

Undocumented Students
Alabama, H.B.* 56, 2011 Leg., Reg. Sess. (Ala. 2011); ALA. CODE §31-13-8 (added section barring undocumented students from enrolling in or attending any institutions of postsecondary education; enjoined by federal district court, October 2011).
Arizona, S.C.R. 1031, §3, Proposition 300, approved election Nov. 7, 2006, eff. Dec. 7, 2006 (Ariz. 2006); ARIZ. REV. STAT. ANN. §15-1803 (amended to ban in-state tuition for undocumented students).
Florida, S.B.** 2040 and H.B 7089 (proposed)—would give law enforcement the ability to check the documented status of people under criminal investigation if there is "reasonable suspicion." It would also make being undocumented a state crime. (Did not pass.)
Georgia, S.B. 492, 149th Gen. Assemb., Reg. Sess. (Ga. 2008); GA. CODE ANN. §20-3-66(d) (amended to ban in-state tuition for undocumented students).
Indiana, H.B. 1402, 2011 Gen. Assemb., Reg. Sess. (Ind. 2011); IND. CODE ANN. §21-14-11 (added Ch. 11 to title 21, banning in-state tuition for undocumented students).
New Hampshire, H.B 1383 (signed into law, June 18, 2012). Requires students paying in-state tuition rates to sign an affidavit attesting they are legal residents of U.S.
Ohio, 129th General Assembly File No. 28, H.B. 153, §101.01; O.R.C. 3333.31 (D), (E) (2011) (banning in-state tuition for undocumented students).
Montana, 2011 Mont. Laws 1238 (ratified by state ballot measure, November 2012; amending MONT. CODE ANN. §20-25-502 [2009], eff. Jan. 2013) (enjoined by federal court, June 2014).
South Carolina, H.B. 4400, 117th Gen. Assemb. Reg. Sess. (S.C. 2008); S.C. CODE ANN. §59-101-430 (added section 430 to bar undocumented students from attending public institutions of higher learning, and also bar them from being able to receive in-state tuition).

Immigration Policy
SB 1070 AZ (2010)—"Papers please" law.
Secure Fence Act 2006—border across Southwestern United States to keep Mexicans out.
Proposition 187 CA (1994)—attack on immigrant, civil, and educational rights.

Pedagogy
HB 2281 AZ (2010)—ban on ethnic studies in public schools.

Linguistic Policy Restrictions
Proposition 227 CA (1998)—ban on bilingual education.
Proposition 203 in AZ (2000).
Question 2 MA (2002).
Horne v. Flores, 129 S.Ct. 2579 (AZ-2009).

Higher Education and Affirmative Action Policy
SP-1 policy, UC Regents (CA-1995).
Proposition 209 (CA-1996).
Hopwood v. Texas, 78 F.3d 932 (5th Cir.) (TX-1996).
Initiative 200 (WA-1998).
One Florida Initiative (1999).
Smith v. University of Washington Law School (WA-2002).
Grutter v. Bollinger (2003)
Proposal 2 (MI-2006).
Federal court upholds *Grutter* (2009).
Fisher v. University of Texas, Austin (2013).

*House Bill
**Senate Bill

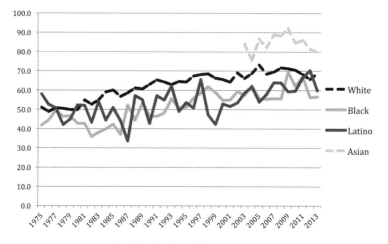

Figure 10.2. Percent of High School Graduates Who Have Had an Immediate Transition to College by Race/Ethnicity, 1975-2014
Source: U.S. Department of Commerce, U.S. Census Bureau, *Current Population Survey (CPS)*, October Supplement, 1975-2014 (2014).

Americans across two generations, following up on an original sample of 684 respondents from 1970. The researchers interviewed the respondents' children (n = 784) to examine various factors related to social and economic progress. They examined measures of progress, which included: socioeconomic status, language use, neighborhood integration, educational attainment, and civic engagement. They found minimal economic progress after the second generation, and educational attainment stalled after the third and fourth generations. Limited economic and educational mobility was attributed to insufficient funding in school systems that serve Mexican American students (Telles and Ortiz 2008). These data confirm the struggle for P–12 school equity (see, for example, Valenzuela 1999; Contreras 2011). This lack of equity helps to explain low college transition, retention, and completion rates among underserved and underrepresented minority students. Mexican American students continue to experience limited access to school resources (e.g., most advanced technology), highly qualified teachers, and a rigorous college-going curriculum, and they live in highly segregated communities where they attend underperforming Hispanic-serving schools.

Problems of inequity within schools and districts remain a salient concern, as deep gaps in funding exist across and within school districts in the United States. These gaps appear to be the greatest in districts and states with high Mexican American and Black population concentrations. Funding gaps include, but are not limited to, those affecting access to programmatic offerings and rigorous curriculum content, access to adequate facilities, access to highly qualified teachers, and access to technology.

Challenges to the inequities that Mexican American students experience in schools continue in the courts. In *Rodriguez et al. v. San Antonio Independent School District* (1971), parents alleged in a class-action suit that the State of Texas's system of funding schools based on local property taxes violated equal protection to students in poor districts under the Equal Protection Clause of the Fourteenth Amendment. The parents initially won, with the Texas district court ruling Texas's school finance system unconstitutional. However, in 1973, the U.S. Supreme Court reversed the lower court decision, preserving Texas's school finance policy (*Rodriguez II: San Antonio Independent School District et al. v. Rodriguez et al.*, 411 U.S. 1 [1973]). In the opinion, the Supreme Court noted: "Though education is one of the most important services performed by the state, it is not within the limited category of rights recognized by this Court as guaranteed by the Constitution" (36 L. Ed. 2d 16). In the past forty years, over forty-five states have witnessed school finance litigation (Reyes and Rodriguez 2004). The discourse around public school financing has now become a discussion of adequacy; finance equity is based on the resources necessary to provide an "adequate" education to all students (Satz 2007).

These funding constraints yield two unfavorable outcomes in districts serving high concentrations of foreign-born and native-born Mexican students: English language learners (ELLs) being taught by underqualified personnel and low National Assessment of Educational Progress (NAEP) scores demonstrating underperformance in math (U.S. Department of Education 2013).

ELLs continue to be ill-served in the educational system, as evident in their consistent underperformance on state and federal exams. These data are a reflection of the neglect they encounter in schools. Such neglect ranges from their not receiving bilingual services in schools to being taught by paraeducators (staff members with less certification/training in curriculum content than teachers) in the classroom (Contreras et al. 2008; Gibson, Gándara, and Koyama 2004). As a result, ELLs score lower on statewide exams and are less likely than their peers to graduate high school and transition to college (Gándara and Contreras 2009; Rumberger and Gándara 2004). Not only is there a pattern of low achievement, but there is also an undercurrent of low expectations for low-income, first-

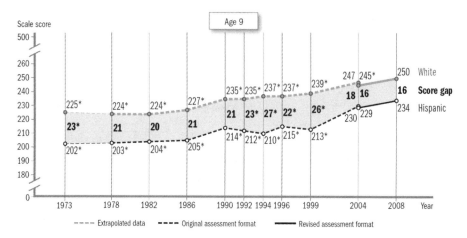

Figure 10.3. NAEP Scores, Math
Source: U.S. Department of Education, Instutite of Education Sciences, National Center for Education Statistics, National Assessment of Educational Progress (NAEP), various years, 1973-2008 Long-Term Trend Mathematics Assessments.
Notes: Score gaps are calculated based on differences between unrounded average scores. "Hispanic" includes Latino. The "White" race category excludes Hispanic origin.
*Significantly different (*p* <.05) from 2008.

generation Mexican American students that is exacerbated by inequities in funding and powerfully impacts their academic performance, particularly in testing outcomes.

The NAEP scores in math for nine-year-old students show the early gaps between Latinos and Whites that persist as students progress through the educational pathways (see figure 10.3). Further, these test score gaps illustrate the uneven performance among Latino students very early in the educational experience.

While NAEP scores show uneven achievement, very few academic supports are built into the educational infrastructure in primary grades to ensure that students are caught up to grade level in critical content areas such as math. As a result, many Mexican American students continue on a path of uneven achievement, which ultimately affects their level of engagement in school. Table 10.2 shows the number of high school students nationally who took advanced placement (AP) courses in academic year 2009–2010. The data highlight uneven access to AP courses (mathematics, science, foreign language, and other AP subjects) in the nation's high schools by race/ethnicity. Latino students make up 25.1 percent of public school enrollment

Table 10.2. Access to Rigorous Advanced Placement (AP) Courses in High School, by Race/Ethnicity, 2009–2010

		American Indian/ Alaska Native	Asian/ Pacific Islander	Chicano/ Latino	Black	White	Total
Courses	Sex	Percent (n)	Percent (n)	Percent (n)	Percent (n)	Percent (n)	(n)
AP Mathematics	Male	.005 (1153)	16.5 (40731)	9.7 (23999)	6.1 (15146)	68.3 (168893)	247417
	Female	.006 (1547)	16.2 (38916)	10.5 (25258)	9.7 (23411)	65 (156017)	240128
	Total	.006 (2700)	16.3 (79647)	10.1 (49257)	7.9 (38558)	66.6 (324910)	487545
AP Science	Male	.006 (1406)	17.4 (41707)	10.6 (25365)	6.9 (16562)	66.8 (160126)	239745
	Female	.007 (1664)	16.4 (41774)	11.4 (29007)	8.8 (22311)	64.2 (163243)	254347
	Total	.006 (3070)	16.9 (83481)	11 (54371)	7.9 (38872)	65.4 (323369)	494092
AP Foreign Language	Male	.004 (233)	13 (8483)	42.7 (27955)	5.6 (3637)	45.6 (29843)	65502
	Female	.006 (625)	11.7 (12794)	42.4 (46439)	7 (7712)	44.4 (48690)	109581
	Total	.005 (857)	12.2 (21277)	42.5 (74394)	6.5 (11349)	44.9 (78533)	175083
AP Other Subjects	Male	.006 (4255)	11.4 (77889)	14.4 (98070)	8.6 (58550)	63.4 (433036)	683164
	Female	.007 (6223)	9.8 (90160)	14.9 (136660)	11.3 (103996)	62.9 (577937)	919336
	Total	.007 (10447)	10.5 (168049)	14.6 (234730)	10.1 (162546)	63.1 (1010973)	1602500

Source: Office of Civil Rights, Civil Rights Data Collection, June 2011, U.S. Department of Education, National Center for Education Statistics.

in 2013, but only 13 percent enroll in AP courses (Solórzano and Ornelas 2004). Thus, Chicano/Latino students are approximately 6 times less likely than their White peers to be enrolled in an AP mathematics or science course, and 4.3 times less likely to be enrolled in other AP subject courses. Interesting patterns can be observed in table 10.2. Chicana/Latina females are more likely to take AP courses than Chicano/Latino males and are twice as likely as their male counterparts to take AP foreign language courses.

Tremendous variation also exists in the number and content of AP courses offered in high schools. For example, Solórzano and Ornelas (2004) found that Mexican American students had far less access to AP and honors classes than White students, even when courses were offered in their Los Angeles high schools (e.g., Mexican Americans constituted 78 percent of school enrollment but only 13 percent of AP class enrollment). Low transition rates to college enrollment are due in large part to these students' poor preparation associated with persistent inequitable opportunities (Gándara and Contreras 2009; see chapter 3).

Accountability Frameworks and Their Role in Inhibiting Opportunities to Learn

No Child Left Behind (NCLB) is part of a high-stakes accountability system that focuses on student assessment and outcomes, using standardized measures. This approach to education, with an emphasis on testing, places the onus of achievement on the student and has adversely impacted Mexican American students throughout the K–12 system. Under this accountability framework, there is very little consideration for the educational context or resources, and how these impact students as they navigate their schooling experience. This accountability framework, which began under the Bush administration in 2000, has extended into the Obama administration, with an ongoing high-stakes orientation toward accountability and outcomes. This framework fails to take into account the role of inequity in school systems, especially regarding adequate funding of resources that are positively associated with academic performance, as one observes in upper-middle-class communities.

The more recent implementation of the Common Core Standards for curricula, like accountability policies that came before, does very little to address persistent inequities present for Mexican American and other underrepresented youth in the United States. As I observed in prior work on this subject:

The underlying assumptions of the present accountability framework are that attaching consequences to education reform will raise student achievement. The approach does not solve the *education* and *opportunity gap* that exists for Latino students. (Contreras 2011, 58)

As a result of NCLB, states continue to rely on statewide assessment mechanisms, as well as exit exams, as a requirement for high school graduation. Several key cases have been filed on behalf of students to challenge the required use of tests in schools. In Florida, for example, the case of *Debra P. v. Turlington* (1984) involved African American students who challenged the high school graduation test requirement for a diploma. The plaintiff argued that the exam was being administered without notice to students and then used as a mechanism to segregate African American students into remedial courses in high school. The key rulings from this case, in favor of the students, included: (1) the court required schools to provide adequate notice regarding the test administration schedule; and (2) the court ruled that students must be exposed to a curriculum that reflects the content of the exam.

The state of Texas has also been a battleground for challenging a high-stakes accountability framework. The Mexican American Legal Defense and Educational Fund (MALDEF) filed a class action suit against the state, in *American GI Forum v. Texas Education Agency* (2000), challenging the TAAS (Texas Academic Assessment System) graduation requirement. The plaintiff's central argument was one of disparate impact—the testing requirement had a racially discriminatory impact on Latino and African American students because they had unequal access to resources in schools. While the court acknowledged that the TAAS exam had a disparate impact on Latino and African American students, as evidenced by their low passing rates when compared to their White peers, the court believed the TAAS exam was not intended to negatively affect Latino and African American students (Moran 2000; Valencia 2000). This ruling raises important questions on the disparate impact exams have on Mexican American students and whether using tests as a requirement for graduation is equitable. In Texas, this has led to the increased use of end-of-course requirements and an alternate pathway to high school graduation. Over the last decade, in twenty-eight states that have used exit exams as a requirement for graduation, they have not been shown to minimize the achievement gap or raise the high school graduation rate (Moran 2000). Such assessments are misaligned with the original intent of the Elementary and Secondary Education Act of 1965 (ESEA, now known as No

Child Left Behind), which emphasizes equal access to educational services. The original Elementary and Secondary Education Act did not include a strong emphasis on "rigorous assessment," as seen in the case of NCLB. Rigorous assessment has translated into "punitive" assessment, where the onus of achievement disparities is placed on the student. Exit exams are the prime example of the punitive approach to assessment that NCLB promotes.

Policy reforms over the past fifty years represent a complex backdrop for understanding the educational plight of Mexican American students. NCLB, for example, has called for accountability and led to a proliferation of exams for students without an infrastructure in place to ensure that all students are taught and can meet grade-level benchmarks. This reform resulted in over fourteen years of heightened accountability without targeting or altering sources of inequity (e.g., teacher quality, resource allocation, school quality) for Mexican American students.

The current educational reform effort, the Common Core Standards Initiative, represents a national effort for encouraging U.S. states and territories to adopt and focus on critical thinking skills and cognitive development across a uniform set of goals. While the potential impact of a Common Core Standards system is unknown, the intent of this reform still fits under the umbrella of the NCLB policy framework that places the onus of achievement on the student. If persistent inequities are not addressed in the accountability frameworks designed to raise student academic achievement, reforms are not likely to show measurable success because infrastructure will continue to be limited in addressing the educational needs of Mexican American students. Policy initiatives have historically and continually approached education reform narrowly rather than holistically, in a way that addresses the needs of every child for the purpose of success in school.

Federal and State Intervention Programs

Federal and state intervention programs historically and currently play a critical role in providing college information, promoting college readiness, and facilitating access to vital academic resources for Mexican American students (Contreras, Flores-Ragade, Lee, and McGuire 2011; Gándara and Bial 2001; Gándara and Contreras 2009). These programs have served to complement the resources not fully present or adequate in formal schooling experiences for Mexican American and underrepresented students. Federal programs such as TRIO, GEAR UP, Talent Search, and Upward Bound[2] have served as vital resources for underrepresented youth from first-generation, low-income backgrounds who are more likely to attend low-resource schools.

State intervention programs, such as the PUENTE Project, provide students with access to role models and ongoing support as they transition from middle school to high school, and then to college. Such systemic approaches across key segments of the educational continuum are not present for Mexican American students in the formal K–12 system. Although making a considerable difference in high school graduation rates and the transition to college, the need for programs such as PUENTE or MESA[3] is far greater than their ability to meet it.

Federal programs are often the primary source of college information and preparation for Mexican American students. While these intervention programs have provided decades of academic support and motivation for Mexican American and other underrepresented students, these programs struggle with federal and state funding. And while these efforts were not intended to replace education services in public education systems, they provide a critical function when underserved students do not receive proper services in schools. The struggle for funding is manifest in table 10.3, which illustrates federal allocations for the TRIO programs over the past decade.

The TRIO program funding levels convey a trend of declining support since 2004 that shows diminishing priority for such programs. From 2004 to 2012, data show a steep decrease in funding allocation for training, in number of awards, and in number of participants. In effect, from their inception to the present, TRIO programs have been severely cut. Between FY 2005 and FYI 2012, TRIO programs lost more than $70 million in funding and, as a result, serve fewer students. Beginning in the 2013–2014 program year, individual grant awards will be reduced by 5.2 percent.

These reductions in public funding for federal programs are particularly devastating for already underrepresented and underserved youth (Contreras et al. 2011). Effective TRIO programs that show successful educational outcomes, and undergo regular internal and external evaluations (Olsen et al. 2008), have been able to raise parent awareness and advocacy in schools, while providing an inspirational and supportive environment in which students achieve academic success and thrive.

Table 10.3. Funding Levels for Federal TRIO Programs, 2002–2012

	2002	*2003*	*2004*	*2005*
Funding allocation for training	$6,762,255	$7,500,188	$5,299,275	$5,299,275
Number of awards	29	29	13	13
Number of participants	4,164	4,416	3,688	3,688
Average award	$233,181	$258,627	$407,637	$407,637
Average number of participants	149	158	284	284
Average cost per participant	$1,555	$1,632	$1,437	$1,437

Source: U.S. Department of Education Office of Postsecondary Education.
Notes: (1) The FY 2002 funding includes $287,573 for a grant for the National TRIO Clearinghouse. Since this project does not provide training to TRIO project staff, the average number of participants per project and the cost per participant exclude this grant award. (2) The FY 2003 funding includes $293,324 for a grant for the National TRIO Clearinghouse. Since this project does not provide training to TRIO project staff, the average number of participants per project and the cost per participant exclude this grant award.

The Role of Parents in Intervention Programs and Higher Education

Intervention programs that target parents and families have also been one of the primary entry points for Mexican American parents to engage with their children in higher education (Gándara and Bial 2001; Gándara and Contreras 2009). Local pathway projects (e.g., Long Beach's Seamless Pathway Project) represent the potential for engaging parents earlier in the college planning efforts of their children. Select K-12 programs such as PUENTE, Upward Bound (TRIO programs), and community partnerships extend into higher education and have distinct parent components and efforts. Parent intervention programs such as PIQE (the Parent Institute for Quality Education) work to empower parents to be advocates for their children by sponsoring parent training institutes and ongoing education programs for Latino and multilingual parents. PIQE also encourages parents to acquire English language skills and seek degree options so they have greater work opportunities. PIQE is now an international model for engaging parents. Formal evaluations of this program have found that it impacts parental support, student academic engagement, completion of A–G courses (refers to the high school courses required for entrance into college) at higher rates for California college admissions, high school graduation, and the rate of students transitioning to college (Chrispeels, Bolívar, and Vaca 2008; Chrispeels, Gonzalez, and Arellano 2004).

2006	2007	2008	2009	2010	2011	2012
$3,331,222	$3,331,222	$4,274,802	$4,274,802	$3,641,500	$3,528,612	$1,399,998
8	8	10	10	10	10	6
2,600	2,600	3,125	3,125	2,500	2,500	1,161
$416,403	$416,403	$427,480	$427,480	$364,150	$352,861	$233,333
325	325	313	313	250	250	194
$1,281	$1,281	$1,368	$1,368	$1,457	$1,411	$1,206

While intervention programs may represent viable ways to increase parent participation and partnerships with colleges, the reality remains that most low-income Mexican American students do not have access to these intervention programs. The challenge, therefore, is to make relevant programmatic features (such as academic supports, ongoing parent involvement, and education engagement activities) part of the institutional infrastructure (Dance 2009). Yet, as of now, there is no policy agenda to better incorporate parents into the postsecondary landscape.

The Rising Cost of College

The rising cost of attending college has many students choosing to attend two-year institutions as their primary entry point into higher education. Over the past decade, tuition has increased well over 25 percent in public four-year colleges (College Board 2012). In addition, most of the increases in college costs have occurred in states with the largest concentration of Mexican American and Latino students, such as California and Texas. "In fall 2010, 13% of all FTE enrollments in degree-granting public institutions were in California colleges and universities. California, Texas, Florida, and New York enrolled one-third of all FTE students attending public institutions in the United States" (College Board 2012). Over 58 percent of Latino students begin postsecondary education in community

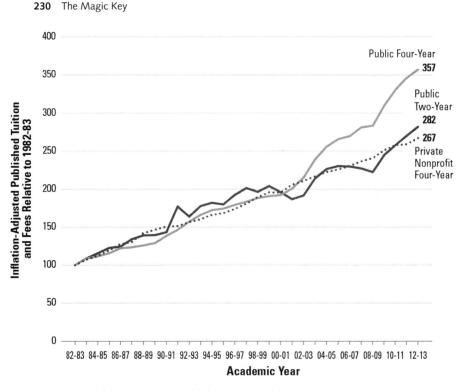

Figure 10.4. Inflation-Adjusted Published Tuition and Fees Relative to 1982-83, 1982-83 to 2012-13 (1982-83 = 100)
Source: College Board (2012).

colleges, largely because of the high cost of attending a four-year institution (Contreras 2011). In 2012–2013, the lowest published tuition and fees for public two-year colleges were in California, where students pay an average of $1,418 annually to attend a community college (College Board 2012). This presents challenges for college completion, as many Latino students who begin postsecondary education in the community college sector do not transfer to four-year institutions, nor do they earn their bachelor's degree. A huge drop-off in college enrollment thus occurs, in part due to financial reasons and the decision to attend the lowest-cost postsecondary option. Figure 10.4 shows inflation-adjusted tuition and fees for the years 1982–2013 for public two- and four-year colleges and universities and private nonprofit four-year higher education institutions. The steep upward curve shows that four-year public institutions experienced the greatest tuition increases over the time period.

The rising cost of tuition at public four-year colleges and universities is

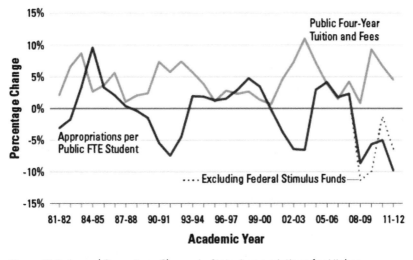

Figure 10.5. Annual Percentage Change in State Appropriations for Higher Education per Full-Time Equivalent (FTE) Student and Percentage Change in Inflation-Adjusted Tuition and Fees at Public Four-Year Institutions, 1981–82 to 2011–12
Source: College Board (2012).

cause for concern, as students are bearing the burden of the current economic recession. Rising tuition levels are happening at a time when state budgets are shrinking, and states have responded by diminishing their investment in higher education (see figure 10.5 for the annual percentage change in state appropriations). Many states have seen a significant decline in annual state appropriations for higher education institutions. Such declines in public support for higher education ultimately affect tuition and college costs, and influence student perceptions of access to higher education. Student perceptions of cost and affordability play a direct role in their willingness to enroll in public higher education, and particularly the higher-cost option of a four-year institution (Perna 2006). In order for greater numbers of Mexican American students to enroll in and graduate from college, cost controls must be an integral part of the policy agenda. Affordability is the single greatest concern among Mexican American parents when thinking about their child's enrollment in college (Contreras 2011; Zarate and Fabienke 2007). Although the public two-year sector has lower tuition rates overall, the trend for community college expense is also steadily on the rise, illustrating the overall increasing cost of attending public institutions of higher education in the United States.

The Role of Parents in College Financing

Nationally, parents play a significant role in college financing, although parents' ability to pay for tuition has diminished (Steelman and Powell 1991; Cunningham and Santiago 2008; Perna and Li 2006; Payea, Baum, and Kurose 2013). Since many Mexican American and other low-income Latino parents are less educated, have lower-paying jobs, and have less disposable income, they are also less likely to have additional resources to finance higher education for their children (Zarate and Pachon 2006). Further, due to a limited amount of disposable income, larger family sizes, and greater levels of economic instability, Mexican American parents are not likely to initiate college savings accounts or participate in payment plans. The recent economic decline, a result of the national housing crisis, has left the Mexican American community with significant declines in household wealth (Taylor, Kochhar, Fry, Velasco, and Motel 2011). High rates of poverty (28 percent) compared to the U.S. population (16 percent), and lower median annual personal earnings of $20,000, compared to $29,000 for the U.S. population, leave Mexican American families with limited monetary resources. Yet, despite these limitations, many Mexican American parents help their children at the postsecondary level by allowing them to continue to live at home while attending college—this is particularly true for those students who are single parents (Fry 2004). Financial support is an important resource in attending and completing college, along with parent support for student college choice. Further, parents play a key role in supporting students once enrolled in college.

Moving from Affirmative Action to Equitable Access and Outcomes

Affirmative action policy was enacted to ensure equal access to opportunity structures (public sectors, institutions, agencies) for communities that had been historically underserved and underrepresented. Executive Order 10925, signed by President Kennedy in 1961, was this nation's first attempt to rectify the impact of discrimination against historically disadvantaged minority groups (e.g., Mexican Americans, Puerto Ricans, Black/African Americans, and Native Americans/American Indians) by U.S. institutions and agencies. Affirmative action is often instituted in employment, housing, and educational contexts to counter or prevent discriminatory practice, promote fair and equal access to opportunity, and increase diversity and inclusion.

The landmark Supreme Court case *University of California v. Bakke* (1978) was significant in that it preserved the right to claim race as one of several factors to be considered in the college admission process. In the decision, the court ruled the use of a quota system (i.e., a certain number of spots reserved for minorities) unconstitutional, but recognized diversity as a compelling government interest. It permitted the use of race-based considerations in the admission process, so long as race was considered amongst a variety of factors that promoted diversity (i.e., a holistic view). However, the 1990s began two decades of ongoing struggle, as litigation and state policy initiatives attacked the use of affirmative action policy. Such initiatives have led to repeated examination of this issue by the Supreme Court in the *Grutter v. Bollinger* and *Gratz v. Bollinger* (2003) and *Fisher v. University of Texas at Austin* (2013) cases.

Figure 10.1 outlines the expansive timeline of anti–affirmative action policies over the past two decades and conveys the overall need for reconceptualizing affirmative action as a means of raising the pool of historically underrepresented groups in public institutions. Two misunderstandings related to affirmative action policies are: that inequities do *not* exist in schools and major public sectors of American society, and that current admissions policies and practices address diversity adequately. One of the more significant examples of this is the valuing of academic merit, which places increased importance on academic achievement, standardized test scores, and grades in advanced course work. The social construction of academic merit is rooted in privilege and fails to acknowledge the fact that first-generation, low-income students, of whom a majority are Mexican American, are less likely to have the course offerings that could earn them a GPA exceeding a 4.0 (which can occur with taking AP classes) (Contreras 2005, 2011; R. Parrish 2006). A holistic review of student admissions applications has been enacted in states like California and Texas, which have large Mexican American concentrations; however, such institutional efforts fall short of achieving equitable access to selective institutions. Now, institutional segregation at the higher education level has reemerged, which scholars have predicted will have a "cascading effect" (Gándara 2000; Loury et al. 2003), where less-competitive institutions admit and enroll students from historically underrepresented groups (see chapter 3).

Even though affirmative action is repeatedly challenged in the courts, this policy alone has not resulted in optimal levels of diversity in higher education; instead, there is far less than parity between underrepresented groups and the general population (Santos, Cabrera, and Fosnacht

2010). Levels of diversity have remained a challenge even under affirmative action. Minority student representation has been far lower in higher education institutions than, for example, the levels of representation that Mexican Americans and Latinos have at the K–12 level. There simply is no substitute, in affirming our commitments to the inclusion of Mexican Americans, for including racial/ethnic, generational, and income-status considerations in admission decisions (Orfield and Miller 1998; Campbell and Kane 1998; Contreras 2005).

In June 2013, in *Fisher v. University of Texas*, affirmative action was once again center stage. The Supreme Court, in a 7-1 ruling, negated the lower appellate court decision in favor of the University, noting that the University did not apply strict scrutiny in admissions practices. The court did not, however, take on the legality of using race as a factor in admissions decisions, thereby leaving the *Grutter* ruling intact. But this ruling remains a challenge for universities seeking to diversify their student body, as it places the onus on the institution to narrowly tailor any use of race in admissions.

Recommendations

Targeted supports for Mexican American students throughout the educational pathways are critical for increasing the overall success of students and ensuring economic mobility. Political bodies such as Obama's President's Advisory Commission on Educational Excellence for Hispanics have the potential to influence policy by implementing tangible recommendations to alter the level of investment in low-income Mexican American students in the United States. Yet, although similar special commissions have been in existence for over fifty years, we still see minimal changes in resource investments and education service delivery for Mexican American students. Greater equity in opportunity indicators for K–12 students (Oakes, Mendoza, and Silver 2004) is a step forward in measuring progress toward equitable educational access in schools that will ultimately prepare students to transition to higher education.

As approaches to achieving greater Mexican American student equity, I extend my prior recommendations to include:

1. *Address the unequal resources that exist across schools and districts.* Education is a civil and human right for our nation's youth. Since Mexican American youth are the largest demographic in this age group, inequi-

ties (as defined by student characteristics such as low-income, first-generation, parents with less than high school education) in schools that serve them must be addressed to raise achievement, persistence, and high school graduation rates, and enhance preparation for college. Since some of the biggest resource inequalities center on teachers (teacher quality, their expectations of students, cultural/ethnic and economic awareness), increasing teacher training across districts serving high concentrations of Mexican American students is one tangible way to address this issue in schools.

2. *Eliminate the use of punitive approaches to testing.* Punitive approaches to assessment inappropriately place the onus of achievement on the student, and fail to acknowledge systemic inequities that persist in schools serving large concentrations of Mexican American students. In the twenty-eight states that have implemented exit exams since the inception of NCLB, student achievement has not risen. Rather, state exams are merely altered if passing rates are far too low. The notion that one exam can seal the fate of a high school student, by determining whether or not he or she receives a diploma, continues to be ineffective public policy (Reardon, Atteberry, Arshan, and Kurlaender 2009; Contreras 2010).

3. *Support intervention programs as a complement to K–12 systems.* Intervention programs at the federal and state levels provide a critical resource in mentorship, academic support, cultural empowerment, and motivation to transition to college. These programs have played an important role in compensating for resources not present in public school districts that serve high concentrations of Mexican American students (Contreras et al. 2011)—resources that *are* present in districts where parents have higher education and income levels (e.g., state-of-the-art technology, books, highly paid and qualified teachers) (Reyes and Rodriguez 2004; Gándara and Contreras 2009). At a time when federal and state governments should be enhancing their level of investment in such efforts, there is a move away from supporting them. Ongoing support for intervention programs will cost far less than having to invest in these youth later into adulthood, particularly if they fail to graduate from college.

4. *Institute cost controls for public four-year colleges.* Controls on tuition increases are necessary to ensure that all young adults have access to public institutions and graduate with their degree. A college degree provides students with longer-term employment options, decreases unemployment rates, provides economic buffers to weather economic

downturns, and increases public revenues through tax receipts. State priorities have shifted away from investing in higher education, despite the fact that resources invested now are a direct investment in the future of states and their workforces. Limited state financing for higher education jeopardizes the ability of states to sustain their economies with domestic workers. Further, expanding finance options beyond loans (the primary option offered to college students) to include such options as work-study, state financial aid programs for low-income students, and merit scholarships would open the doors to higher education for Mexican American students, who are more likely to be debt averse compared to their college-going peers (Cunningham and Santiago 2008).

5. *Restore affirmative action policies for achieving greater postsecondary access and equity.* Historically, affirmative action was a step toward opening public institutions to earlier generations of historically underrepresented and underserved students, allowing them greater access to postsecondary institutions through the admissions process. While diversity was not the sole variable in admissions, the fact that institutions could emphasize and act upon the severe underrepresentation of historically underrepresented groups "affirmatively" resulted in a modest increase of representation and targeted programmatic efforts that countered discrimination.

The Need for a Policy Agenda for Mexican American Students

Creating a policy agenda for Mexican American students is critical to raising the overall status of a community that continues to be largely excluded from equitable access to public education services in the United States (Menchaca 1995). The future of Mexican American and underserved low-income Latino students is closely intertwined with the fate of the nation, as demographic trends show that the majority of students in public schools in California and the southwestern states are Mexican American, and Mexican Americans are the fastest-growing Hispanic subgroup population throughout the country. The services that the public enjoys will rest upon the shoulders of a population that may not be prepared to support the social and service infrastructure if the current pathway of educational achievement and attainment is not altered (Gándara and Contreras 2009; Contreras 2011). An equity agenda for Mexican American students is an investment in the short and long term, and a proactive approach to ensuring that the United States remains viable economically. We simply cannot afford to lose the current or next generation of students to populate only low-wage or low-skilled jobs, because our nation's ability to sustain itself rests upon the shoulders of the current generation of Mexican American students.

Notes

Foreword

1. Desilver 2013.

Chapter 1: Locked Doors, Closed Opportunities

1. We describe four population groups as historically underrepresented, based on their historical incorporation through marginalization and oppression: African Americans (enslavement), Mexican Americans (conquered in northern Mexico and stripped of all civil rights), Puerto Ricans (colonization), and Native Americans/American Indians (mass extermination and banishment to reservations). These historical modes of incorporation have contributed to a stereotypical gaze that shapes the opportunities and policies of these groups differently than those of other groups.

2. "Mexican American"/"Chicano"/"Chicana" will be used throughout the book interchangeably. "Chicano" is a term that many speculate has multiple origins, but many agree the term was one adopted by Mexican American activists that emerged with a political movement (*el movimiento*, in the 1960s–1970s) for social justice and self-determination. It is also important to note that identity is fluid and varies by geographic region. In the five states that were originally northern Mexico (California, Colorado, Texas, New Mexico, and Arizona), Mexican-origin people have extensive generational roots and perceive their identity as Hispanos, Americans of Mexican heritage or descent, Mexicanos, Americans, Tejanos, etc. The term "Hispanic" is used typically when referencing U.S. government data, since that is the category in use in U.S. Census and National Center for Education Statistics data collection and reports.

3. For the purpose of this book, and consistent with the federal standards for racial and ethnic data, we use the terms "Hispanic" and "Latino" interchangeably. Though often used interchangeably in American English, they are not identical terms, and in certain contexts the choice between them can be significant. This book uses the terms interchangeably, especially by staying true to direct quotes

and/or in citing empirical data, in which "Hispanic" is almost always used. "Hispanic," from the Latin word for "Spain," has the broader reference, potentially encompassing all Spanish-speaking peoples in both hemispheres and emphasizing the common denominator of language among communities that sometimes have little else in common. "Latino" is a political construct that challenges hegemonic notions of a singular European Spanish ancestry. Of the two, only "Hispanic" can be used in referring to Spain and its history and culture; a native of Spain residing in the United States is a Hispanic, not a Latino. Yet one cannot substitute "Latino" in the phrase "the Hispanic influence on native Mexican cultures" without garbling the meaning. The basis of Latinos'/Hispanics' identification as "others" in U.S. society is through a nationalism and/or ethnicity grounded in their country of origin, whether born there or not. This creates the constant potential for transnational identities fed by very active international circular migrations, supporting such broad and (to many) obscure notions as cultural citizenship and other postcolonialist perspectives. Last, an effort to use nonsexist language has included the use of "Latina/o" to acknowledge both female and male groups. "Latina" usually refers to feminine, while "Latino" is usually a masculine form. For the sake of simplicity, "Latino" was used by some authors when referring to the total population and is inclusive of both male and female.

   4. P–14 = Preschool through a two-year degree
     P–16 = Preschool through a four-year degree
     P–20 = Preschool through a graduate degree (most inclusive of all possible stages of education)
     K–14 = Kindergarten through a two-year degree
     K–16 = Kindergarten through a four-year degree
     K–20 = Kindergarten through a graduate degree

"The P–16 movement formally began in 1995 in Georgia, and 41 states now have some form of P–16 initiatives or councils. The titles of these initiatives vary from K–16 to P–16 to P–20, but they all fall within a common definition of state-level efforts to move to an integrated system of education stretching from early childhood through a four-year college degree. The ultimate goal of a P–16 system is to acknowledge the interdependency and common goals of all levels of education and to create a 'seamless' system of education" (Davis and Hoffman 2008, 126). "The traditional missions of K–12 and postsecondary education have been different in important ways. K–12 has emphasized universality, a common mission, and uniform standards. Higher education has emphasized selectivity, diverse missions, and standards which vary among programs and institutions. When postsecondary enrollment was optional, differences such as these were relatively inconsequential. But growing aspirations for higher education have fueled the P–20 (pre-school through graduate study) movement, which seeks to make the transition from one level of education to the next more transparent and 'seamless'" (127).

   5. The term "racial/ethnic" is meant as an alternative to either "minority," which is disparaging, or "Third World," which has an international connotation. In contrast to simply "ethnic," which usually refers to groups that are culturally distinct but members of the dominant White society, "racial/ethnic" refers to people who are both culturally and racially distinct. In the United States racial-

ethnics have historically shared certain common conditions as oppressed and internally colonized people. In this book "racial/ethnic" will refer to historically underrepresented groups, including African Americans, Mexican Americans, Puerto Ricans, and Native Americans/American Indians.

6. On May 11, 2010, Arizona Governor Jan Brewer signed House Bill 2281 (also known as HB 2281 and A.R.S. §15-112), which prohibits a school district or charter school from including in its program of instruction any courses or classes that (1) promote the overthrow of the federal or state government or the Constitution, (2) promote resentment toward any race or class (e.g., racism and classism), (3) advocate ethnic solidarity instead of individualism, and (4) are designed for a certain ethnicity. Research that acknowledges the benefits of ethnic studies has been produced to counter this perspective, but as of this writing, its impact has not been determined (Cabrera, Milem, Jaquette, and Marx 2014).

7. We draw on multiple perspectives. Intersectionality as a critical race theorizing lens to understand power relations in educational institutions is not employed in all chapters due to study limitations (Baca Zinn and Dill 1994; Collins 2000; Crenshaw 1991).

Chapter 2: History's Prism in Education

1. In this chapter "Mexican" and "Mexican American" will be used interchangeably except when indicating a particular generation, in which case usage will be clear in the text.

2. The one exception to this statement is the 1930 census, which included "Mexican" under the category "Other Races." Enumerators were instructed that "all persons born in Mexico, or having parents born in Mexico, who are definitely not White, Negro, Indian, Chinese, or Japanese should be returned as Mexican" (U.S. Department of Commerce 1933, 27).

3. The term "caste" in this context is not parallel to that of the Hindu religion; rather, the word "*casta*" referred to any mixture, such as what occurred in New Spain between Spaniards and Native Americans during the colonial era.

4. The long period of Spanish conquest and reign (late 1400s to early 1800s) had a devastating effect on Native Americans. In this chapter the term "Native American" denotes a member of any of the native Indian tribes of the Americas as defined in the *Compact Oxford English Dictionary*, 3rd ed., 2005. Abuses of the *encomienda* (a system in which Natives were forced to work Spaniards' lands), de facto enslavement, and forced relocation into missions permanently altered the demographics of the Americas. Close contact between Europeans and Native Americans resulted in alarmingly high rates of Native American mortality, particularly from smallpox and other infectious diseases. The Council of Indies, located in Spain, governed all colonial activities. The council issued reforms such as the 1573 Royal Orders for New Discoveries, prohibiting explorers from conquering and physically harming Native Americans. However, the distance from authorities in Spain, opportunities for exploitation, and religious zeal limited the effectiveness of these reforms (D. J. Weber 1992).

5. The Brothers of St. Mary founded a school for young men in San Antonio

in 1852. The academy quickly became St. Mary's University and offered advanced study that included Latin, history, algebra, and philosophy. In 1888 the Brothers of St. Mary also opened the San Fernando Cathedral School as a preparatory school. The Brothers of the Holy Cross came to Austin in the early 1870s and founded St. Edward's Academy for boys. The school expanded and was chartered by the State of Texas as St. Edward's College in 1885. Schools for boys were also founded in Brownsville (1872), Houston (1899), and Waco (1899) (Castañeda 1958).

6. See Ruiz and Tiano (1987); Ruiz (1987); and Ruiz, Jones, Wood, May, and Borstelmann (2005).

7. A recent challenge to educational opportunities and access for youth resides in the phenomenon of children brought to the United States as infants or young children who remained undocumented. As they reach high school age and discover that they are not documented, they see little future for themselves and are at risk for deportation along with their undocumented parents. In order to offer hope and opportunities for these children, the Development, Relief and Education of Alien Minors (DREAM) Act would allow them to enroll in college or enlist in the military and have a pathway to permanent residency.

8. In most states, the DREAM Act also permits undocumented students to pay in-state versus international student tuition, a significant saving. The requirements for the DREAM Act are lengthy and strict.

Chapter 3: Trend Analyses from 1971 to 2012 on Mexican American/Chicano Freshmen

1. I use "Mexican American/Chicano" ethnic identifiers together and the terms individually because students have identified with both categories in the national surveys used for the trend data from 1971–2012 presented in this chapter. Different researchers opted to use one specific term or the other in the literature; federal reports typically use "Hispanic-origin" and do not show trends for "Mexican Americans."

2. The Higher Education Research Institute, UCLA, houses the Cooperative Institutional Research Program and issues regular annual reports on its surveys that are available at the website heri.ucla.edu for download. Individual campuses also received their own reports on their students in relation to comparison campuses as part of data services provided through the program.

3. Low-income status was calculated as a function of the poverty threshold for each specific year, multiplied by 200 percent.

Chapter 4: An Intersectional Lens

1. Intersectionality is grounded in Black feminist scholarship and activism (e.g., Collins 2000; Crenshaw 1991) and has been used across a significant number of disciplines.

Chapter 5: Parental Educational and Gender Expectations

1. See http://newscenter.berkeley.edu/2012/12/11/study-shows-mexican-amer ican-toddlers-lag-in-literacy-skills-excel-in-social-skills/, which reviews Jung, Fuller, and Galindo (2012).

2. Maxine Baca Zinn and Barbara Wells (2000) cogently address the limitations of family studies, as the field tends to root an understanding of Latino families in a problem-orientation framework. The authors describe several flaws in the analytic categories used to study Latino families:

1. Diversity and heterogeneity within Latino families have been ignored.
2. The findings for Mexican-origin families have been generalized to all Latinos.
3. Hispanics are officially defined as an ethnic group, and are also defined as a separate racialized group.
4. Yet native-born and immigrant Latinos are subordinated in similar ways.
5. Definitional and measurement flaws include inconsistent definitions of the concepts of familism and extended family systems.

Because of inadequate conceptualization of structural factors such as SES, segmented labor markets, and institutional discrimination and racism associated with differences in family development and processes, knowledge production has been limited in advancing our understanding of the role of Mexican American families in promoting educational options for their children. Gender-role stereotypes of Latinas as submissive underachievers and caretakers of elder and younger family members are often reinforced by family, school personnel, and media and contribute to Latinas' oftentimes poor educational performance (Romo and Falbo 1996; Ginorio and Huston 2001).

3. The Higher Education Act of 1965 (Pub. L. 89-329) (HEA) was legislation signed into United States law on November 8, 1965, as part of President Lyndon Johnson's Great Society domestic agenda. The law was intended "to strengthen the educational resources of our colleges and universities and to provide financial assistance for students in postsecondary and higher education." It increased federal money given to universities, created scholarships, gave low-interest loans to students, and established a National Teachers Corps.

Chapter 6: Examining the Influence of K–12 School Experiences on the Higher Education Pathway

1. For comparison purposes, in 2007, among Latinas age eighteen years and over, those with less than a high school diploma represent the largest group and are the most likely to be the poorest in any racial/ethnic category. For example, 2008 U.S. Census Bureau data show that among U.S.-born Latinas with no high school completion, their expected median annual earnings are $21,182 versus median earnings of $35,644 with some college or more (Fry 2010).

2. Language growing up was predominantly English, with 19.6 percent reporting Spanish only. About 37 percent of respondents reported that their English was

limited when they entered school. In a question regarding whether parents' lack of English skills influenced their schooling, 38.7 percent said yes.

3. Movimiento Estudiantil Chicano de Aztlán (MEChA) is a student organization that promotes higher education, *cultura*, and *historia*. MEChA was founded on the principles of self-determination for the liberation of Mexican American people. Members believe that political involvement and education are the avenue for change in our society. See http://www.nationalmecha.org/about.html.

Chapter 7: The Ivory Tower Is Still White

1. "Students of color" is used in this chapter to indicate students educated in racialized contexts who at some level share oppression in predominantly White college environments. These include Black, Latina/o, Native American, and Asian/Pacific Islander.

2. We use the term "Latina/o" to refer to a pan-ethnic identity including anyone of Latin American descent.

Chapter 9: Mexican American Males' Pathways to Higher Education

Portions of this chapter were first published in Sáenz and Ponjuan 2011 and Sáenz and Ponjuan 2012.

1. This chapter uses the words "Latino" and "Hispanic" interchangeably. Unless otherwise noted, all references to Whites and African Americans refer to non-Hispanics.

2. "Colleges" refers to public and private two-year and four-year postsecondary educational institutions.

3. The U.S. Census Bureau defined the six Hispanic ethnic subgroups as: Mexican, Puerto Rican, Cuban, Spanish-speaking Central or South American countries, and other Hispanic/Latino, regardless of race. Central American totals exclude Mexican.

4. Two pathways outside the labor force include the military and prison. Latino males comprise 11.2 percent of enlisted military persons within the Department of Defense, which includes all the armed forces and the Coast Guard (Office of the Deputy Under Secretary of Defense 2012). A close examination of the military appointments of Latino males indicates that they are still underrepresented in the military in proportion to the dramatic growth of the Latino population over the last forty years. According to a U.S. Department of Defense report, racial/ethnic minority officers are still underrepresented in military officer appointments in comparison to other race/ethnic groups (Office of the Deputy Under Secretary of Defense 2012).

Not all Latino males are eligible to serve in the military, because a large percentage are high school dropouts or have a nonpermanent immigration status. The lack of a basic high school degree credential suggests some Latino males are less likely to pursue a career in the military and hold military officer appointments, or pursue four-year degrees after military service is over—especially Mexican American males. Unfortunately, the Department of Defense report did not provide specific ethnic demographic subgroup information, which hinders our ability to closely examine the percentages of Mexican American males who participate in the military branches.

In contrast, an unfavorable alternative is incarceration. In 2011, 21.5 percent (331,500) of all state and federal prisoners, or one in five of all U.S. prisoners, were Latino males (Carson and Sabol 2012). Data show that "Hispanic males were imprisoned at 2 to 3 times the rate of white males in 2011" (Carson and Sabol 2012, 8). Although the rate of Latino males entering the judicial system remains lower than that of Black males, they are approximately four times more likely than White males to be imprisoned during their lifetime (Bonczar and Beck 1997). The U.S. Bureau of Justice Statistics also shows that the rate of incarceration for Latino males is 1.2 percent, compared to .05 percent of White males (Carson and Sabol 2012).

College-age (eighteen- to twenty-four years old) Latino males make up 3.5 percent of prisoners, compared to only 1 percent of such White males. These rates of incarceration raise serious concerns, as this age cohort faces daunting roadblocks to a college education, with limited options for reentry into the skilled labor force. Formerly incarcerated individuals have tremendous difficulty reentering the workforce or systems of higher education after a criminal conviction (Prager 2007; Rios 2011). For Mexican Americans, intersecting these challenges are additional considerations of race, ethnicity, gender, SES, citizenship status, and other coconstitutive identities, which thicken the barriers to educational attainment. Some argue that society is failing to help the most vulnerable and at-risk male youths. Rios (2011) states, "I argue that punitive social control is embedded in the everyday lives of marginalized youth and the state has not abandoned the poor but instead has punitively asserted itself into various institutions in the community" (35). It stands to reason, since Mexican American males represent such a large percentage of Latino male youth, that they have a higher probability than other Latino males to experience punitive social control—prison.

While these numbers and percentages are significant, and underscore the harsh realities that Latino males face within the correctional system, the actual number of incarcerated Latinos may be higher than what is accounted for due to inconsistencies by reporting agencies, which oftentimes do not recognize Latinos as distinct subgroups. It can also be assumed that Latinos are frequently counted by racial phenotype, such as White or Black (Carson and Sabol 2012).

Chapter 10: The Role of Educational Policy in Mexican American College Transition and Completion

1. This chapter draws extensively from my previous work and extends the discourse with new data. For further discussion on these topics, see Contreras (2011) and Gándara and Contreras (2009).

2. The TRIO program, GEAR UP, Talent Search, and Upward Bound are federally funded national programs, incubated by the civil rights movement, and are designed to assist low-income first-generation students with academic support in

middle and high school, and enable more minority students to make the transition to college.

3. The PUENTE program is a statewide mentorship program that started in California to assist high school and community college students as they enter and complete four-year institutions. MESA, also a California program and sponsored by the University of California, stands for Math Engineering Science Achievement, and is designed to assist low-income first-generation students in gaining access to and success in STEM courses in high school.

Bibliography

Acevedo-Garcia, D. 2000. "A Conceptual Framework of the Role of Residential Segregation in the Epidemiology of Infectious Diseases." *Social Science and Medicine* 51 (8): 1143–1161.

Acevedo-Garcia, D., T. Osypuk, N. McArdle, and D. Williams. 2008. "Towards a Policy Relevant Analysis of Geographic and Racial/Ethnic Disparities in Child Health." *Health Affairs* 27 (2): 321–333.

Aguilar, M. A. 1996. "Promoting the Educational Achievement of Mexican American Young Women." *Social Work in Education* 18 (3): 145–156.

Akerlund, M., and M. Cheung. 2000. "Teaching beyond the Deficit Model." *Journal of Social Work Education* 36 (2): 279–292.

Alba, R. D., and D. E. Lavin. 1981. "Community Colleges and Tracking in Higher Education." *Sociology of Education* 54 (4): 223–237.

Alexander, K. L., and D. O. Entwisle. 1988. *Achievement in the First 2 Years of School: Patterns and Processes. Monographs of the Society for Research in Child Development* 53, no. 2.

Alfonso, M. 2006. "The Impact of Community College Attendance on Baccalaureate Attainment." *Research in Higher Education* 47 (8): 873–903.

Allen, W. R. 1985. "Black Students, White Campus: Structural, Interpersonal, and Psychological Correlates of Success." *Journal of Negro Education* 54 (2): 134–147.

Allen, W. R., E. Kimura-Walsh, and K. Griffin. 2009. *Towards a Brighter Tomorrow: College Barriers, Hopes and Plans of Black, Latino/a and Asian American Students in California*. Charlotte, NC: IAP, Information Age Pub.

Allen, W. R., and D. G. Solórzano. 2001. "Affirmative Action, Educational Equity, and Campus Racial Climate: A Case Study of the University of Michigan Law School." *Berkeley La Raza Law Journal* 12 (2): 237–363.

Almaguer, T. 1993. "Chicano Men: A Cartography of Homosexual Identity and Behavior." In *The Lesbian and Gay Studies Reader*, ed. H. Abelove, M. A. Barale, and D. M. Halperin, pp. 255–273. New York: Routledge.

———. 1994. *Racial Fault Lines: The Historical Origins of White Supremacy in California*. Berkeley: University of California Press.

Alva, S. A. 1991. "Academic Invulnerability among Mexican American Students: The Importance of Protective Resources and Appraisals." *Hispanic Journal of Behavioral Sciences* 13 (1): 18–34.

Alvarez, R. 1986. "The Lemon Grove Incident: The Nation's First Successful Desegregation Court Case." *Journal of San Diego History* 32 (2): 116–135.

Amaro, H. 1995. "Love, Sex, and Power: Considering Women's Realities in HIV Prevention." *American Psychologist* 30 (6): 437–447.

American Association of Colleges for Teacher Education (AACTE). 2013. *The Changing Teacher Preparation Profession: A Report from AACTE's Professional Education Data System (PEDS)*. Washington, DC: AACTE.

Ancis, J., J. Mohr, and W. Sedlacek. 2000. "Student Perceptions of Campus Cultural Climate by Race." *Journal of Counseling and Development* 78 (2): 180–185.

Anthias, F. 2013. "Intersectional What? Social Divisions, Intersectionality, and Levels of Analysis." *Ethnicities* 13 (1): 3–19.

antonio, a. l. 2001. "Diversity and the Influence of Friendship Groups in College." *Review of Higher Education* 25 (1): 63–89.

Antrop-González, R., and A. De Jesús. 2006. "Toward a Theory of Critical Care in Urban Small School Reform: Examining Structures and Pedagogies of Caring in Two Latino Community Based Schools." *International Journal of Qualitative Studies in Education* 19 (4): 409–433.

Anzaldúa, G. 1987. *Borderlands/La Frontera: The New Mestiza*. San Francisco: Aunt Lute Books.

Arciniega, G. M., T. C. Anderson, Z. G. Tovar-Blank, and T. J. G. Tracey. 2008. "Toward a Fuller Conception of Machismo: Development of a Traditional Machismo and *Caballerismo* Scale." *Journal of Counseling Psychology* 55 (1): 19–33.

Arellano, L. 2011. "Capitalizing Baccalaureate Degree Attainment: Revealing the Path of the Latina/o Scholar." PhD diss., University of California, Los Angeles.

Armendariz, A. L. 2000. "The Impact of Racial Prejudice on the Socialization of Mexican American Students in the Public Schools." *Equity and Excellence in Education* 33 (3): 59–63.

Artiles, A. J., B. Harry, D. Reschly, and P. Chinn. 2002. "Over-identification of Students of Color in Special Education: A Critical Overview." *Multicultural Perspectives* 4 (1): 3–10.

Artiles, A. J., R. Rueda, J. J. Salazar, and I. Higareda. 2002. "English-Language Learner Representation in Special Education in California Urban School Districts." In *Racial Inequity in Special Education*, ed. D. J. Losen and G. Orfield, pp. 117–136. Cambridge, MA: Harvard Education Press.

Ascher, C. 1985. "Helping Hispanic Students to Complete High School and Enter College." *The Urban Review* 17 (1): 65–72.

Astin, A. W. 1982. *Final Report of the Commission on the Higher Education of Minorities*. Los Angeles: Higher Education Research Institute.

Aud, S., M. Fox, and A. KewalRamani. 2010. *Status and Trends in the Education of Racial and Ethnic Groups*. Publication no. NCES 2010-015. U.S. Department of Education, National Center for Education Statistics. Washington, DC: U.S. Government Printing Office.

Aud, S., W. Hussar, G. Kena, K. Bianco, L. Frohlich, J. Kemp, and K. Tahan. 2011. *The Condition of Education 2011*. Publication no. NCES 2011-033. National Center for Education Statistics. Washington, DC: U.S. Department of Education.

Aud, S., W. Hussar, G. Kena, F. Johnson, and E. Roth. 2012. *The Condition of Education 2012*. Publication no. NCES 2012-045. National Center for Education Statistics, Institute of Education Sciences. Washington, DC: U.S. Department of Education.

Aud, S., A. Rathbun, S. Flicker-Wilkinson, P. Kristapovich, X. Wang, J. Zhang, and L. Notter. 2013. *The Condition of Education 2013*. Publication no. NCES 2013-037. Washington, DC: Department of Education, National Center for Education Statistics. http://nces.ed.gov/pubsearch/pubsinfo.asp?pubid=2013037.

Auerbach, S. 2002. "Why Do They Give the Good Classes to Some and Not to Others? Latino Parent Narratives of Struggle in a College Access Program." *Teachers College Record* 104 (7): 1369–1392.

Azmitia, M., C. R. Cooper, E. E. Garcia, and N. Dunbar. 1996. "The Ecology of Family Guidance in Low-Income Mexican-American and European-American Families." *Social Development* 5 (1): 1–23.

Baca Zinn, M. 1995. "Social Science Theorizing for Latino Families in the Age of Diversity." In *Understanding Latino Families: Scholarship, Policy and Practice*, ed. R. E. Zambrana, pp. 177–189. Thousand Oaks, CA: Sage.

Baca Zinn, M., and B. T. Dill. 1994. *Women of Color in U.S. Society*. Philadelphia: Temple University Press.

Baca Zinn, M., and B. Wells. 2000. "Diversity within Latino Families: New Lessons for Family Social Science." In *Handbook of Family Diversity*, ed. D. H. Demo, K. R. Allen, and M. A. Fine, pp. 252–273. New York: Oxford University Press.

Balfanz, R., J. M. Bridgeland, L. A. Moore, and J. H. Fox. 2010. "Building a Grad Nation: Progress and Challenge in Ending the High School Dropout Epidemic." Baltimore: Civic Enterprises; Everyone Graduates at Johns Hopkins University.

Ball, S. J., and C. Vincent. 1998. "I Heard It on the Grapevine: Hot Knowledge and School Choice." *British Journal of Sociology of Education* 19 (3): 377–400.

Bandura, A. 1991. "Social Cognitive Theory of Self-Regulation." *Organizational Behavior and Human Decision Processes* 50 (2): 248–287.

Banks, T. L. 2006. "Mestizaje and the Mexican Mestizo Self: No Hay Sangre Negra, So There Is No Blackness." *Southern California Interdisciplinary Law Journal* 15 (2): 199–234.

Barajas, F. P. 2012. *Curious Unions: Mexican American Workers and Resistance in Oxnard, California, 1898–1961*. Lincoln: University of Nebraska Press.

Barerra, M. 1979. *Race and Class in the Southwest*. South Bend, IN: University of Notre Dame Press.

Barnett, E. A. 2011. "Faculty Validation and Persistence among Nontraditional Community College Students." *Enrollment Management Journal* 5 (2): 97–117.

Behnken, B. D. 2011. *Fighting Their Own Battles: Mexican Americans, African Americans, and the Struggle for Civil Rights in Texas*. Chapel Hill: University of North Carolina Press.

Belfield, C. R., and T. Bailey. 2011. "The Benefits of Attending Community College: A Review of the Evidence." *Community College Review* 39 (1): 46–68.

Bender, S. 2003. *Greasers and Gringos*. New York: New York University Press.

Berger, M. 1947. "Education in Texas during the Spanish and Mexican Periods." *Southwestern Historical Quarterly* 51 (1): 41–53.

Bernstein, S. 2011. *Bridges of Reform: Interracial Civil Rights Activism in Twentieth-Century Los Angeles*. New York: Oxford University Press.

Bettie, J. 2003. *Women without Class: Girls, Race, and Identity*. Berkeley: University of California Press.

Bieschke, K. J., J. A. Hardy, R. E. Fassinger, and J. M. Croteau. 2008. "Intersecting Identities of Gender-Transgressive Sexual Minorities: Toward a New Paradigm of Affirmative Psychology." In *Biennial Review of Counseling Psychology: Volume 1*, ed. B. Walsh, pp. 177–208. Washington, DC: Psychology Press.

Bivens, D. 1995. *Internalized Racism: A Definition*. Boston: Women's Theological Center.

Blanton, C. K. 2006. "George I. Sánchez, Ideology, and Whiteness in the Making of the Mexican American Civil Rights Movement, 1930–1960." *Journal of Southern History* 72 (3): 569–604.

Bonczar, T. P., and A. J. Beck. 1997. *Bureau of Justice Statistics Special Report: Lifetime Likelihood of Going to State or Federal Prison*. Washington, DC: U.S. Department of Justice.

Bonilla-Silva, E. 2006. *Racism without Racists: Color-Blind Racism and the Persistence of Racial Inequality in the United States*. Lanham, MD: Rowman and Littlefield.

Bourdieu, P. 1986. "The Forms of Capital." In *Handbook of Theory and Research for Sociology of Education*, ed. J. G. Richardson, pp. 241–258. New York: Greenwood Press.

Bourdieu, P., and J. C. Passeron. 1977. *Reproduction in Education, Society, and Culture*. London: Sage.

Bowen, W. G., M. M. Chingos, and M. S. MacPherson. 2009. *Crossing the Finish Line: Completing College at America's Public Universities*. Princeton, NJ: Princeton University Press.

Bowleg, L. 2008. "When Black + Lesbian + Woman ≠ Black Lesbian Woman: The Methodological Challenges of Qualitative and Quantitative Intersectionality Research." *Sex Roles* 59 (5–6): 312–325.

Bowles, S., and H. Gintis. 1976. *Schooling in Capitalist America: Educational Reform and Contradictions of Economic Life*. New York: Basic Books.

Brick, K., A. E. Challinor, and M. R. Rosenblum. 2011. *Mexican and Central American Immigrants in the United States*. Washington, DC: Migration Policy Institute.

Brooks-Gunn, J., and L. B. Markman. 2005. "The Contributions of Parenting to Ethnic and Racial Gaps in School Readiness." *The Future of Children* 15 (1): 139–168.

Brown, A., and E. Patten. 2013. *Hispanics of Mexican Origin in the United States, 2011*. Washington, DC: Pew Research Hispanic Trends Project. http://www.pewhispanic.org/2013/06/19/hispanics-of-mexican-origin-in-the-united-states-2011/.

Burciaga, R. 2007. "Chicana Ph.D. Students Living Nepantla: Educación and Aspirations beyond the Doctorate." PhD diss., University of California, Los Angeles (UCLA).

Bureau of Labor Statistics. 2014. "Employed Persons by Detailed Occupation,

Sex, Race, and Hispanic or Latino Ethnicity." Labor Force Statistics from the Current Population Survey. Last modified February 26. http://www.bls.gov/cps/cpsaat11.htm.

Burns, J. A. 1908. *The Catholic School System in the United States: Its Principles, Origin, and Establishment.* New York: Benziger Brothers.

Cabrera, A. F., and A. Nora. 1994. "College Students' Perceptions of Prejudice and Discrimination and Their Feelings of Alienation." *Review of Education, Pedagogy, and Cultural Studies* 16 (3–4): 387–409.

Cabrera, N. L. 2012. "Exposing Whiteness in Higher Education: White Male College Students Minimizing Racism, Claiming Victimization, and Recreating White Supremacy." *Race Ethnicity and Education* 17 (1): 30–55.

———. 2014. "But We're Not Laughing: White Male College Students' Racial Joking and What This Says about 'Post-Racial' Discourse." *Journal of College Student Development* 55 (1): 1–15.

Cabrera, N. L., F. Milem, O. Jaquette, and R. W. Marx. 2014. "Missing the (Student Achievement) Forest For All the (Political) Trees: Empiricism and the Mexican American Studies Controversy in Tucson." *American Educational Research Journal* 51 (6): 1084–1118.

Cabrera, N. L., and A. M. Padilla. 2004. "Entering and Succeeding in the 'Culture of College': The Story of Two Mexican Heritage Students." *Hispanic Journal of Behavioral Sciences* 26 (2): 152–170.

Cabrera, N. L., and B. G. Valencia. 2012. "Campus Racial Climate: Microaggressions and Counterspaces for Latina/o Students." Paper presented at the annual meeting of the NASPA — Student Affairs Administrators in Higher Education, Phoenix, AZ.

Caldera, Y. M., J. Fitzpatrick, and K. S. Wampler. 2002. "Coparenting in Intact Mexican American Families: Mothers' and Fathers' Perceptions." In *Latino Children and Families in the United States: Current Research and Future Directions*, ed. J. M. Contreras, K. A. Kerns, and A. M. Neal-Barnett, pp. 107–131. Westport, CT: Praeger Publishers.

Calderón, D., D. Delgado Bernal, L. Pérez Huber, M. C. Malagón, and V. N. Vélez. 2012. "A Chicana Feminist Epistemology Revisited: Cultivating Ideas a Generation Later." *Harvard Educational Review* 82 (4): 513–567.

Campa, B. 2010. "Critical Resilience, Schooling Processes, and the Academic Success of Mexican Americans in a Community College." *Hispanic Journal of Behavioral Sciences* 32 (3): 429–455.

Campbell, A., and K. Kane. 1998. *School-Based Teacher Education: Telling Tales from a Fictional Primary School.* London: David Fulton Publishers.

Camras, M. 2004. "Investing in Social Capital: Afterschool Activities and Social Affiliation in Immigrant Youth." *Afterschool Matters Occasional Paper*, Fall/Winter, pp. 20–46. Retrieved from http://repository.wellesley.edu/cgi/viewcontent.cgi?article=1005&context=afterschoolmatters.

Canino, G., and R. E. Roberts. 2001. "Suicidal Behavior among Latino Youth." *Suicide and Life-Threatening Behavior* 31 (s1): 122–131.

Carnevale, A. P., and J. Strohl. 2013. *Separate and Unequal: How Higher Education Reinforces the Intergenerational Reproduction of White Racial Privilege.* Washington, DC: Georgetown University, Center on Education and the Workforce.

Carson, E. A., and W. J. Sabol. 2012. *Prisoners in 2011.* Washington, DC: Department of Justice. http://www.bjs.gov/content/pub/pdf/p11.pdf.

Carter, T. P. 1970. *Mexican Americans in School: A History of Educational Neglect.* New York: College Entrance Examination Board.

Carter, T. P., and R. D. Segura. 1979. *Mexican Americans in School: A Decade of Change.* New York: College Entrance Examination Board.

Castañeda, C. E. 1958. *The Church in Texas since Independence, 1836–1950. Supplement, 1936–1950.* Vol. 7 of *Our Catholic Heritage in Texas, 1519–1936.* Austin: Von Boeckmann-Jones Co.

Ceja, M. 2004. "Chicana College Aspirations and the Role of Parents: Developing Educational Resiliency." *Journal of Hispanic Higher Education* 3 (4): 338–362.

Chacón, M. A., and E. G. Cohen. 1982. *Chicanas in Postsecondary Education.* Stanford, CA: Center for Research on Women, Stanford University.

Chacón, M. A., E. G. Cohen, M. M. Camarena, and S. Strover. 1983. "Chicanas in Postsecondary Education." *La Red/The Net, Newsletter of the National Chicano Council on Higher Education* 65 (Winter Supplement): 3–24.

Chacón, M. A., E. G. Cohen, and S. Strover. 1986. "Chicanas and Chicanos: Barriers to Progress in Higher Education." In *Latino College Students,* ed. M. A. Olivas, pp. 296–324. New York: Teachers College Press.

Chavez, E. L., and E. R. Oetting. 1994. "Dropout and Delinquency: Mexican-American and Caucasian Non-Hispanic Youth." *Journal of Clinical Child Psychology* 23 (1): 47–55.

Chickering, A. W., and L. Reisser. 1993. *Education and Identity.* 2nd ed. San Francisco: Jossey-Bass.

Cho, S., K. W. Crenshaw, and L. McCall. 2013. "Toward a Field of Intersectionality Studies: Theory, Applications, and Praxis." *Signs* 38 (4): 785–810.

Chrispeels, J. H., J. M. Bolívar, and R. C. Vaca. 2008. *Parent Institute for Quality Education High School Study.* Research Progress Report #2. Parent Institute for Quality Education. http://www.piqe.org/research/Dr_Chrispeels_PIQE_2nd_year_report_07-07-08.pdf.

Chrispeels, J. H., M. Gonzalez, and B. Arellano. 2004. *Evaluation of the Effectiveness of the Parent Institute for Quality Education in Los Angeles Unified School District.* Evaluation Report. http://www.bridgingworlds.org/P-20/ChrispeelsPIQE evaluation.pdf.

Cobas, J. A., J. Duany, and J. R. Feagin. 2009. *How the United States Racializes Latinos: White Hegemony and Its Consequences.* Boulder, CO: *Paradigm Publishers.*

Cofresi, N. I. 1999. "Gender Roles in Transition among Professional Puerto Rican Women." *Frontiers* 20 (1): 161–178.

Coleman, J. S. 1988. "Social Capital in the Creation of Human Capital." *American Journal of Sociology* 94 (Supplement): S95–S120.

Coleman-Burns, P. 1989. "African American Women: Education for What?" *Sex Roles* 21 (1/2): 145–160.

College Board. 2012. *Trends in College Pricing 2012.* http://trends.collegeboard.org/sites/default/files/college-pricing-2012-full-report_0.pdf.

Collins, P. H. 2000. *Black Feminist Thought: Knowledge, Consciousness, and the Politics of Empowerment.* New York: Routledge.

Conchas, G. Q. 2006. *The Color of Success: Race and High-Achieving Urban Youth.* New York: Teachers College Press.

Conchas, G. Q., and K. A. Goyette. 2001. "The Race Is Not Even: Minority Education in a Post–Affirmative Action Era." *Harvard Journal of Hispanic Policy* 13 (7): 87–102.

Contreras, F. 2005. "Access, Achievement, and Social Capital: Standardized Exams and the Latino College-Bound Population." *Journal of Hispanic Higher Education* 4 (3): 197–214.

———. 2010. "The Role of High Stakes Testing and Accountability in Educating Latinos." In *Handbook of Latinos and Education: Research, Theory, and Practice*, ed. E. G. Murillo et al., pp. 194–209. New York: Routledge.

———. 2011. *Achieving Equity for Latino Students.* New York: Teachers College Press.

Contreras, F., et al. 2008. *Understanding Opportunities to Learn for Latino Students in Washington.* Report prepared for the Washington State Commission on Hispanic Affairs and Washington State Legislature under HB 2687. http://www.governor.wa.gov/oeo/educators/hispanic_ach_gap_report.pdf.

Contreras, F., A. Flores-Ragade, J. Lee, and K. McGuire. 2011. *The Latino College Completion Agenda: Research and Context Brief.* Latino Edition. College Board Advocacy and Policy Center. http://media.collegeboard.com/digitalServices/public/pdf/rd/context_brief_latino_2011.pdf.

Cooper, C. R. 2001. "Bridging Multiple Worlds: Inclusive, Selective, and Competitive Programs, Latino Youth, and Pathways to College. Affirmative Development of Ethnic Minority Students." *The CEIC Review: A Catalyst for Merging Research, Policy, and Practice* 9 (14–15): 22.

Corbett, C., and C. Hill. 2012. *Graduating to a Pay Gap: The Earnings of Women and Men One Year after College Graduation.* Washington, DC: American Association of University Women. Retrieved from http://www.aauw.org/research/graduating-to-a-pay-gap/.

Covarrubias, A. 2011. "Quantitative Intersectionality: A Critical Race Analysis of the Chicana/o Educational Pipeline." *Journal of Latinos and Education* 10 (2): 86–105.

Crenshaw, K. 1991. "Mapping the Margins: Intersectionality, Identity Politics, and Violence Against Women of Color, 43 *Stanford Law Review* 1241–99 (1991). Mapping the Margins: Intersectionality, Identity Politics, and Violence Against Women of Color, 43 *Stanford Law Review* 1241–99 (1991).Mapping the Margins: Intersectionality, Identity Politics and Violence against Women." *Stanford Law Review* 43 (6): 1241–1299.

Crisp, G., and A. M. Núñez. 2011. "Modeling Transfer among Underrepresented Minority and Non-Minority Community College Students Pursuing a 4-Year Degree." Paper presented at the annual meeting of the Association for the Study of Higher Education, Charlotte, NC, November.

Crosnoe, R., C. Riegle-Crumb, S. Field, K. Frank, and C. Muller. 2008. "Peer Group Contexts of Girls' and Boys' Academic Experiences." *Child Development* 79 (1): 139–155.

Cross, W. E., Jr. 1971. "Toward a Psychology of Black Liberation: The Negro to Black Conversion Experience." *Black World* 20 (9): 13–27.

Cruz, B. 2002. "Don Juan and Rebels under Palm Trees: Depictions of Latin Americans in U.S. History Textbooks." *Critique of Anthropology* 22 (3): 323–342.

Cuádraz, G. H. 2005. "Chicanas and Higher Education: Three Decades of Literature and Thought." *Journal of Hispanic Higher Education* 4 (3): 215–234.

Cuellar, M. 2012. "Latina/o Student Success in Higher Education: Models of Empowerment at Hispanic-Serving Institutions (HSIs), Emerging HSIs, and Non-HSIs." PhD diss., University of California, Los Angeles.

Cunningham, A. F., and D. A. Santiago. 2008. *Student Aversion to Borrowing: Who Borrows and Who Doesn't.* Washington, DC: Institute for Higher Education Policy and Excelencia in Education.

Dance, L. J. 2009. "Racial, Ethnic, and Gender Disparities in Early School Leaving (Dropping Out)." In *Emerging Intersections: Race, Class, and Gender in Theory, Policy, and Practice*, ed. B. T. Dill and R. E. Zambrana, pp. 180–202. New Brunswick, NJ: Rutgers University Press.

Dávila, A. A. 2001. *Latinos, Inc.: The Marketing and Making of a People.* Berkeley: University of California Press.

Dávila, B. 2014. "Critical Race Theory, Disability Microaggressions, and Latina/o Student Experiences in Special Education." *Race, Ethnicity and Education*, November 17, pp. 1–26.

Davis, R. P., and J. F. Hoffman. 2008. "Higher Education and the P-16 Movement: What Is to Be Done?" *Thought & Action*, Fall, 123–134.

"'Deadly Trend' of Hispanic Worker Deaths on Top of Agenda at OSHA." 2002. *Labor Relations Week* 16, no. 41 (October 17): 1257.

DeAngelo, L., R. Franke, S. Hurtado, J. H. Pryor, and S. Tran. 2011. *Completing College: Assessing Graduation Rates at Four-Year Institutions.* Los Angeles: Higher Education Research Institute.

De Jesús, A. 2005. "Theoretical Perspectives on the Underachievement of Latino Students in US Schools: Toward a Framework for Culturally Additive Schooling." In *Latino Education: An Agenda for Community Action Research*, ed. P. Pedraza and M. Rivera, pp. 343–371. Mahwah, NJ: Lawrence Erlbaum Associates.

De Jesús, A., and R. Antrop-González. 2006. "Instrumental Relationships and High Expectations: Exploring Critical Care in Two Latino Community Based Schools." *Journal of Intercultural Education* 17 (3): 281–299.

De La Cancela, V. 1993. "'Coolin': The Psychosocial Communication of African and Latino Men." *Urban League Review* 16 (2): 33–44.

de la Torre, A., and B. M. Pesquera. 1993. *Building with Our Hands: New Directions in Chicana Studies.* Berkeley: University of California Press.

del Castillo, R. G. 1990. *The Treaty of Guadalupe Hidalgo: A Legacy of Conflict.* Norman: University of Oklahoma Press.

———, ed. 2008. *World War II and Mexican American Civil Rights.* Austin: University of Texas Press.

De León, A. 1983. *They Call Them Greasers: Anglo Attitudes toward Mexicans in Texas, 1821–1900.* Austin: University of Texas Press.

Delgado Bernal, D. 2001. "Learning and Living Pedagogies of the Home: The Mestiza Consciousness of Chicana Students." *International Journal of Qualitative Studies in Education* 14 (5): 623–639.

Delgado Bernal, D., C. A. Elenes, F. E. Godinez, and S. Villenas. 2006. *Chicana/*

Latina Education in Everyday Life: Feminista Perspectives on Pedagogy and Epistemology. Albany: State University of New York Press.

Delgado Gaitan, C. 1992. "School Matters in the Mexican-American Home: Socializing Children to Education." *American Educational Research Journal* 29 (3): 495–513.

Delpit, L. D. 2006. *Other People's Children: Cultural Conflict in the Classroom.* New York: New Press.

DeNavas-Walt, C., B. D. Proctor, and J. C. Smith. 2011. *Income, Poverty, and Health Insurance Coverage in the United States: 2010.* Washington, DC: United States Census Bureau.

Denner, J., D. Kirby, K. Coyle, and C. Brindis. 2001. "The Protective Role of Social Capital and Cultural Norms in Latino Communities: A Study of Adolescent Births." *Hispanic Journal of Behavioral Sciences* 23 (3): 3–21.

Desilver, D. 2013. "U.S. Income Inequality, On Rise for Decades, Is Now Highest since 1928." *FactTank: News in the Numbers.* Pew Research Center. http://www.pewresearch.org/fact-tank/2013/12/05/u-s-income-inequality-on-rise-for-decades-is-now-highest-since-1928/.

Dey, E. L., S. Hurtado, B. S. Rhee, K. K. Inkelas, L. A. Wimsatt, and F. Guan. 1997. *Improving Research on Postsecondary Student Outcomes: A Review of the Strengths and Limitations of National Data Resources.* Ann Arbor, MI: National Center for Postsecondary Improvement.

Diaz, Y., and R. E. Zambrana. 2011. "Understanding Contextual Influences on Parenting and Child Behavior in the Assessment and Treatment of ADHD in Latino Children." In *Latina/o Adolescent Psychology and Mental Health,* vol. 1, *Early to Middle Childhood: Development and Context,* ed. N. Cabrera, F. Villarruel, and H. Fitzgerald, pp. 83–108. Santa Barbara, CA: ABC-CLIO.

Dill, B. T., A. E. McLaughlin, and A. D. Nieves. 2012. "Future Directions of Feminist Research: Intersectionality." In *Handbook of Feminist Research: Theory and Praxis,* ed. S. N. Hesse-Biber, pp. 629–637. Thousand Oaks, CA: Sage Publications.

Dill, B. T., S. M. Nettles, and L. Weber. 2001. "Defining the Work of the Consortium: What Do We Mean by Intersections?" *Connections: Newsletter of the Consortium on Race, Gender & Ethnicity,* Spring, p. 4. Retrieved from http://www.crge.umd.edu/pdf/RC2001_spring.pdf.

Dill, B. T., and R. E. Zambrana. 2009. "Critical Thinking about Inequality: An Emerging Lens." In *Emerging Intersections: Race, Class, and Gender in Theory, Policy, and Practice,* ed. B. T. Dill and R. E. Zambrana, pp. 1–21. New Brunswick, NJ: Rutgers University Press.

DiPrete, T. A., and C. Buchmann. 2013. *The Rise of Women: The Growing Gender Gap in Education and What It Means for American Schools.* New York: Russell Sage Foundation.

Donato, R. 1997. *The Other Struggle for Equal Schools: Mexican Americans during the Civil Rights Era.* Albany: State University of New York Press.

———. 2007. *Mexicanos and Hispanos in Colorado Schools and Communities, 1920–1960.* Albany: State University of New York Press.

Donato, R. G., and J. S. Hanson. 2012. "Legally White, Socially 'Mexican': The

Politics of De Jure and De Facto School Segregation in the American Southwest." *Harvard Educational Review* 82 (2): 202–225.

Dougherty, K. 2001. *The Contradictory College: The Conflicting Origins, Impacts, and Futures of Community Colleges.* Albany: State University of New York Press.

Douglass, J. A. 2010. "From Chaos to Order and Back? A Revisionist Reflection on the California Master Plan for Higher Education@50 and Thoughts about Its Future." University of California, Berkeley, Research & Occasional Paper Series. *CSHE* 7, no. 10 (May): 1–20.

D'Souza, D. 1991. *Illiberal Education.* New York: Vintage Books.

———. 1995. *The End of Racism: Principles for a Multiracial Society.* New York: Free Press.

DuBois, W. 1903. "The Talented Tenth." In *The Negro Problem: A Series of Articles by Representative Negroes of To-day.* New York: James Pott and Company.

Dunn, L. 1968. "Special Education for the Mildly Mentally Retarded: Is Much of It Justifiable?" *Exceptional Children* 35 (1): 5–22.

Duster, T. 1993. "The Diversity of California at Berkeley: An Emerging Reformulation of 'Competence' in an Increasingly Multicultural World." In *Beyond a Dream Deferred: Multicultural Education and the Politics of Excellence,* ed. B. W. Thompson and S. Tyagi, pp. 231–255. Minneapolis: University of Minnesota Press.

Eagan, M. K., S. Hurtado, M. J. Chang, G. A. Garcia, F. A. Herrera, and J. C. Garibay. 2013. "Making a Difference in Science Education: The Impact of Undergraduate Research Programs." *American Educational Research Journal* 50 (4): 683–713.

Eby, F. E., ed. 1918. *Education in Texas: Source Materials.* Austin: University of Texas Press.

Engberg, M. E., and S. Hurtado. 2011. "Developing Pluralistic Skills and Dispositions in College: Examining Racial/Ethnic Group Differences." *Journal of Higher Education* 82 (4): 416–443.

Ennis, S. R., M. Ríos-Vargas, and N. G. Albert. 2011. *The Hispanic Population: 2010.* U.S. Census Bureau publication no. C2010BR-04. Washington, DC: U.S. Department of Commerce, Economics and Statistics Administration.

Escobedo, T. H. 1981. *Education and Chicanos: Issues and Research.* Los Angeles: Spanish Speaking Mental Health Research Center.

Esparza, M., and E. J. Olmos. 2006. *Walkout.* Aired March 18. New York: Home Box Office Films. DVD.

Espino, M. M. 2012. "Seeking the 'Truth' in the Stories We Tell: The Role of Critical Race Epistemology in Higher Education Research." *Review of Higher Education* 36 (1): 31–67.

———. 2014. "Exploring the Role of Community Cultural Wealth in Graduate School Access and Persistence of Mexican American PhDs." *American Journal of Education* 120 (4): 545–574.

Espinoza, G., C. Gillen-O'Neel, N. A. Gonzales, and A. J. Fuligni. 2013. "Friend Affiliations and School Adjustment among Mexican-American Adolescents: The Moderating Role of Peer and Parent Support." *Journal of Youth and Adolescence* 43 (12): 1969–1981.

Espinoza, R. 2011. *Pivotal Moments: How Educators Can Put All Students on a Path to College.* Cambridge, MA: Harvard Education Press.

Evans, N. J., and E. M. Broido. 2002. "The Experiences of Lesbian and Bisexual Women in College Residence Halls: Implications for Addressing Homophobia and Heterosexism." *Journal of Lesbian Studies* 6 (3/4): 29–42.

Farkas, G. 2003. "Racial Disparities and Discrimination in Education: What Do We Know, How Do We Know It, and What Do We Need to Know?" *Teachers College Record* 105 (6): 1119–1146.

Faulstich Orellana, M. 2003. *In Other Words: En Otras Palabras: Learning from Bilingual Kids' Translating/Interpreting Experiences.* Evanston, IL: Northwestern University, School of Education and Social Policy.

Feagin, J. R., and J. A. Cobas. 2014. *Latinos Facing Racism: Discrimination, Resistance, and Endurance.* Boulder, CO: Paradigm Publishers.

Feagin, J. R., H. Vera, and N. Imani. 1996. *The Agony of Education: Black Students at White Colleges and Universities.* New York: Routledge.

Ferdman, B. M., and P. I. Gallegos. 2001. "Racial Identity Development and Latinos in the United States." In *New Perspectives on Racial Identity Development*, ed. C. L. Wijeyesinghe and B. W. Jackson, pp. 32–66. New York: New York University Press.

Ferri, B. A., and D. J. Connor. 2005. "In the Shadow of Brown: Special Education and Overrepresentation of Students of Color." *Remedial and Special Education* 26 (2): 93–100.

Fischer, M. 2007. "Settling into Campus Life: Differences by Race/Ethnicity in College Involvement and Outcomes." *Journal of Higher Education* 78 (2): 124–161.

Flores, L. H. 2001. "Thirty Years of Chicano and Chicana Studies." In *Color-Line to Borderlands: The Matrix of American Ethnic Studies*, ed. J. E. Butler, pp. 203–223. Seattle: University of Washington Press.

Flores, S. M., and J. Chapa. 2009. "Latino Immigrant Access to Higher Education in a Bipolar Context of Reception." *Journal of Hispanic Higher Education* 8 (1): 90–109.

Flores, Y. 2006. "La Salud: Latina Adolescents Constructing Identities, Negotiating Health Decisions." In *Latina Girls: Voices of Adolescent Strength in the United States*, ed. J. Denner and B. Guzman, pp. 199–211. New York: New York University Press.

Flores Carmona, J. 2010. "Transgenerational Educación: Latina Mothers' Everyday Pedagogies of Cultural Citizenship in Salt Lake City, Utah." PhD diss., University of Utah.

Foley, N. 1997. *The White Scourge: Mexicans, Blacks, and Poor Whites in Texas Cotton Culture.* Berkeley: University of California Press.

———. 2010. *Quest for Equality: The Failed Promise of Black-Brown Solidarity.* Cambridge, MA: Harvard University Press.

Ford Foundation. 1968. "A Mexican-American Legal Defense and Education Fund." A proposal to the Ford Foundation prepared under the auspices of the NAACP Legal Defense & Educational Fund, Inc. Modified Proposal. Grant No. 68-248. New York: Ford Foundation Archives.

Franco, J. L., L. Sabattini, and F. J. Crosby. 2004. "Anticipating Work and Family:

Exploring the Associations among Gender-Related Ideologies, Values, and Behaviors in Latino and White Families in the United States." *Journal of Social Issues* 60 (4): 755–766.

Franke, R. 2012. "Towards the Education Nation: Revisiting the Impact of Financial Aid, College Experience, and Institutional Context on Baccalaureate Degree Attainment Using a Propensity Score Matching, Multilevel Modeling Approach." PhD diss., University of California, Los Angeles.

Fry, R. 2003. *Hispanic Youth Dropping Out of U.S. Schools: Measuring the Challenge*. Washington, DC: Pew Hispanic Research Center.

———. 2004. *Latino Youth Finishing College: The Role of Selective Pathways*. Washington, DC: Pew Hispanic Research Center.

———. 2005a. *The Higher Dropout Rates of Foreign-Born Teens: The Role of Schooling Abroad*. Washington, DC: Pew Hispanic Research Center.

———. 2005b. *Recent Changes in the Entry of Hispanic and White Youth into College*. Washington, DC: Pew Hispanic Research Center.

———. 2010. *Hispanics, High School Dropouts and the GED*. Washington, DC: Pew Hispanic Research Center.

———. 2011. *Hispanic College Enrollment Spikes: Narrowing Gaps with Other Groups*. Washington, DC: Pew Hispanic Research Center.

Fry, R., and M. H. Lopez. 2012. "Hispanic Student Enrollments Reach New Highs in 2011: Now Largest Minority Group on Four-Year College Campuses." Washington, DC: Pew Hispanic Research Center. http://www.pewhispanic .org/2012/08/20/hispanic-student-enrollments-reach-new-highs-in-2011/.

Fry, R., and P. Taylor. 2013. *Hispanic High School Graduates Pass Whites in Rate of College Enrollment*. Washington, DC: Pew Hispanic Research Center.

Fuligni, A. J. 2007. *Contesting Stereotypes and Creating Identities: Social Categories, Social Identities, and Education Participation*. New York: Russell Sage.

Gallegos, B. P. 1992. *Literacy, Education, and Society in New Mexico, 1693–1821*. Albuquerque: University of New Mexico Press.

Gammel, H. P. N. 1898. *The Laws of Texas, 1822–1897*. 10 vols. Austin: Gammel Book Company.

Gándara, P. 1979. "Early Environmental Correlates of High Academic Attainment in Mexican Americans from Low Socioeconomic Backgrounds." PhD diss., University of California, Los Angeles (UCLA).

———. 1980. *Chicano Scholars: Against All Odds*. Santa Monica, CA: The RAND Corporation.

———. 1982. "Passing through the Eye of the Needle: High-Achieving Chicanas." *Hispanic Journal of Behavioral Science* 4 (2): 167–179.

———. 1995. *Over the Ivy Walls: The Educational Mobility of Low-Income Chicanos*. Albany: State University of New York Press.

———. 1997. *Review of Research on the Instruction of Limited English Proficient Students: A Report to the California Legislature*. Davis: University of California Linguistic Minority Research Institute.

———. 1998. "Final Report of the Evaluation of High School Puente: 1994–1998." Carnegie Corporation of New York. http://www.aypf.org/publications /rmaa/pdfs/HighSchoPuente.pdf.

———. 1999a. *Priming the Pump: Strategies for Increasing the Achievement of Under-represented Minority Undergraduates*. New York: College Board.

———. 1999b. "Telling Stories Of Success: Cultural Capital and the Educational Mobility of Chicano Students." *Latino Studies Journal* 10 (1): 38–54.

———. 2000. "Latinos and Higher Education: A California Perspective." Paper presented to the Chicano/Latino Public Policy Seminar, Sacramento, CA, February 1–2.

Gándara, P., and D. Bial. 2001. *Paving the Way to Higher Education: K–12 Intervention Programs for Underrepresented Youth*. Washington, DC: National Postsecondary Education Cooperative.

Gándara, P., and F. Contreras. 2009. *The Latino Education Crisis*. Cambridge, MA: Harvard University Press.

Garces, L. M. 2012. "Racial Diversity, Legitimacy, and the Citizenry: The Impact of Affirmative Action Bans on Graduate School Enrollment." *Review of Higher Education* 36 (1): 93–132.

Garcia, A. M., ed. 1997. *Chicana Feminist Thought: The Basic Historical Writings*. New York: Routledge Press.

García, D. G., and T. J. Yosso. 2013. "Strictly in the Capacity of Servant: The Interconnection between Residential and School Segregation in Oxnard, California, 1934–1954." *History of Education Quarterly* 53 (1): 64–89.

García, D. G., T. J. Yosso, and F. Barajas. 2012. "'A Few of the Brightest, Cleanest Mexican Children': School Segregation as a Form of Mundane Racism." *Harvard Educational Review* 82 (1): 1–25.

Garcia, I. M. 1998. *Chicanismo: The Forging of a Militant Ethos among Mexican Americans*. Tucson: University of Arizona Press.

García, M. 1989. *Mexican Americans: Leadership, Ideology, and Identity, 1930–1960*. New Haven, CT: Yale University Press.

García, M., and S. Castro. 2011. *Blowout!: Sal Castro and the Chicano Struggle for Educational Justice*. Chapel Hill: University of North Carolina Press.

García-Coll, C., K. Crnic, G. Lamberty, B. H. Wasik, R. Jenkins, H. V. García, and H. P. McAdoo. 1996. "An Integrative Model for the Study of Developmental Competencies in Minority Children." *Child Development* 67 (5): 1891–1914.

Garza, H. 1993. "Second-Class Academics: Chicano/Latino Faculty in U.S. Universities." In *Building a Diverse Faculty: New Directions for Teaching and Learning*, ed. J. Gainen and R. Boice, pp. 31–42. San Francisco: Jossey-Bass.

Garza, R. 2009. "Latino and White High School Students' Perceptions of Caring Behaviors: Are We Culturally Responsive to Our Students?" *Urban Education* 44 (3): 297–321.

Gibson, M. A., P. Gándara, and J. P. Koyama, eds. 2004. *School Connections: U.S. Mexican Youth, Peers, and School Achievement*. New York: Teachers College Press.

Ginorio, A., and M. Huston. 2001. *Si Se Puede! Yes, We Can: Latinas in School*. Washington, DC: American Association of University Women Educational Foundation.

Gladwell, M. 2011. *Outliers: The Story of Success*. New York: Little, Brown & Company.

Gloria, A. M., and J. Castellanos. 2003. "Latina/o and African American Students at Predominantly White Institutions." In *The Majority in the Minority: Expand-*

ing the Representation of Latina/o Faculty, Administrators and Students in Higher Education, ed. J. Castellanos and L. Jones, pp. 71–92. Sterling, VA: Stylus.

Gómez, L. E. 2007. *Manifest Destinies: The Making of the Mexican American Race*. New York: New York University Press.

González, A. 2001. *Mexican Americans and the US Economy: Quest for Buenos Días*. Tucson: University of Arizona Press.

Gonzalez, G. 1990. *Chicano Education in the Era of Segregation*. Philadelphia: Balch Institute Press.

Gonzalez, J. 2000. *Harvest of Empire: A History of Latinos in America*. New York: Viking Press.

González, K. P. 2002. "Campus Culture and the Experiences of Chicano Students in a Predominantly White University." *Urban Education* 37 (2): 193–218.

Gonzalez-Barrera, A., and M. H. Lopez. 2013. *A Demographic Portrait of Mexican-Origin Hispanics in the United States*. Washington, DC: Pew Hispanic Research Center.

Grebler, L., J. W. Moore, and R. C. Guzman. 1970. *The Mexican-American People: The Nation's Second Largest Minority*. New York: Free Press.

Gregory, A., R. J. Skiba, and P. A. Noguera. 2010. "The Achievement Gap and the Discipline Gap: Two Sides of the Same Coin?" *Educational Researcher* 39 (1): 59–68.

Griffin, K. A., and R. J. Reddick. 2011. "Surveillance and Sacrifice: Gender Differences in the Mentoring Patterns of Black Professors at Predominantly White Research Universities." *American Educational Research Journal* 48 (5): 1032–1057.

Gugliemo, T. A. 2006. "Fighting for Caucasian Rights: Mexicans, Mexican Americans, and the Transnational Struggle for Civil Rights in World War II Texas." *Journal of American History* 92 (4): 1212–1237.

Guinier, L., and S. Sturm. 2001. *Who's Qualified: A New Democracy Forum on the Future of Affirmative Action*. Boston: Beacon Press.

Gurian, M., and K. Stevens. 2005. *The Minds of Boys*. San Francisco: Jossey-Bass.

Gurin, P., E. L. Dey, S. Hurtado, and G. Gurin. 2002. "Diversity and Higher Education: Theory and Impact on Educational Outcomes." *Harvard Educational Review* 72 (3): 330–366.

Gutiérrez, E. 2008. *Fertile Matters: The Politics of Mexican-Origin Women's Reproduction*. Austin: University of Texas Press.

Gutiérrez, R. A. 1991. *When Jesus Came the Corn Mothers Went Away: Marriage, Sexuality and Power in New Mexico, 1500–1846*. Stanford, CA: Stanford University Press.

Guzmán, G., and V. M. MacDonald. 2013. "'Non-White on Arrival': The Mexican Consul, Racial Segregation, and the Transnational Fight for Educational Equality, 1915–1919." Paper presented at the History of Education Society, Nashville, TN, November 2.

Hannon, L., R. DeFina, and S. Bruch. 2013. "The Relationship between Skin Tone and School Suspension for African Americans." http://www88.homepage.villanova.edu/lance.hannon/ColorismSuspension.pdf.

Hardiman, R. 2001. "Reflections on White Identity Development Theory." In *New Perspectives on Racial Identity Development*, ed. C. L. Wijeyesinghe and B. W. Jackson, pp. 108–128. New York: New York University Press.

Haro, C. M. 1983. "Chicanos and Higher Education: A Review of Selected Literature." *Aztlan* 14 (1): 35–77.

Harper, S. R., and S. Hurtado. 2007. "Nine Themes in Campus Racial Climates and Implications for Institutional Transformation." In *Responding to the Realities of Race on Campus: New Directions for Student Services*, ed. S. R. Harper and L. D. Patton, pp. 7–24. San Francisco: Jossey-Bass.

Harry, B., and J. K. Klingner. 2006. *Why Are So Many Minority Students in Special Education? Understanding Race & Disability in Schools.* New York: Teachers College Press.

Harvard Educational Review. 2012. "Symposium: Chicano Feminist Epistemology: Past, Present, and Future." *Harvard Educational Review* 82 (4): 511–512.

Hayes-Bautista, D. E. 2004. *La Nueva California: Latinos in the Golden State.* Berkeley: University of California Press.

Helms, J., ed. 1990. *Black and White Identity: Theory, Research, and Practice.* Westport, CT: Praeger.

Higginbotham, E. 1980. "Educated Black Women: An Exploration into Life Chances and Choice." PhD diss., Brandeis University.

Horne, T. 2010. "Findings by the State Superintendent of Public Instruction of Violation by Tucson Unified School District Pursuant to A.R.S. §15-112(B)," December 30. Phoenix: Arizona Department of Education. Retrieved from https://www.azag.gov/sites/default/files/sites/all/docs/TUSD_Ethnic_Studies_Findings.pdf.

Horsman, R. 1981. *Race and Manifest Destiny: The Origins of American Racial Anglo-Saxonism.* Cambridge, MA: Harvard University Press.

Huang, Y. P., and L. Y. Flores. 2011. "Exploring the Validity of the Problem-Solving Inventory with Mexican American High School Students." *Journal of Career Assessment* 19 (4): 431–441.

Hurtado, A. 1996. *The Color of Privilege: Three Blasphemies on Race and Feminism.* Ann Arbor: University of Michigan Press.

———. 2003. *Voicing Chicana Feminisms: Young Women Speak Out on Sexuality and Identity.* New York: New York University Press.

Hurtado, S. 1992. "The Campus Racial Climate: Contexts of Conflict." *Journal of Higher Education* 63 (5): 539–569.

———. 1994a. "The Graduate School Racial Climate and Academic Self-Concept among Minority Graduate Students in the 1970s." *American Journal of Education* 102 (3): 330–351.

———. 1994b. "The Institutional Climate for Talented Latino Students." *Research in Higher Education* 35 (1): 21–41.

———. 2003. *Preparing College Students for a Diverse Democracy.* Final report to the U.S. Department of Education, Office of Educational Research and Improvement, Field Initiated Studies Program. Ann Arbor: Center for the Study of Higher and Postsecondary Education, University of Michigan. http://www.umich.edu/~divdemo/031819.FIS_report_Wed_rev.pdf.

Hurtado, S., C. L. Alvarez, C. Guillermo-Wann, M. Cuellar, and L. Arellano. 2012. "A Model for Diverse Learning Environments: The Scholarship on Creating and Assessing Conditions for Student Success." In *Higher Education:*

Handbook of Theory and Research, vol. 27, ed. J. C. Smart and M. B. Paulsen, pp. 41–122. New York: Springer.

Hurtado, S., and D. F. Carter. 1997. "Effects of College Transition and Perceptions of the Campus Racial Climate on Latino College Students' Sense of Belonging." *Sociology of Education* 70 (4): 324–345.

Hurtado, S., D. F. Carter, and A. Spuler. 1996. "Latino Student Transition to College: Assessing Difficulties and Factors in Successful Adjustment." *Research in Higher Education* 37 (2): 135–157.

Hurtado, S., M. Cuellar, and C. Guillermo-Wann. 2011. "Quantitative Measures of Students' Sense of Validation: Advancing the Study of Diverse Learning Environments." *Enrollment Management Journal* 5 (2): 53–71.

Hurtado, S., M. K. Eagan, M. C. Tran, C. B. Newman, M. J. Chang, and P. Velasco. 2011. "'We Do Science Here': Underrepresented Minority Student Interactions with Faculty in Different College Contexts." *Journal of Social Issues* 67 (3): 555–581.

Hurtado, S., J. Gasiewski, and C. L. Alvarez. 2014. *The Climate for Diversity at Cornell University: Student Experiences*. Los Angeles: Higher Education Research Institute. http://diversity.cornell.edu/sites/default/files/Qualitative-Study-of-Student-Climate-Full-Report.pdf.

Hurtado, S., K. A. Griffin, L. Arellano, and M. Cuellar. 2008. "Assessing the Value of Climate Assessments: Progress and Future Directions." *Journal of Diversity in Higher Education* 1 (4): 204–221.

Hurtado, S., J. F. Milem, A. R. Clayton-Pederson, and W. Allen. 1998. "Enhancing Campus Climates for Racial/Ethnic Diversity: Educational Policy and Practice." *Review of Higher Education* 21 (3): 279–302.

———. 1999. *Enacting Diverse Learning Environments: Improving the Campus Climate for Racial/Ethnic Diversity in Higher Education*. ASHE-ERIC Series. San Francisco: Jossey-Bass.

Hurtado, S., and L. Ponjuan. 2005. "Latino Educational Outcomes and the Campus Climate." *Journal of Hispanic Higher Education* 4 (3): 235–251.

Hurtado, S., and A. Ruiz. 2012. *The Climate for Underrepresented Groups and Diversity on Campus*. HERI Research Brief. Los Angeles: Higher Education Research Institute. http://heri.ucla.edu/briefs/urmbriefreport.pdf.

Hurtado, S., A. Ruiz, and H. Whang. 2012. "Assessing Students' Social Responsibility and Commitment to Public Service." Paper presented at the Association for Institutional Research Annual Forum, New Orleans, LA.

Hurtado, S., V. B. Sáenz, J. L. Santos, and N. L. Cabrera. 2008. *Advancing in Higher Education: A Portrait of Latina/o College Freshmen at Four-Year Institutions, 1975–2006*. Los Angeles: Higher Education Research Institute.

Hyams, M. 2006. "La Escuela: Young Latina Women Negotiating Identities in School." In *Latina Girls: Voices of Adolescent Strength in the United States*, ed. J. Denner and B. Guzman, pp. 93–108. New York: New York University Press.

Jackson, B. W. 2001. "Black Identity Development: Further Analysis and Elaboration." In *New Perspectives on Racial Identity Development*, ed. C. L. Wijeyesinghe and B. W. Jackson, pp. 8–31. New York: New York University Press.

Johnson, V. D. 2003. "Cultural Group Perceptions of Racial Climates in Residence Halls." *NASPA Journal* 41 (1): 114–134.

Jones, L., J. Castellanos, and D. Cole. 2002. "Examining the Ethnic Minority Student's Experience at Predominantly White Institutions: A Case Study." *Journal of Hispanic Higher Education* 1 (1): 19–39.

Jung, S., B. G. Fuller, and C. Galindo. 2012. "Family Functioning and Early Learning Practices in Immigrant Homes." *Child Development* 83 (5): 1510–1526.

Justice Center. 2011. *Breaking Schools' Rules: A Statewide Study of How School Discipline Relates to Students' Success and Juvenile Justice Involvement*. New York: Council of State Governments. http://csgjusticecenter.org/wp-content/up loads/2012/08/Breaking_Schools_Rules_Report_Final.pdf.

Kaestle, C. 1983. *Pillars of the Republic: Common Schools and American Society*. New York: Hill and Wang.

Kaiser, C. R., and J. S. Pratt-Hyatt. 2009. "Distributing Prejudice Unequally: Do Whites Direct Their Prejudice toward Strongly Identified Minorities?" *Journal of Personality and Social Psychology* 96 (2): 432–445.

Kaiser, C. R., and C. L. Wilkins. 2010. "Group Identity and Prejudice: Theoretical and Empirical Advances and Implications." *Journal of Social Issues* 66 (3): 461–476.

Kanellos, N. 1997. *Hispanic Firsts: 500 Years of Extraordinary Achievement*. Detroit: Visible Ink Press.

Karabel, J. 1972. "Community Colleges and Social Stratification." *Harvard Educational Review* 42 (4): 251–262.

Kelly, B. T., and A. Torres. 2006. "Campus Safety: Perceptions and Experiences of Woman Students." *Journal of College Student Development* 47 (1): 20–36.

KewalRamani, A., L. Gilbertson, M. A. Fox, and S. Provasnik. 2007. *Status and Trends in the Education of Racial and Ethnic Minorities*. Publication no. NCES 2007-039. National Center for Education Statistics, Institute of Education Sciences, U.S. Department of Education. Washington, DC: U.S. Government Printing Office.

Kochhar, R. 2005. *The Occupational Status and Mobility of Hispanics*. Washington, DC: Pew Hispanic Research Center. http://pewhispanic.org/files/reports/59 .pdf.

Kozol, J. 1991. *Savage Inequalities*. New York: HarperCollins.

Labaree, D. 1997. "Public Goods, Private Goods: The American Struggle over Educational Goals." *American Educational Research Journal* 34 (1): 39–81.

Landale, N. S., R. S. Oropesa, and C. Bradatan. 2006. "Hispanic Families in the United States: Family Structure and Process in an Era of Family Change." In *Hispanics and the Future of America*, ed. M. Tienda and F. Mitchell, pp. 138–178. Washington, DC: National Academies Press.

Langhout, R. D., F. Rosselli, and J. Feinstein. 2007. "Assessing Classism in Academic Settings." *Review of Higher Education* 30 (2): 145–184.

Lareau, A. 2003. *Unequal Childhoods: Class, Race and Family Life*. Berkeley: University of California Press.

———. 2014. "Schools, Housing, and the Reproduction of Inequality." In *Choosing Homes, Choosing Schools: Residential Segregation and the Search for a Good School*, ed. A. Lareau and K. Goyette, pp. 169–206. New York: Russell Sage Publications.

Lareau, A., and E. M. Horvat. 1999. "Moments of Social Inclusion and Exclusion:

Race, Class, and Cultural Capital in Family-School Relationships." *Sociology of Education* 72 (1): 37–53.

Lee, V. E., and D. T. Burkam. 2002. *Inequality at the Starting Gate: Social Background Differences in Achievement as Children Begin School.* Washington, DC: Economic Policy Institute.

León, D. J., and D. McNeil. 1992. "A Precursor to Affirmative Action: Californios and Mexicans in the University of California, 1870–72." *Perspectives in Mexican American Studies* 3 (July): 179–206.

Levin, S., C. van Laar, and W. Foote. 2006. "Ethnic Segregation and Perceived Discrimination in College: Mutual Influences and Effects on Social and Academic Life." *Journal of Applied Social Psychology* 36 (6): 1471–1501.

Levin, S., C. van Laar, and J. Sidanius. 2003. "The Effects of Ingroup and Outgroup Friendships on Ethnic Attitudes in College: A Longitudinal Study." *Group Processes and Intergroup Relations* 6 (1): 76–92.

Lipschütz, A. 1944. *Indoamericanismo y el Problema Racial en las Americas.* Santiago de Chile: Editorial Nascimiento.

Livingston, G., K. Park, and S. Fox. 2009. *Latinas Online, 2006–2008: Narrowing the Gap.* Washington, DC: Pew Hispanic Research Center.

Locks, A. M., S. Hurtado, N. A. Bowman, and L. Oseguera. 2008. "Extending Notions of Campus Climate and Diversity to Students' Transition to College." *Review of Higher Education* 31 (3): 257–285.

López, I. F. H. 1997. *White by Law: The Legal Construction of Race.* New York: New York University Press.

———. 2003. *Racism on Trial: The Chicano Fight for Justice.* Cambridge, MA: Belknap Press of Harvard University Press.

Lopez, M. H. 2009. *Latinos and Education: Explaining the Attainment Gap.* Washington, DC: Pew Hispanic Research Center.

Lopez, M. L., and C. Stack. 2001. "Social Capital and the Culture of Power: Lessons from the Field." In *Social Capital and Poor Communities,* ed. S. Saegert, J. Thomson, and M. Warren, pp. 31–59. New York: Russell Sage Foundation.

Losen, D. J., and G. Orfield. 2002. *Racial Inequity in Special Education.* Cambridge, MA: Harvard Education Press.

Loury, G. C., N. Glazer, J. F. Kain, T. J. Kane, D. Massey, M. Tienda, and B. Bucks. 2003. Amicus Brief of Social Scientists for Respondents, *Grutter v. Bollinger* and *Gratz v. Bollinger.* U.S. Supreme Court Nos. 02-241 and 02-516.

Loza, P. P. 2003. "A System at Risk: College Outreach Programs and the Educational Neglect of Underachieving Latino High School Students." *Urban Review* 35 (1): 43–57.

MacDonald, V. M. 2001. "Hispanic, Latino, Chicano, or 'Other'?: Deconstructing the Relationship between Historians and Hispanic-American Educational History." *History of Education Quarterly* 41 (3): 365–413.

———. 2004. *Latino Education in the United States: A Narrated History from 1513–2000.* New York: Palgrave MacMillan.

———. 2011a. "Beyond El Movimiento: Latino Student Culture Building in the Pre–Civil Rights Twentieth Century." Paper presented at annual meeting of the Organization of American Historians, Houston, TX, November.

———. 2011b. "'A Few Chosen Mexicans': High School Access and Opportunity in the World War II Era for Southwestern Mexican Americans, 1920s–1950s." Paper presented at the History of Education Society Annual Meeting, Chicago, November.

MacDonald, V. M., J. Botti, and L. H. Clark. 2007. "From Visibility to Autonomy: Latinos and Higher Education in the U.S., 1965–2005." *Harvard Educational Review* 77 (4): 474–504.

MacDonald, V. M., and T. Garcia. 2003. "Historical Perspectives on Latino Access to Higher Education, 1848–1990." In *The Majority in the Minority: Expanding the Representation of Latino/a Faculty, Administrators and Students in Higher Education*, ed. J. Castellanos and L. Jones, pp. 15–46. Sterling, VA: Stylus Press.

MacDonald, V. M., and B. P. Hoffman. 2012. "Compromising *La Causa*? The Ford Foundation and Chicano Intellectual Nationalism in the Creation of Chicano History, 1963–1977." *History of Education Quarterly* 52 (3): 251–281.

MacLeod, J. 1995. *Ain't No Makin' It: Aspirations and Attainment in a Low-Income Neighborhood*. Boulder, CO: Westview Press.

Malagon, M. 2010. "All the Losers Go There: Challenging the Deficit Educational Discourse of Chicano Racialized Masculinity in a Continuation High School." *Educational Foundations* 24 (1): 59–76.

Maldonado, C., and E. I. Farmer. 2006. "Examining Latinos Involvement in the Workforce and Postsecondary Technical Education in the United States." *Journal of Career and Technical Education* 22 (2): 1–13.

Malkin, M. 2003. "Reconquistador." *Front Page Magazine*, September 1. http://archive.frontpagemag.com/readArticle.aspx?ARTID=16591.

Marlino, D., and F. Wilson. 2006. "Career Expectations and Goals of Latina Adolescents: Results from a Nationwide Study." In *Latina Girls: Voices of Adolescent Strength in the United States*, ed. J. Denner and B. Guzman, pp. 123–137. New York: New York University Press.

Martinez, G. A. 1997. " Teaching, Scholarship, and Service: Practicing Latcrit Theory: The Legal Construction of Race: Mexican Americans and Whiteness." *Harvard Latino Law Review* 2 (Fall): 321–347.

Martinez, J. J., and J. C. L. Alire. 1999. "The Influence of the Roman Catholic Church in New Mexico under Mexican Administration." In *Seeds of Struggle/Harvest of Faith: The Papers of the Archdiocese of Santa Fe Cuarto Centennial Conference: The History of the Catholic Church in New Mexico*, ed. T. J. Steele, P. Rhetts, and B. Awalt, pp. 329–344. Albuquerque, NM: LPD Press.

Martínez, M. E. 2008. *Genealogical Fictions: Limpieza de Sangre, Religion, and Gender in Colonial Mexico*. Stanford, CA: Stanford University Press.

Massey, D. S., R. E. Zambrana, and S. Alonzo Bell. 1995. "Contemporary Issues in Latino Families: Future Directions for Research, Policy, and Practice." In *Understanding Latino Families*, ed. Ruth E. Zambrana, pp. 190–203. Thousand Oaks, CA: Sage.

Maxwell-Jolly, J., and P. C. Gándara. 2006. "Critical Issues in the Preparation of Teachers for English Learners." In *Crucial Issues in California Education 2000*, ed. E. Burr et al., pp. 103–119. Berkeley, CA: PACE.

Mayhew, M. J., H. E. Grunwald, and E. L. Dey. 2005. "Curriculum Matters: Creating a Positive Climate for Diversity from the Student Perspective." *Research in Higher Education* 46 (4): 389–412.

McDonough, P. M. 1997. *Choosing Colleges: How Schools and Social Class Structure Opportunity*. Albany: State University of New York Press.

McKenna, T., and I. F. Ortiz. 1987. *The Broken Web: The Educational Experiences of Hispanic American Women*. Claremont, CA: Tomas Rivera Center, and Berkeley, CA: Floricanto Press.

McLachlan, G. J., and T. Krishnan. 1997. *The EM Algorithm and Extensions*. New York: Wiley Press.

McLoyd, V. C., A. M. Cauce, D. Takeuchi, and L. Wilson. 2000. "Marital Processes and Parental Socialization in Families of Color: A Decade Review of Research." *Journal of Marriage and the Family* 62 (4): 1070–1093.

Mehan, H. 1996. *Constructing School Success: The Consequences of Untracking Low-Achieving Students*. New York: Cambridge University Press.

Menchaca, M. 1995. *The Mexican Outsiders: A Community History of Marginalization and Discrimination in California*. Austin: University of Texas Press.

———. 2001. *Recovering History, Constructing Race: The Indian, Black, and White Roots of Mexican Americans*. Austin: University of Texas Press.

Mendez et al. v. Westminster School District. 1946. 64 F.Supp. 544. http://law.justia .com/cases/federal/district-courts/FSupp/64/544/1952972/.

Merskin, D. 2007. "Three Faces of Eva: Perpetuation of the Hot-Latina Stereotype in Desperate Housewives." *Howard Journal of Communications* 18 (2): 133–151.

Milem, J. F., M. J. Chang, and a. l. antonio. 2005. *Making Diversity Work on Campus: A Research-Based Perspective*. Washington, DC: Association of American Colleges and Universities.

Milner, H. R. 2013. "Why Are Students of Color (Still) Punished More Severely and Frequently than White Students?" *Urban Education* 48 (4): 483–489.

Mirande, A. 1985. *The Chicano Experience: An Alternative Perspective*. Notre Dame, IN: University of Notre Dame Press.

Mirande, A., and E. Enriquez. 1979. *La Chicana: The Mexican American Woman*. Chicago: University of Chicago Press.

Molina, K. 2008. "Women of Color in Higher Education: Resistance and Hegemonic Academic Culture." *Feminist Collections* 29 (1): 1–6.

Moll, L., C. Amanti, D. Neff, and N. Gonzales. 1992. "Funds of Knowledge for Teaching: Using a Qualitative Approach to Connect Homes and Classrooms." *Theory into Practice* 31 (2): 132–141.

Montejano, D. 2010. *Quixote's Soldiers: A Local History of the Chicano Movement, 1966–1981*. Austin: University of Texas Press.

Montoya, M. 1994. "Mascaras, Trenzas, y Grenas: Un/Masking the Self While Un/Braiding Latina Stories and Legal Discourse." *Chicano-Latino Law Review* 15 (1): 1–37.

Morales, E. 1996. "Gender Roles among Latino Gay and Bisexual Men: Implications for Family and Couple Relationships." In *Lesbians and Gays in Couples and Families: A Handbook for Therapists*, ed. J. Laird and R. J. Green, pp. 272–297. San Francisco: Jossey-Bass.

Moran, R. 2000. "Sorting and Reforming: High-Stakes Testing in the Public Schools." *Akron Law Review* 34 (107): 1–29.

Moreno, J. F., ed. 1999. *The Elusive Quest for Equality: 150 Years of Chicano/Chicana Education.* Cambridge, MA: Harvard Educational Review.

Mörner, M. 1967. *Race Mixture in the History of Latin America.* Boston: Little, Brown & Company.

Motel, S., and E. Patten. 2012. *The 10 Largest Hispanic Origin Groups: Characteristics, Rankings, Top Counties.* Washington, DC: Pew Hispanic Research Center.

———. 2013. *Statistical Portrait of Hispanics in the United States, 2011.* Washington, DC: Pew Hispanic Research Center.

Muñoz, C. 1989. *Youth, Identity, Power: The Chicano Movement.* New York: Verso.

Muñoz, L. K. 2001. "Separate but Equal?: A Case Study of *Romo v. Laird* and Mexican American Education." *OAH Magazine of History* 15 (2): 28–34.

———. 2013. "*Romo v. Laird*: Mexican American Segregation and the Politics of Belonging in Arizona." *Western Legal History* 26 (1 & 2): 97–132.

Museus, S. D., A. H. Nichols, and A. D. Lambert. 2008. "Racial Differences in the Effects of Campus Racial Climate on Degree Completion: A Structural Equation Model." *Review of Higher Education* 32 (1): 107–134.

National Center for Education Statistics. 2008. *Digest of Education Statistics, 2007.* Publication no. NCES 2008-022. Washington, DC: NCES, U.S. Department of Education.

———. 2010. *Digest of Education Statistics, 2009.* Publication no. NCES 2010-013. Washington, DC: U.S. Department of Education. http://nces.ed.gov/pubs2010/2010013_0.pdf.

———. 2013. *The Condition of Education 2013.* Publication no. NCES 2013-037. Washington, DC: U.S. Department of Education.

National Women's Law Center (NWLC) and Mexican American Legal Defense and Educational Fund (MALDEF). 2009. *Listening to Latinas: Barriers to High School Graduation.* Washington, DC: National Women's Law Center.

Navarro, A. 1995. *Mexican American Youth Organizations: Avant-Garde of the Chicano Movement in Texas.* Austin: University of Texas Press.

———. 1998. *The Cristal Experiment: A Chicano Struggle for Community Control.* Madison: University of Wisconsin Press.

Nero, C. I. 2005. "Why Are the Gay Ghettos White?" In *Black Queer Studies: A Critical Anthology*, ed. E. P. Johnson and M. G. Henderson, pp. 228–245. Durham, NC: Duke University Press.

Ngai, M. 2005. *Impossible Subjects: Illegal Aliens and the Making of Modern America.* Princeton, NJ: Princeton University Press.

Nieto, S. 1999. *The Light in Their Eyes.* New York: Teachers College Press.

Nieto-Phillips, J. M. 2004. *The Language of Blood: The Making of Spanish American Identity in New Mexico, 1880s–1990s.* Albuquerque: University of New Mexico Press.

Nineteenth and Twentieth Annual Reports of the Territorial Superintendent of Public Instruction to the Governor of New Mexico for the Years 1909–1910. 1911. Santa Fe: New Mexican Printing Co.

Noddings, N. 1984. *Caring: A Feminine Approach to Ethics and Moral Education.* Berkeley: University of California Press.

Noguera, P. A. 2003. "The Trouble with Black Boys: The Role and Influence of

Environmental and Cultural Factors on the Academic Performance of African American Males." *Urban Education* 38 (4): 431–459.

———. 2006. "Education, Immigration and the Future of Latinos in the United States." *Journal of Latino Studies* 5 (2): 45–58.

Nora, A. 2003. "Access to Higher Education for Hispanic Students: Real or Illusory?" In *The Majority in the Minority: Expanding the Representation of Latina/o Faculty, Administrators and Students in Higher Education*, ed. J. Castellanos and L. Jones, pp. 47–68. Sterling, VA: Stylus.

Nora, A., and Á. F. Cabrera. 1996. "The Role of Perceptions of Prejudice and Discrimination on the Adjustment of Minority Students to College." *Journal of Higher Education* 67 (2): 119–148.

Norton, M. I., and S. R. Sommers. 2011. "Whites See Racism as a Zero-Sum Game That They Are Now Losing." *Perspectives in Psychological Science* 6 (3): 215–218.

Núñez, A. M. 2009. "Latino Students' Transitions to College: A Social and Intercultural Capital Perspective." *Harvard Educational Review* 79 (1): 22–48.

———. 2011. "Counterspaces and Connections in College Transitions: First-Generation Latino Students' Perspectives on Chicano Studies." *Journal of College Student Development* 52 (6): 639–655.

———. 2014a. "Advancing an Intersectionality Framework in Higher Education: Power and Latino Postsecondary Opportunity." In *Higher Education: Handbook of Theory and Research*, vol. 29, ed. M. B. Paulsen, pp. 33–92. New York: Springer.

———. 2014b. "Employing Multilevel Intersectionality in Educational Research: Latino Identities, Contexts, and College Access." *Educational Researcher* 43 (2): 85–92.

Núñez, A. M., and G. Crisp. 2012. "Ethnic Diversity and Latino/a College Access: A Comparison of Mexican American and Puerto Rican Beginning College Students." *Journal of Diversity in Higher Education* 5 (2): 78–95.

Núñez, A. M., S. Hurtado, and E. C. Galdeano. Forthcoming 2015. *Hispanic-Serving Institutions: Advancing Research and Transformative Practice*. New York: Routledge.

Núñez, A. M., and D. Kim. 2012. "Building a Multicontextual Model of Latino College Enrollment: Student, School, and State-Level Effects." *Review of Higher Education* 35 (2): 237–263.

Núñez, A. M., P. McDonough, M. Ceja, and D. Solórzano. 2008. "Diversity Within: Latino College Choice and Ethnic Comparisons." In *Racism in Post-Race America: New Theories, New Directions*, ed. C. Gallagher, pp. 267–284. Chapel Hill, NC: Social Forces Publishing.

Oakes, J. 2005. *Keeping Track: How Schools Structure Inequality*. 2nd ed. New Haven, CT: Yale University Press.

Oakes, J., J. Mendoza, and D. Silver. 2004. "California Opportunity Indicators: Informing and Monitoring California's Progress toward Equitable College Access." UCACCORD Public Policy Series. http://ucaccord.gseis.ucla.edu/publications/pdf/Indicators2004.pdf.

Obama, B. 2009. "The American Graduation Initiative." Speech presented at War-

ren, MI, July 14. http://www.whitehouse.gov/the_press_office/Remarks-by-the
-President-on-the-American-Graduation-Initiative-in-Warren-MI/.

Ochoa, G. 2013. *Academic Profiling: Latinos, Asian Americans, and the Achievement Gap.* Minneapolis: University of Minnesota Press.

Office of the Deputy Under Secretary of Defense. 2012. *2011 Demographics: Profile of the Military Community.* Washington, DC: Department of Defense. http://www.militaryonesource.mil/12038/MOS/Reports/2011_Demographics _Report.pdf.

Olivas, M. A. 2006. *Colored Men and Hombres Aquí: Hernandez v. Texas and the Emergence of Mexican American Lawyering.* Hispanic Civil Rights Series. Houston: Arte Publico Press.

Olsen, R., N. Seftor, T. Silva, D. Myers, D. DesRoches, and J. Young. 2008. *Upward Bound Math-Science: Program Description and Interim Impacts.* Princeton, NJ: Mathematica Policy Research, Inc.

Ong, P., and J. Rickles. 2004. "The Continued Nexus between School and Residential Segregation." *Asian American Law Journal* 11 (2): 260–275. http:// scholarship.law.berkeley.edu/cgi/viewcontent.cgi?article=1103&context=aalj.

Orfield, G., and N. Gordon. 2001. *Schools More Separate: Consequences of a Decade of Desegregation.* Cambridge, MA: Harvard University, Civil Rights Project.

Orfield, G., D. Losen, J. Wald, and C. Swanson. 2004. *Losing Our Future: How Minority Youth Are Being Left Behind by the Graduation Rate Crisis.* Cambridge, MA: Civil Rights Project at Harvard University.

Orfield, G., and E. Miller. 1998. *Chilling Admissions: The Affirmative Action Crisis and the Search for Alternatives.* Cambridge, MA: Harvard Education Publishing Group.

Orozco, C. E. 2009. *No Mexicans, Women, or Dogs Allowed: The Rise of the Mexican American Civil Rights Movement.* Austin: University of Texas Press.

Orozco, V. 2003. "Latinas and the Undergraduate Experience: ¡No Estamos Solas!" In *The Majority in the Minority: Expanding the Representation of Latina/o Faculty, Administrators and Students in Higher Education,* ed. J. Castellanos and L. Jones, pp. 127–138. Sterling, VA: Stylus.

Ortiz, V., and E. Telles. 2012. "Racial Identity and Racial Treatment of Mexican Americans." *Race and Social Problems* 4 (1): 41–56.

Oseguera, L., G. Conchas, and E. Mosqueda. 2011. "Beyond Family and Ethnic Culture: Understanding the Preconditions for the Potential Realization of Social Capital." *Youth and Society* 43 (3): 1136–1167.

Outcalt, C. L., and T. E. Skewes-Cox. 2002. "Involvement, Interaction, and Satisfaction: The Human Environment at HBCUs." *Review of Higher Education* 25 (3): 331–347.

Palmer, P. 1983. "White Women/Black Women: The Dualism of Female Identity and Experience in the United States." *Feminist Studies* 9 (1): 151–170.

Parrish, R. 2006. "The Meritocracy Myth: A Dollars & Sense Interview with Lani Guinier." *Dollars & Sense,* January/February, pp. 24–26.

Parrish, T. 2002. "Racial Disparities in the Identification, Funding, and Provision of Special Education." In *Racial Inequity in Special Education,* ed. D. J. Losen and G. Orfield, pp. 15–37. Cambridge, MA: Harvard Education Press.

Passel, J. S. 2006. *The Size and Characteristics of the Unauthorized Migrant Popula-*

tion in the U.S.: Estimates Based on the March 2005 Current Population Survey. Washington, DC: Pew Hispanic Research Center. http://pewhispanic.org/files /reports/61.pdf.

Passel, J. S., D. Cohn, and A. Gonzalez-Barrera. 2012. *Net Migration from Mexico Falls to Zero—and Perhaps Less.* Washington, DC: Pew Hispanic Research Center.

Patton, L. D., ed. 2010. *Cultural Centers in Higher Education: Perspectives on Identity, Theory, and Practice.* Sterling, VA: Stylus.

Payea, K., S. Baum, and C. Kurose. 2013. *How Students and Parents Pay for College.* Trends in Higher Education Series. College Board Advocacy & Policy Center Analysis Brief. http://trends.collegeboard.org/sites/default/files/analysis -brief-how-students-parents-pay-college.pdf.

Pérez, D. J., L. Fortuna, and M. Alegría. 2008. "Prevalence and Correlates of Everyday Discrimination among US Latinos." *Journal of Community Psychology* 36 (4): 421–433.

Perez, D., W. M. Sribney, and M. A. Rodríguez. 2009. "Perceived Discrimination and Self-Reported Quality of Care among Latinos in the United States." *Journal of General Internal Medicine* 24 (3): 548–554.

Pérez Huber, L. 2010. "Beautifully Powerful: A LatCrit Reflection on Coming to an Epistemological Consciousness and the Power of *Testimonio.*" *Journal of Gender, Social Policy & the Law* 18 (3): 839–851.

Pérez Huber, L., R. N. Johnson, and R. Kohli. 2006. "Naming Racism: A Conceptual Look at Internalized Racism in U.S. Schools." *Chicano Latino* 26 (Spring): 183–206.

Perlmann, J. 2010. "The Importance of Raising Mexican American High School Graduation Rates." In *Helping Young Refugees and Immigrants Succeed: Public Policy, Aid, and Education,* ed. G. Sonnert and G. Holton, pp. 167–175. New York: Palgrave Macmillan.

Perna, L. W. 2006. "Understanding the Relationship between Information about College Prices and Financial Aid and Students' College-Related Behaviors." *American Behavioral Scientist* 49 (12): 1620–1635.

Perna, L. W., and C. Li. 2006. "College Affordability: Implications for College Opportunity." *NASFAA Journal of Student Financial Aid* 36 (1): 7–24.

Pewewardy, C., and B. Frey. 2002. "Surveying the Landscape: Perceptions of Multicultural Support Services and Racial Climate at a Predominantly White University." *Journal of Negro Education* 71 (1/2): 77–95.

Pew Hispanic Research Center. 2004. *Latino Teens Staying in High School: A Challenge for All Generations.* Washington, DC: Pew Hispanic Research Center.

———. 2011. *The Mexican-American Boom: Births Overtake Immigration.* Washington, DC: Pew Hispanic Research Center.

Picca, L., and J. Feagin. 2007. *Two-Faced Racism: Whites in the Backstage and Frontstage.* London: Routledge.

Pitt, L. 1966. *The Decline of the Californios: A Social History of the Spanish-Speaking Californians, 1846–1890.* Berkeley: University of California Press.

Pizarro, M. 2005. *Chicanas and Chicanos in School: Racial Profiling, Identity Battles, and Empowerment.* Austin: University of Texas Press.

Pollack, W. 1998. *Real Boys: Rescuing Our Sons from the Myths of Boyhood*. New York: Random House.

Ponjuan, L. 2011. "Recruiting and Retaining Latino Faculty Members: The Missing Piece to Latino Student Success." *Thought & Action* 27 (Fall): 99–110.

Portes, A. 1998. "Social Capital: Its Origins and Applications in Modern Sociology." *Annual Reviews in Sociology* 22: 1–24.

———. 2001. "The Resilient Importance of Class: A Nominalist Interpretation." In *Political Power and Social Theory, Volume 14*, ed. D. E. Davis, pp. 249–284. Bingley, UK: Emerald Group Publishing Limited.

Portes, A., and P. Fernández-Kelly. 2008. "No Margin for Error: Educational and Occupational Achievement among Disadvantaged Children of Immigrants." *ANNALS of the American Academy of Political and Social Science* 620 (1): 12–36.

Prager, D. 2007. *Marked: Race, Crime, and Finding Work in an Era of Mass Incarceration*. Chicago: University of Chicago Press.

Pryor, J., S. Hurtado, V. B. Sáenz, J. L. Santos, and W. S. Korn. 2007. *The American Freshman: Forty-Year Trends*. Los Angeles: Higher Education Research Institute.

Public Broadcasting Service. 1996. *Chicano!* Part 3, *History of the Mexican American Civil Rights Movement*. Film.

Putnam, R. D. 2000. *Bowling Alone: The Collapse and Revival of American Community*. New York: Simon & Schuster.

Pycior, J. L. 1997. *LBJ & Mexican Americans: The Paradox of Power*. Austin: University of Texas Press.

Quinones, J. G. 1990. *Chicano Politics: Reality and Promise, 1940–1990*. Albuquerque: University of New Mexico Press.

Ramírez, E. 2013. "Examining Latino/as' Graduate School Choice Process: An Intersectionality Perspective." *Journal of Hispanic Higher Education* 12 (1): 23–36.

Ramírez, R. L., and R. E. Casper. 1999. *What It Means to Be a Man: Reflections on Puerto Rican Masculinity*. New Brunswick, NJ: Rutgers University Press.

Ramos, C. 2001. "The Educational Legacy of Racially Restrictive Covenants: Their Long Term Impact on Mexican Americans." *The Scholar: St. Mary's Law Review on Minority Issues* 4 (1): 149–184.

Rankin, S. R. 2004. "Campus Climate for Lesbian, Gay, Bisexual, and Transgender People." *The Diversity Factor* 12 (1): 18–23.

Rankin, S. R., and R. D. Reason. 2005. "Differing Perceptions: How Students of Color and White Students Perceive Campus Climate for Underrepresented Groups." *Journal of College Student Development* 46 (1): 43–61.

Raudenbush, S. W., and A. S. Bryk. 2002. *Hierarchical Linear Models: Applications and Data Analysis Methods*. 2nd ed. Newbury Park, CA: Sage.

Reardon, S. F., A. Atteberry, N. Arshan, and M. Kurlaender. 2009. "Effects of the California High School Exit Exam on Student Persistence, Achievement, and Graduation." Working paper #2009-12. Institute for Research on Education Policy & Practice, Stanford University. http://tinyurl.com/cahsee-report-2009.

Reese, L., S. Balzano, R. Gallimore, and C. Goldenberg. 1995. "The Concept of Educación: Latino Family Values and American Schooling." *International Journal of Educational Research* 23 (1): 57–81.

Rendón, L. 1994. "Validating Culturally Diverse Students: Toward a New Model of Learning and Student Development." *Innovative Higher Education* 19 (1): 33–51.

———. 2002. "Community College Puente: A Validating Model of Education." *Journal of Educational Policy* 16 (4): 642–667.

Rendón Linares, L., and S. Muñoz. 2011. "Revisiting Validation Theory: Theoretical Foundations, Applications, and Extensions." *Enrollment Management Journal* 5 (2): 12–33.

Report of the Public Schools of El Paso, Texas, 1905–1906 for the Scholastic year, Commencing September 4, 1905, and Ending May 5, 1906. Monroe C. Gutman Library Special Collections, Harvard Graduate School of Education.

Reyes, A. H., and G. Rodriguez. 2004. "School Finance: Raising Questions for Urban Schools." *Education and Urban Society* 37 (1): 3–21.

Reyes, X. A. 2006. "Cien Porciento Puertorriquena (One Hundred Percent Puerto Rican): Latina High School Students Forge Identity." In *Latina Girls: Voices of Adolescent Strength in the United States,* ed. J. Denner and B. Guzman, pp. 157–168. New York: New York University Press.

Rios, V. M. 2011. *Punished: Policing the Lives of Black and Latino Boys.* New York: New York University Press.

Rivas-Rodriguez, M., ed. 2005. *Mexican Americans and World War II.* Austin: University of Texas Press.

Rochin, R. I., and D. N. Valdes, eds. 2000. *Voices of a New Chicana/o History.* East Lansing: Michigan State University Press.

Rodríguez, C. E. 2000. *Changing Race: Latinos, the Census, and the History of Ethnicity in the United States.* New York: New York University Press.

Rodriguez, R., and P. Gonzales. 1997. "Deconstructing Machismo." San Francisco Chronicle Features, June 20. http://www.azteca.net/aztec/literat/macho.html.

Rodriguez II: San Antonio Independent School District et al. v. Rodriguez et al. 1973. 411 U.S. 1; 36 L. Ed. 2d 16. https://bulk.resource.org/courts.gov/c/US/411/411 .US.1.71-1332.html.

Rolón-Dow, R. 2005. "Critical Care: A Color(full) Analysis of Care Narratives in the Schooling Experiences of Puerto Rican Girls." *American Educational Research Journal* 42 (1): 77–111.

Romero, R. C., and L. F. Fernandez. 2012. *Doss v. Bernal: Ending Mexican Apartheid in Orange County.* Research Report No. 14. Los Angeles: UCLA Chicano Studies Research Center.

Romo, H., and T. Falbo, eds. 1996. *Latino High School Graduation: Defying the Odds.* Austin: University of Texas Press.

Romo, L. F., E. S. Lefkowitz, M. Sigman, and T. K. Au. 2002. "A Longitudinal Study of Maternal Messages about Dating and Sexuality and Their Influence on Latino Adolescents." *Society for Adolescent Medicine* 31 (1): 59–69.

Rosales, F. A. 1996. *Chicano!: The History of the Mexican American Civil Rights Movement.* Houston: Arte Publico Press.

Ruiz, V. L. 1987. *Cannery Women, Cannery Lives: Mexican Women, Unionization, and the California Food Processing Industry, 1930–1950.* Albuquerque: University of New Mexico Press.

Ruiz, V. L., J. Jones, P. Wood, E. May, and T. Borstelmann. 2005. *Created Equal: A Social and Political History of the United States*. New York: Longman.

Ruiz, V. L., and V. S. Korrol. 2005. *Latina Legacies: Identity, Biography, and Community*. Cary, NC: Oxford University Press.

Ruiz, V. L., and S. Tiano. 1987. *Women on the U.S.-Mexico Border: Responses to Change*. Winchester, MA: Allen and Unwin.

Ruiz Alvarado, A., and S. Hurtado. 2015. "Salience at the Intersection: Latina/o Identities across Different Campus Contexts." In *Intersectionality in Education Research*, ed. D. J. Davis, R. J. Brunn, and J. L. Olive. Sterling, VA: Stylus Publishing, LLC.

Rumberger, R., and P. Gándara. 2004. "Seeking Equity in the Education of California's English Learners." *Teachers College Record* 106 (10): 2031–2055.

Ryan, C., D. Huebner, R. M. Díaz, and J. Sanchez. 2009. "Family Rejection as a Predictor of Negative Health Outcomes in White and Latino Lesbian, Gay, and Bisexual Young Adults." *Pediatrics* 123 (1): 346–352.

Sabia, J. J. 2002. "Segregation Now, Segregation Tomorrow, Segregation Forever." *Front Page Magazine*, December 11. http://www.frontpagemag.com/Articles/ReadArticle.asp?ID=5033.

Sáenz, V. B., H. N. Ngai, and S. Hurtado. 2007. "Factors Influencing Positive Interactions across Race for African American, Asian American, Latino and White College Students." *Research in Higher Education* 48 (1): 1–38.

Sáenz, V. B., and L. Ponjuan. 2009. "The Vanishing Latino Male in Higher Education." *Journal of Hispanic Higher Education* 8 (1): 54–89.

———. 2011. *Men of Color: Ensuring the Academic Success of Latino Males in Higher Education*. Washington, DC: Institute for Higher Education Policy. http://www.ihep.org/assets/files/publications/m-r/(Brief)_Men_of_Color_Latinos.pdf.

———. 2012. "Latino Males: Improving College Access and Degree Completion—A New National Imperative." San Antonio: AAHHE, Educational Testing Services, and University of Texas–San Antonio.

Sánchez, G. I., and V. Strickland. 1948. "Spanish Name Spells Discrimination." *The Nation's Schools* 41, no. 1 (January): 22–24.

Sánchez, G. J. 1995. *Becoming Mexican American: Ethnicity, Culture, and Identity in Chicano Los Angeles, 1900–1945*. New York: Oxford University Press.

Sandoval, C. 2000. *Methodology of the Oppressed*. Minneapolis: University of Minnesota Press.

San Miguel, G., Jr. 1987. *Let Them All Take Heed: Mexican Americans and the Campaign for Educational Equality in Texas, 1910–1981*. Austin: University of Texas Press.

———. 2001. *Brown Not White: School Integration and the Chicano Movement in Houston*. College Station: Texas A&M University Press.

———. 2013. *Chicana/o Struggles for Education*. College Station: Texas A&M University Press.

San Miguel, G., Jr., and R. R. Valencia. 1998. "From the Treaty of Guadalupe Hidalgo to Hopwood: The Educational Plight and Struggle of Mexican Americans in the Southwest." *Harvard Educational Review* 68 (3): 353–412.

Santillana, R. 1989. "'Rosita the Riveter': Midwest Mexican American Women during World War II, 1941–1945." *Perspectives in Mexican American Studies* 2 (1): 115–146.

Santos, J. L., N. L. Cabrera, and K. J. Fosnacht. 2010. "Is 'Race-Neutral' Really Race-Neutral?: Adverse Impact towards Underrepresented Minorities in the UC System." *Journal of Higher Education* 81 (6): 675–701.

Sarkisian, N., M. Gerena, and N. Gerstel. 2006. "Extended Family Ties among Mexicans, Puerto Ricans, and Whites: Superintegration or Disintegration?" *Family Relations* 55 (3): 331–344.

Satz, D. 2007. "Equality, Adequacy, and Education for Citizenship." *Ethics* 117 (July): 623–648.

Saylor, E. S., and E. Aries. 1999. "Ethnic Identity and Change in Social Context." *Journal of Social Psychology* 139 (5): 549–566.

Shaffer, S., and L. Gordon. 2006. "What Is the Impact of 'Boys Will Be Boys'?" Presentation at the 2006 annual conference of the Mid-Atlantic Equity Center, Bethesda, MD, March 24.

Skiba, R. 2000. *Zero Tolerance, Zero Evidence: An Analysis of School Disciplinary Practice.* Bloomington: Education Policy Center, Indiana University.

Sleeter, C. E. 2011. *The Academic and Social Value of Ethnic Studies: A Research Review.* Washington, DC: National Education Association.

Snyder, H. N., and M. H. Swahn. 2004. "Juvenile Suicides, 1981–1998." *Youth Violence Research Bulletin*, March. Retrieved from https://www.ncjrs.gov/html /ojjdp/196978/contents.html.

Snyder, T. D. 2012. *Digest of Education Statistics, 2012.* "Table 143. Percentage of Students at or above Selected National Assessment of Educational Progress (NAEP) Reading Achievement Levels, by Grade and Selected Student Characteristics: Selected Years, 1998 through 2011." http://nces.ed.gov/programs /digest/d12/tables/dt12_143.asp.

Soldatenko, M. T. 2009. *Chicano Studies: The Genesis of a Discipline.* Tucson: University of Arizona Press.

Solórzano, D. G. 1997. "Images and Words That Wound: Critical Race Theory, Racial Stereotyping, and Teacher Education." *Teacher Education Quarterly* 24 (3): 5–19.

Solórzano, D. G., W. Allen, and G. Carroll. 2002. "A Case Study of Racial Microaggressions and Campus Racial Climate at the University of California, Berkeley." *UCLA Chicano/Latino Law Review* 23 (15): 15–112.

Solórzano, D. G., M. Ceja, and T. Yosso. 2000. "Critical Race Theory, Racial Microaggressions, and Campus Racial Climate: The Experiences of African American College Students." *Journal of Negro Education* 69 (1/2): 60–73.

Solórzano, D. G., and D. Delgado Bernal. 2001. "Examining Transformational Resistance through a Critical Race and LatCrit Theory Framework: Chicana and Chicano Students in an Urban Context." *Urban Education* 36 (3): 308–342.

Solórzano, D. G., and A. Ornelas. 2002. "A Critical Race Analysis of Advanced Placement Classes: A Case of Educational Inequality." *Journal of Latinos and Education* 1 (4): 215–229.

———. 2004. "A Critical Race Analysis of Latina/o and African American Advanced Placement Enrollment in Public High Schools." *High School Journal* 87, no. 3 (February/March): 15–26.

Solórzano, D. G., and T. J. Yosso. 2000. "Toward a Critical Race Theory of Chicana and Chicano Education." In *Charting Terrains of Chicana(o)/Latina(o) Education*, ed. C. Tejada, C. Martinez, and Z. Leonardo, pp. 35–65. Cresskill, NJ: Hampton Press, Inc.

Stanton-Salazar, R. D. 1997. "A Social Capital Framework for Understanding the Socialization of Racial Minority Children and Youth." *Harvard Educational Review* 67 (1): 1–39.

———. 2001. *Manufacturing Hope and Despair: The School and Kin Support Networks of U.S. Mexican Youth*. New York: Teachers College Press.

———. 2010. "A Social Capital Framework for the Study of Institutional Agents and Their Role in the Empowerment of Low-Status Students and Youth." *Youth and Society* 43 (3): 1–44.

Stebleton, M. J., R. Huesman, and A. Kuzhabekova. 2010. "Do I Belong Here? Exploring Immigrant College Student Responses on the SERU Survey Sense of Belonging/Satisfaction Factor." CSHE Research and Occasional Paper Series, Berkeley, CA. *Center for Studies in Higher Education* 13 (10): 1–13.

Steelman, L. C., and B. Powell. 1991. "Sponsoring the Next Generation: Parental Willingness to Pay for Higher Education." *American Journal of Sociology* 96 (6): 1505–1529.

Stoney, S., and J. Batalova. 2013. *Mexican Immigration in the United States*. Washington, DC: Migration Policy Institute.

Suarez-Orozco, C., and M. Suarez-Orozco. 1995. *Immigration, Family Life, and Achievement Motivation among Latino Adolescents*. Stanford, CA: Stanford University Press.

Suarez-Orozco, M., and M. M. Paez, eds. 2002. *Latinos: Remaking America*. Berkeley: University of California Press.

Sue, D. W. 2010. *Microaggressions in Everyday Life: Race, Gender, and Sexual Orientation*. Hoboken, NJ: Wiley Press.

Sweet, J. 1997. "The Iberian Roots of American Racist Thought." *William and Mary Quarterly* 54 (1): 143–166.

Tatum, B. D. 2003. *"Why Are All The Black Kids Sitting Together in the Cafeteria?": And Other Conversations about Race*. New York: Basic Books.

Taylor, P., R. Kochhar, R. Fry, G. Velasco, and S. Motel. 2011. *Wealth Gaps Rise to Record Highs between Whites, Blacks, Hispanics*. Washington, DC: Pew Hispanic Research Center.

Telles, E. E., and E. Murgia. 1990. "Phenotypic Discrimination and Income Differences among Mexican Americans." *Social Science Quarterly* 71 (4): 682–696.

Telles, E. E., and V. Ortiz. 2008. *Generations of Exclusion: Mexican Americans, Assimilation and Race*. New York: Russell Sage Foundation.

Teranishi, R., W. Allen, and D. G. Solórzano. 2004. "Opportunity at the Crossroads: Racial Inequality, School Segregation, and Higher Education in California." *Teachers College Record* 106 (11): 2224–2245.

Thernstrom, S., and A. Thernstrom. 1997. *America in Black and White: One Nation Indivisible*. New York: Simon & Schuster.

Tierney, W. G. 1992. "An Anthropological Analysis of Student Participation in College." *Journal of Higher Education* 63 (6): 603–618.

Timberlake, J. M. 2007. "Racial and Ethnic Inequality in the Duration of Children's Exposures to Neighborhood Poverty and Affluence." *Social Problems* 54 (3): 319–342.

Tinto, V. 1975. "Dropouts from Higher Education: A Theoretical Synthesis of the Recent Literature." *Review of Educational Research* 45 (1): 89–125.

———. 1993. *Leaving College: Rethinking the Causes and Cures of Student Attrition.* 2nd ed. Chicago: University of Chicago Press.

Toro-Morn, M. I. 2008. "Beyond Gender Dichotomies: Toward a New Century of Gendered Scholarship in the Latino/a Experience." In *Latinas/os in the United States: Changing the Face of America*, ed. H. Rodríguez, S. Rogelio, and C. Menjívar, pp. 277–293. New York: Springer.

Torres, J. B., V. S. H. Solberg, and A. H. Carlstrom. 2002. "The Myth of Sameness among Latino Men and Their Machismo." *American Journal of Orthopsychiatry* 72 (2): 163–181.

Torres, V. 1999. "Validation of the Bicultural Orientation Model for Hispanic College Students." *Journal of College Student Development* 40 (3): 285–298.

———. 2003. "Influences of Ethnic Identity Development of Latino College Students in the First Two Years of College." *Journal of College Student Development* 44 (4): 532–547.

Trujillo, C. M. 1991. *Chicana Lesbians: The Girls Our Mothers Warned Us About.* Chicago: Third Women Press.

Tuck, R. 1946. *Not with the Fist: Mexican-Americans in a Southwest City.* New York: Harcourt Brace.

Twenty-Seventh and Twenty-Eighth Annual Reports of the State Superintendent of Public Instruction to the Governor of New Mexico for the Years of 1917–1918. 1918. Albuquerque, NM: Central Printing Co.

U.S. Census Bureau. 2010. *The Hispanic Population: 2010.* Washington, DC: U.S. Department of Commerce, Economics and Statistics Administration.

———. 2011. *The Hispanic Population: 2010.* "Table 6. Educational Attainment of the Population 25 Years and Over by Sex and Hispanic Origin Type: 2010." Retrieved from https://www.census.gov/population/hispanic/data/2010.html.

———. 2012a. *Current Population Survey, Annual Social and Economic Supplement, 2011.* Washington, DC: U.S. Department of Commerce, Economics and Statistics Administration.

———. 2012b. *Hispanic Population in the United States: 2011.* "Table 6. Educational Attainment of the Population 25 Years and Over by Sex and Hispanic Origin Type: 2011." Retrieved from https://www.census.gov/population/hispanic/data/2011.html.

———. 2012c. *Hispanic Population in the United States: 2011.* "Table 7. Nativity and Citizenship Status by Sex, Hispanic Origin, and Race: 2011." Retrieved from https://www.census.gov/population/hispanic/data/2011.html.

———. 2012d. *Hispanic Population in the United States: 2011.* "Table 8. Nativity and Citizenship Status by Sex and Hispanic Origin Type: 2011." Retrieved from https://www.census.gov/population/hispanic/data/2011.html.

———. 2012e. *Hispanic Population in the United States: 2011.* "Table 16. Labor Force and Employment Status of the Civilian Population 16 Years and Over by Sex and Hispanic Origin Type: 2011." Retrieved from https://www.census.gov/population/hispanic/data/2011.html.

————. 2012 f. *Hispanic Population in the United States: 2011.* "Table 17. Occupation of the Civilian Employed Population 16 Years and Over by Sex, Hispanic Origin, and Race: 2011." Retrieved from https://www.census.gov/population/hispanic/data/2011.html.

————. 2012g. *Hispanic Population in the United States: 2011.* "Table 18. Occupation of the Civilian Employed Population 16 Years and Over by Sex and Hispanic Origin Type: 2011." Retrieved from https://www.census.gov/population/hispanic/data/2011.html.

————. 2012h. *Hispanic Population in the United States: 2011.* "Table 21. Earnings of Full-Time, Year-Round Workers 15 Years and Over by Sex, Hispanic Origin, and Race: 2010." Retrieved from https://www.census.gov/population/hispanic/data/2011.html.

————. 2012i. *Hispanic Population in the United States: 2011.* "Table 22. Earnings of Full-Time, Year-Round Workers 15 Years and Over by Sex and Hispanic Origin Type: 2010." Retrieved from https://www.census.gov/population/hispanic/data/2011.html.

————. 2012j. *Hispanic Population in the United States: 2011.* "Table 25. Poverty Status of the Population by Sex, Age, Hispanic Origin, and Race: 2010." Retrieved from https://www.census.gov/population/hispanic/data/2011.html.

————. 2013. *Current Population Survey* (March 2013). Washington, DC: U.S. Census Bureau, Population Division, Ethnic and Hispanic Statistics Branch.

U.S. Commission on Civil Rights. 1968. *The Mexican American: A Paper Prepared for the U.S. Commission on Civil Rights.* Primary author and researcher, Helen Rowan. Washington, DC: Government Printing Office.

————. 1971a. *Ethnic Isolation of Mexican Americans in the Public Schools of the Southwest*, Report I. Washington, DC: Government Printing Office.

————. 1971b. *The Unfinished Education: Mexican American Educational Series*, Report II. Washington, DC: Government Printing Office.

————. 1972a. *Excluded Student: Educational Practices Affecting Mexican Americans in the Southwest*, Report III. Washington, DC: Government Printing Office.

————. 1972b. *Mexican American Education in Texas: A Function of Wealth*, Report IV. Washington, DC: Government Printing Office.

————. 1973. *Teachers and Students: Mexican American Education Study: Differences in Teacher Interaction with Mexican American and Anglo Students*, Report V. Washington, DC: Government Printing Office.

————. 1974. *Toward Quality Education for Mexican Americans*, Report VI. Washington, DC: Government Printing Office.

U.S. Department of Commerce. 1933. *General Report, Statistics by Subjects.* Fifteenth Census of the U.S.: 1930, Population. Vol. II. Washington, DC: Government Printing Office.

U.S. Department of Commerce, Census Bureau. 2013. "Table 103.10. Percentage of the Population 3 to 34 years Old Enrolled in School, by Sex, Race/Ethnicity, and Age Group: Selected Years, 1980 through 2012." Prepared May 2013 from *Current Population Survey (CPS), October, Selected Years, 1980 through 2012.* http://nces.ed.gov/programs/digest/d13/tables/dt13_103.10.asp.

U.S. Department of Commerce, 2014, Census Bureau, *Current Population Survey*

(CPS), October Supplement, 1990–2013. See *Digest of Education Statistics* 2014, table 302.20.

U.S. Department of Education. 2010a. National Center for Education Statistics, Integrated Postsecondary Education Data System (IPEDS), Fall 2010, Completions Component.

———. 2010b. *Status and Trends in the Education of Racial and Ethnic Minorities.* Publication no. NCES 2010-015. http://nces.ed.gov/pubs2010/2010015/index .asp.

———. 2013. *National Assessment of Educational Progress (NAEP), Various Years, 1990–2013. Mathematics and Reading Assessments.* Institute of Education Sciences, National Center for Education Statistics. Retrieved from http://nces .ed.gov/nationsreportcard/mathematics/; http://nces.ed.gov/nationsreport card/reading/.

Usher, A. 2012. *What Roles Do Parent Involvement, Family Background, and Culture Play in Student Motivation?* Washington, DC: George Washington University, Center on Education Policy.

Valencia, R. R. 2000. "Inequalities and the Schooling of Minority Students in Texas: Historical and Contemporary Conditions." *Hispanic Journal of Behavioral Sciences* 22 (4): 445–459.

———. 2005. "The Mexican American Struggle for Equal Educational Opportunity in *Mendez v. Westminster*: Helping to Pave the Way for *Brown v. Board of Education.*" *Teachers College Record* 107 (3): 389–423.

———. 2008. *Chicano Students and the Courts: The Mexican American Legal Struggle for Educational Equality.* New York: New York University Press.

———. 2010. *Dismantling Contemporary Deficit Thinking: Educational Thought and Practice.* New York: Routledge.

Valencia, R. R., and M. Black. 2002. "'Mexican Americans Don't Value Education!'—On the Basis of the Myth, Mythmaking, and Debunking." *Journal of Latinos and Education* 1 (2): 81–103.

Valenzuela, A. 1999. *Subtractive Schooling: U.S.-Mexican Youth and the Politics of Caring.* Albany: State University of New York Press.

Valenzuela, A., and S. M. Dornbusch. 1994. "Familism and Social Capital in the Academic Achievement of Mexican Origin and Anglo Adolescents." *Social Science Quarterly* 75 (1): 18–36.

Vallejo, J. A. 2012. "Socially Mobile Mexican Americans and the Minority Culture of Mobility." *American Behavioral Scientist* 56 (5): 666–681.

Velez, V. N., and L. G. Bedolla. 2012. *Educational Opportunity in San Francisco's Mission Neighborhood: Assessing Critical Conditions for Children and Youth in Mission Promise Neighborhood Schools.* Berkeley, CA: Center for Latino Policy Research.

Velez, W. 1985. "Finishing College: The Effects of College Type." *Sociology of Education* 58 (3): 191–200.

Villalpando, O. 2003. "Self-Segregation or Self-Preservation? A Critical Race Theory and Latina/o Critical Theory Analysis of a Study of Chicana/o College Students." *International Journal of Qualitative Studies in Education* 16 (5): 619–646.

Villenas, S. A. 2006. "Pedagogical Moments in the Borderland: Latina Mothers Teaching and Learning." In *Chicana/Latina Education in Everyday Life: Femi-*

nista Perspectives on Pedagogy and Epistemology, ed. D. Delgado Bernal, C. A. Elenes, F. E. Godinez, and S. Villenas, pp. 147–159. Albany: State University of New York Press.

Villenas, S. A., and M. Moreno. 2001. "To *Valerse por Si Misma* between Race, Capitalism, and Patriarchy: Latina Mother-Daughter Pedagogies in North Carolina." *Qualitative Studies in Education* 14 (5): 671–687.

Viruell-Fuentes, E. A. 2011. " 'It's a Lot of Work': Racialization Processes, Ethnic Identity Formations, and Their Health Implications." *Du Bois Review: Social Science Research on Race* 8 (1): 37–52.

Weber, D. J. 1992. *The Spanish Frontier in North America*. New Haven, CT: Yale University Press.

Weber, L. 2010. *Understanding Race, Class, Gender, and Sexuality*. New York: Oxford University Press.

Whitaker, M. C. 2005. *Race Work: The Rise of Civil Rights in the Urban West*. Lincoln: University of Nebraska Press.

Wijeyesinghe, C. L., and B. W. Jackson, eds. 2001. *New Perspectives on Racial Identity Development*. New York: New York University Press.

Wollenberg, C. M. 1976. *All Deliberate Speed: Segregation and Exclusion in California Schools 1955–1975*. Berkeley: University of California Press.

Wortham, S., E. Hamann, and E. Murillo, eds. 2001. *Education in the New Latino Diaspora: Policy and the Politics of Identity*. Westport, CT: Praeger.

Yin, R. K. 1994. *Case Study Research: Design and Methods*, vol. 5. 2nd ed. Thousand Oaks, CA: Sage Publications.

Yohn, S. 1995. *A Contest of Faiths: Missionary Women and Pluralism in the American Southwest*. Ithaca, NY: Cornell University Press.

Yosso, T. J. 2005. "Whose Culture Has Capital? A Critical Race Theory Discussion of Community Cultural Wealth." *Race Ethnicity and Education* 8 (1): 69–91.

———. 2006. *Critical Race Counterstories along the Chicana/Chicano Educational Pipeline*. New York: Routledge.

Yosso, T. J., W. A. Smith, M. Ceja, and D. G. Solórzano. 2009. "Critical Race Theory, Racial Microaggressions, and Campus Racial Climate for Latina/o Undergraduates." *Harvard Educational Review* 79 (4): 659–690.

Yosso, T. J., and D. G. Solórzano. 2006. "Leaks in the Chicana and Chicano Educational Pipeline." *Latino Policy and Issues Brief*, no. 13. Los Angeles: UCLA Chicano Studies Research Center.

Zambrana, R. E. 1987. "Toward Understanding the Educational Trajectory and Socialization of Latina Women." In *The Broken Web: The Educational Experience of Hispanic American Women*, ed. T. McKenna and F. I. Ortiz, pp. 61–77. Encino, CA: Floricanto Press.

———. 2011. *Latinos in American Society: Families and Communities in Transition*. Ithaca, NY: Cornell University Press.

Zambrana, R. E., C. Dorrington, and S. A. Bell. 1997. "Mexican American Women in Higher Education: A Comparative Study." *Race, Gender & Class* 4 (2): 127–149.

Zambrana, R. E., and V. MacDonald. 2009. "Staggered Inequalities to Access in Higher Education by Gender, Race and Ethnicity." In *Emerging Intersections:*

Race, Class and Gender in Theory, Policy and Practice, ed. B. T. Dill and R. E. Zambrana, pp. 73–100. New Brunswick, NJ: Rutgers University Press.

Zambrana, R. E., and T. Morant. 2009. "Latino Immigrant Children and Inequality in Access to Early Schooling Programs." *Zero to Three* 29 (5): 46–53.

Zambrana, R. E., R. J. Ray, M. Espino, C. Castro, B. Douthirt Cohen, and J. Eliason. 2015. "'Don't Leave Us Behind': The Importance of Mentoring for Underrepresented Minority Faculty." *American Educational Research Journal.*

Zambrana, R. E., and I. E. Zoppi. 2002. "Latina Students: Translating Cultural Wealth into Social Capital to Improve Academic Success." *Journal of Ethnic & Cultural Diversity in Social Work* 11 (1/2): 33–53.

Zapata, J. T. 1988. "Early Identification and Recruitment of Hispanic Teacher Candidates." *Journal of Teacher Education* 39 (1): 19–23.

Zarate, M. E., and D. Fabienke. 2007. "Financial Aid as a Perceived Barrier to College for Latino Students." *American Academic* 3 (January): 129–140.

Zarate, M. E., and H. P. Pachon. 2006. *Perceptions of College Financial Aid among California Latino Youth.* TRPI Policy Brief. Los Angeles: Tomás Rivera Policy Institute, University of Southern California.

Zayas, L. H., R. J. Lester, L. J. Cabassa, and L. R. Fortuna. 2005. "Why Do So Many Latina Teens Attempt Suicide? A Conceptual Model for Research." *American Journal of Orthopsychiatry* 75 (2): 275–287.

Zuberi, T., and E. Bonilla-Silva. 2008. *White Logic, White Methods: Racism and Methodology.* Lanham, MD: Rowman and Littlefield.

Contributing Authors

Ruth E. Zambrana

RUTH ENID ZAMBRANA, PhD, is currently at the University of Maryland as a professor in the Women's Studies Department; director of the Consortium on Race, Gender and Ethnicity; and Adjunct Professor of Family Medicine at the UMD Baltimore School of Medicine, Department of Family Medicine. Dr. Zambrana served as interim director of the U.S. Latina/o Studies Initiative at the University of Maryland, College Park, from 2007 to 2009. She has worked in the areas of health and educational inequalities across the life course among low-income populations for over three decades. Her work focuses on the intersections of gender, race, Hispanic ethnicity, socioeconomic status, and institutional access and their association with the health and life course outcomes of race/ethnic underserved groups. Her scholarship also emphasizes the heterogeneity in life course outcomes based on national origin, gender, and socioeconomic status within and across the Latino population.

Sylvia Hurtado

SYLVIA HURTADO is a professor and former director of the Higher Education Research Institute at UCLA in the Graduate School of Education and Information Studies. Just prior to coming to UCLA, she served as director of the Center for the Study of Higher and Postsecondary Education at the University of Michigan. Dr. Hurtado has published numerous articles and books related to her primary interest in student educational outcomes, campus climates, college impact on student development, Latinas/os in higher education, and diversity in higher education. She has served on numerous editorial boards for journals in education and is past-president of the Association for the Study of Higher Education (ASHE). She obtained her PhD in education from UCLA, EdM from Harvard Graduate School of Education, and AB in Sociology from Princeton University.

Adriana Ruiz Alvarado

ADRIANA RUIZ ALVARADO, PhD, is a postdoctoral scholar in the Higher Education Research Institute at the University of California, Los Angeles. She has a professional background in academic advising and college outreach programs. Her research addresses student enrollment and mobility patterns, persistence of underrepresented students, and issues of campus climate and intergroup relations. She earned her PhD in Higher Education and Organizational Change from UCLA, her MEd in Student Affairs from UCLA, and her BA in Social Welfare from UC Berkeley.

Rebeca Burciaga

REBECA BURCIAGA is an assistant professor of Educational Leadership at San José State University, USA. Her research and teaching focus on educational practices and structures that (re)produce social inequalities for historically marginalized communities and on cultivating asset-based mindsets in teachers and administrators who work with youth of color. Rebeca Burciaga earned her EdM degree at the Harvard Graduate School of Education in Administration, Planning, and Social Policy with an emphasis in Higher Education, and earned her PhD at UCLA in Social Science and Comparative Education. Her dissertation research focused on the pathways from preschool to the professoriate for Chicana PhD students in the field of education. Her dissertation used *testimonio* as methodology and included data from the Survey of Earned Doctorates to provide an overview of Chicana doctoral students' demographics and postgraduate plans for the past twenty-one years. Her work has been recognized and supported by the Spencer Foundation, the American Association of University Women, the Ford Foundation, and the National Institutes of Health.

Nolan L. Cabrera

DR. CABRERA is an assistant professor in the Center for the Study of Higher Education, where he researches the impact the New Start Summer Program has on low-income, first-generation, and racial minority college students. Prior to coming to the University of Arizona, Dr. Cabrera graduated from UCLA, where he worked as a research analyst on projects at the Higher Education Research Institute. His dissertation, "Invisible Racism: Male Hegemonic Whiteness in Higher Education," critically analyzed White, male undergraduates' racial ideologies. Dr. Cabrera's primary research interests include race/racism in higher education, Whiteness formation, diversity, and affirmative action. Prior to his graduate studies, Dr. Cabrera was the director of a Boys & Girls Club in the San Francisco Bay Area. He earned his BA from Stanford University and is originally from McMinnville, Oregon.

Frances Contreras

DR. CONTRERAS researches issues of equity and access for underrepresented students in the education pipeline. She addresses transitions between K–12 and higher education, community college transfer, faculty diversity, affirmative action in higher education, and the role of the public policy arena in higher education access for underserved students of color. In addition to her research and teaching, Dr. Contreras serves on the boards of the *Harvard Journal of Hispanic Policy*, LEAP, and the ACLU of Washington. She earned her PhD in education, Stanford University; MEd, Harvard Graduate School of Education; and BA in history and mass communications, University of California, Berkeley.

Brianne A. Dávila

BRIANNE DÁVILA is an assistant professor of sociology at California State Polytechnic University, Pomona. She earned her doctorate in sociology and Feminist Studies at the University of California, Santa Barbara. She has a master's from the same program and received a bachelor's in sociology with a Spanish minor from Pitzer College in Claremont, California. Her research and teaching interests are sociology of education, Latina/o sociology, and social inequality.

Anthony De Jesús

ANTHONY DE JESÚS is an assistant professor of Social Work and
Latino Community Practice and Director of Field Education for the
new MSW Program at the University of Saint Joseph in West Hart-
ford, Connecticut. Dr. De Jesús has extensive experience as a social
work practitioner, administrator, and researcher in urban schools,
community-based organizations, and institutions of higher education,
and previously served as an assistant professor at the Silberman School
of Social Work at Hunter College and as a researcher and interim director at the Center for Puerto Rican Studies at Hunter College. Dr. De
Jesús holds an EdD in Administration, Planning and Social Policy from
the Harvard Graduate School of Education, an MSW from the Boston
University School of Social Work, and a BSW from Dominican College. Dr. De Jesús's current research focuses on examining models of
pathways into health and social work careers for Latinos, the postsecondary experiences of Latinos within higher education, the effectiveness of cultural competence training in child welfare, and the evaluation
of supportive housing and mental health services provided to formerly
incarcerated women.

Victoria-María MacDonald

VICTORIA-MARÍA MACDONALD, EdD (Harvard University), is currently an assistant professor and unit chair of the Minority and Urban
Education program, Department of Teaching and Learning, Policy and
Leadership, at the University of Maryland, College Park. Her research
examines how historical legacies impact contemporary policy regarding the equal access of Latino and African American students to high-
quality educational institutions at all levels. Her works include *Latino
Education in the United States: A Narrated History from 1513–2000*
(2004); "From Visibility to Autonomy: Latinos and Higher Education
in the United States, 1965–2005" (*Harvard Educational Review*, 2007);
"The United Status of Latinos" (in the *Routledge Handbook of Latino
Education*, 2010); and "Compromising *La Causa*? The Ford Foundation
and Chicano Intellectual Nationalism in the Creation of Chicano History, 1963–1977" (*History of Education Quarterly*, 2012). Professor Mac-
Donald is a former Spencer Foundation postdoctoral fellow from the
National Academy of Education.

Luis Ponjuán

LUIS PONJUÁN, PhD (University of Michigan), is currently an associate professor in the College of Education at Texas A&M University, College Station. He has published research articles focused on the educational pathways of Latino students. In particular, he has published on the educational pathways of Latino males into higher education. In addition, he has published on the educational experiences of undergraduate students of color in pursuing STEM academic degrees and in research lab settings, and explores the work life experiences of faculty of color in higher education institutions. He has earned grant funding from the TG Foundation and the Howard Hughes Medical Institute.

Jason Rivera

JASON RIVERA is a doctoral candidate in the Minority and Urban Education (MUE) program at the University of Maryland, College Park, and a 2014 American Association of Hispanics in Higher Education Ford Fellow. His dissertation examines the factors that contribute to Latino male academic achievement in college. He has a professional background in education, with an emphasis on academic support programs in both K–12 and higher education settings. He earned his MSEd in elementary education from the City University of New York at Staten Island, and his BA in history and political science from Manhattanville College in Purchase, New York.

Victor B. Sáenz

VICTOR B. SÁENZ, PhD (UCLA), is an associate professor in the Department of Educational Administration at the University of Texas at Austin. He is also a faculty affiliate with the UT Center for Mexican American Studies, a faculty fellow with the UT Division of Diversity and Community Engagement, and a faculty associate with the UCLA Higher Education Research Institute. Dr. Sáenz has published in numerous peer-reviewed journals and also has two book projects under way, including one on Latino males in higher education (Stylus Publishing). He has spoken about his research and programmatic work at the White House, on Capitol Hill, and at conferences and meetings across the country, and he continues to work closely with the Institute for Higher Education Policy (IHEP), the College Board's Policy and Advocacy Center, and the American Association of Hispanics in Higher Education (AAHHE) on their efforts to raise awareness about the crisis facing young men of color in education.

Index

Page numbers in italics indicate charts and tables.